Caped Crusaders 101

Caped Crusaders 101

Composition Through Comic Books

JEFFREY KAHAN *and*
STANLEY STEWART

McFarland & Company, Inc., Publishers
Jefferson, North Carolina, and London

All illustrations are by permission of Marvel Comics.

LIBRARY OF CONGRESS CATALOGUING-IN-PUBLICATION DATA

Kahan, Jeffrey, 1964–
   Caped crusaders 101 : composition through
comic books / Jeffrey Kahan and Stanley Stewart.
   p.   cm.
   Includes bibliographical references and index.

   ISBN-13: 978-0-7864-2532-7
   softcover : 50# alkaline paper ∞

   1. Comic books, strips, etc.— United States— History and
criticism.   I. Title: Caped crusaders one hundred one.
II. Title: Caped crusaders one hundred and one.   III. Stewart,
Stanley, 1931–   IV. Title.
   PN6725.K34 2006
   741.50973 — dc22   2005035057

British Library cataloguing data are available

Cover illustration ©2006 Digital Vision

Manufactured in the United States of America

McFarland & Company, Inc., Publishers
 Box 611, Jefferson, North Carolina 28640
  www.mcfarlandpub.com

To
Cory Waxman and Justin Stewart:
For heroism rendered

Acknowledgments

We would like to thank Carol Platt of Marvel Comics for permission to use illustrations, the University of La Verne for their generous research grant, and family and friends for their unwearied support.

Table of Contents

Introduction: Why Comics Can Save Us from Illiteracy

Comic book heroes have saved us from exploding stars, streaking comets, alien invasions, communist conspiracies, banks robbers, and terrorists. So why shouldn't they save the human race from illiteracy? After all, high literary culture aside, comic books are books. And — more to the point of *this* book — they are one of the very few types of books that young Americans willingly pay to read. Can we utilize their obvious appeal to make us all better readers and, ideally, better writers? For as media gurus tell us, something happens to voluntary readers as they navigate the American school system. After exposure to traditional school-mandated literature, many young readers give up reading everything, comic books included. Education sets in, and with it, a kind of reading rigor mortis.

The following pages aim to revive a love of reading. If you read comic books, the following data do not apply to you: According to the National Education Association (NEA) most people do not voluntarily read *anything*— not novels, not short stories, not poems or drama, nor, as Dana Giolia, chair of the NEA, explained, "any book that people read without guns pointed to their heads."[1] And let's not kid ourselves, the problem is real and it is serious: Only 46.7 percent of respondents to a 2004 *Newsweek* survey had read any fiction at all, down from 56.9 percent twenty years ago. And, we are told, young people, irrespective of race and gender, show the least interest in reading. In fact, the steepest decline in literary reading is in the youngest age groups. Over the past twenty years, adults 18–34 have declined from being those most likely to those least likely to

---

1. Malcolm Jones, "Waiting for the Movie: Reading's going out of style, even as publishers go wild." *Newsweek,* July 19, 2004.

read literature, and the rate of decline for the youngest adults 18–24 is 55 percent greater than that of the adult population.

We think the NEA needs to visit a comic book shop. For as we know, there are readers—young readers—so passionate about books that they cherish them like treasures to be handed down to future generations. We are talking about millions of readers: willing readers, habitual readers, readers hooked on character and plot, readers who weigh virtues not simply in terms of winning and losing but in spiritual and moral terms of good and evil; readers who discuss issues and concerns with other readers at conventions, online, and in coffee houses; readers who take pleasure in a suffusion of ethics and aesthetics, paneled in transitions of images and words, drawn from the disparate vocabularies of cuneiform, the printed word, and the cinema.[2] They are comic book readers, and, we argue, each one has the enthusiasm, dedication, motivation, and imaginative skill to make an excellent English major.[3]

Here are some startling and, we think, hopeful, statistics:

Monthly Audience

Magazine	Kid Readers (6–11)	Teen Readers (12–17)
Marvel Comics	20,449,000	10,826,000
DC Comics	14,804,000	5,597,000
Archie	1,000,000	300,000

Although there is a significant drop off in comic book readers once they reach puberty, superhero comics still sell over 16,000,000 copies a month, well in advance of teen magazines such as *Seventeen* (5,269,000 a month) or *Teen People* (5,244,000 a month).[4] Even Stephen King can't match these numbers. The numbers are even more astonishing when we consider the findings of Lawrence A. Breed, who noted that on average one comic book is read by 4.5 different readers.[5] That means that teen comic readers go through some 72 million comics a month, or about 864 million comics a year.

In this book you'll discover that the connections between, say, Spider-

---

2. Hugo Frey and Benjamin Noys have argued that comics have been intellectually marginalized because the medium is a hybrid of text and image and, thus, defies easy categorization. See "History in the Graphic Novel," in *Rethinking History* (London: Routledge, 2002), 255–60; 255.

3. Anne Rubenstein argues that comics compete directly with video games and movies more than with other forms of print media. See *Bad Language, Naked Ladies, and Other Threats to the Nation: A Political History of Comic Books in Mexico* (Durham, N.C.: Duke University Press, 1998), 8. Nonsense! A comic book's direct competition is other comics on the same rack. Video games often feature comic book characters and are, thus, an extension of the comic reader's experience; ditto films, which increasingly cater to comic readers: witness the blockbuster summer films *Spider-Man I* and *II*, *X-Men, Daredevil, Batman Begins*, etc.

4. Simmons Market Research Bureau, Spring 2002 Study.

5. Lawrence A. Breed, *Alcohol in the Comic Book* (M.A. Thesis, San Jose State University, 1979), 4.

Man and Shakespeare are not as remote as you may think. If you love *The Fantastic Four*, we want you to check out *The Fairie Queene*; we want you to connect or reconnect one book with another, to read allusively, intelligently, critically, and, yes, poetically. We're not arguing that comics can or should replace Milton or Shakespeare — or even Stephen King. But, if we can get you to think of comics *as* literature, telling similar stories, expressing similar concerns, then you might see the role that other literature can play in your life.[6]

One legitimate question some of you may ask is exactly how we're defining the comics themselves. When dealing with Spider-Man, for example, should we include just *Spider-Man* comics or include offshoots such as *Spectacular Spider-Man* or *Amazing Spider-Man, Spider-Man Unlimited, Web of Spider-Man*, or *Spider-Man 2099*? What if our web-slinging hero appears in another series, such as *Marvel Team-Up* or *The New Avengers*? What about the newspaper serial, *Amazing Spider-Man*, or the 1960s TV animated series, or the short-lived TV live action show, or the recent *Spider-Man* movies? What about novelizations, video games, board games, or product placements? Can we discuss Spider-Man as a singular character if there are 10 or more Spider-Men engaged in differing adventures running concurrently? When we refer to Spider-Man, can we or should we draw from all of these sources and various media outlets—comics, newspapers, animations, low-budget live-action TV, big-budget live-action film, video games, etc.? Another problem: If Spider-Man, is a prisoner of Dr. Octopus in *Amazing Spider-Man*, how can he in the same time frame be free to fight alongside Iron Man in *The Avengers*? Should we consider these comics as existing in parallel but distinct worlds or simply ignore the special issues and conflate them all under the rubric of "Spider-Man"? Can we discuss Spider-Man as a constant, or should we consider him as ongoing, ever evolving? Let's recall that a myriad of writers and artists have drawn the character and written his stories since he was first crafted by Stan Lee and Steve Ditko in *Amazing Fantasy* #15 way back in 1962. Does it matter that Spider-Man's creators did not and could not envision the new stories of their hero?

To students of literature, these questions are indeed important. Let's start with the most obvious problem: Just who owns Spider-Man? Can or should we have the freedom to change him? Can we give him a new power or take one away? In doing so, are we betraying Lee and Ditko's Spider-Man? Another problem comes when we want to use traditional literary techniques

6. Many programs are attempting to use comics in just this way: A series of educational comics, bowdlerized of obscene language and sexual content, is available from *Crossgeneration Comics*, designed for high school readers. The books come with a teacher's guide, CD ROMs and skill activities. The program is currently being used in seven states nationwide. (See www.crossgen.com)

to examine and ultimately pass judgment upon these characters. In Aristotelian terms, we should value a character for how he matures and grows through the story. But in the comics, how a character develops, grows, matures, is not only unclear; for some characters, it is practically impossible. When we read issues of *Superboy*, *Supergirl*, *The Teen Titans*, *The Young Avengers*, their titles tell us that our heroes must remain always young; no matter how many issues pass, their lives must include all the things that go along with youth, inexperience, immaturity. Eternally 14 or so, these characters cannot, despite their prowess, suffer into any truth without losing the sheen of youth that defines them.

Certainly, our most treasured writers would not be impressed with the open-endedness of the comics. The sixteenth-century Italian poet Tasso, for example, derided the idea of sequels. Once the poem had reached its end, he argued, it was complete and perfect, and to add sequels to continue the action would only introduce imperfection, which would then need to be corrected in yet another sequel, which would introduce more imperfection and so on. Very soon, the reader would be confronted with a massive and forbidding body of work, but one that only weakened the simplicity and clarity of the original. It would be as if we kept covering a statue with layer after layer of clothes. Eventually, the statue itself would disappear from view.

Then again, we might say, who cares what Aristotle or Tasso thought? Certainly William Shakespeare didn't. When his play *Henry VI* became a hit, he wrote not one sequel but three. His *Henry IV* plays inspired two sequels. And, as legend has it, when Queen Elizabeth complained that Shakespeare shouldn't have killed off the comic character Falstaff, he simply brought him back to life in *The Merry Wives of Windsor*.

As for the various media in which comic book heroes appear, the fan is encouraged to integrate all stories into a stable and coherent lore. Let's remember that Kryptonite was first introduced not in *Superman* comics, but on the *Superman* radio series; Spider-Man's foe the Kingpin was not introduced in a *Spider-Man* comic, but on the animated TV series. Further, many of these characters remain remarkably stable in their "backstory"— in fact, the comics often meticulously trace prior appearances, which they detail in helpful, almost scholarly footnotes. Daredevil, for example, might run into Spider-Man and say, "I haven't seen you since we both fought Kingpin," to which the helpful editor might add the following: "As seen in *Spider-Man* #124." Another example: When Frank Miller decided that he wanted to kill off a fairly minor character like Daredevil's sometime love interest, Karen Page, he had to have the approval of Marvel editor Joe Quesada, who had to consider how the death of one of Marvel's characters would affect the larger Marvel Universe. And as for not aging, well, *no* character in literature ages beyond the confines of the text. Further, Aristotle is often misread on the problem of a character's growth; it is not necessary that a character cultivate wisdom. It is the reader who must suffer into truth, who must age, experience, mature, gain and grow in wisdom by reading and reflection.

Some will doubtless say that by bringing Aristotle, Tasso, and Shakespeare into the discussion we're taking comic books too seriously. But comic book readers are serious about comics. And, as we will argue, comics offer serious intellectual arguments on the problems we all face. After all, the comic book world *is* our world. It has the same problems—crime, drugs, racism, nationalism, commercial exploitation — and offers ideological solutions to these problems. Our first chapter, for example, looks at Marvel's attempts in the late 1960s and early 1970s to broaden its comic book line to include African-American heroes. While there were economic and perhaps even altruistic interests at the heart of this project, the result was often a kind of apartheid: black heroes for black villains. Chapter 2 shifts to the comics' varied responses to the brinkmanship of the Cold War and the end game we now refer to as *glasnost*. Our next chapter looks at the comic industry's take on capitalism. Both recent Batman and Spider-Man movies have argued that with great power comes great responsibility, but in terms of business practice, are we talking about a responsibility to the workers or to the shareholders? Chapter 4 traces the concept of the superhero to the philosopher Nietzsche. His superman, however, lacks the restraint of the hero and more closely resembles the typical supervillain. Exploring the concept of the alter ego, we'll argue that what makes the hero truly super is his moral strength, not his muscular articulations. Our next chapter looks at the recent *Daredevil* movie and asks what responses the comic industry had to the tragedy of September 11. In our seventh chapter, we look at prisons in the comics and wonder how they influence the ongoing debate concerning capital punishment. In out conclusion, we ask you, the reader, to join us in a crusade against illiteracy — our weapon of choice, the comic book. To that end, each chapter contains a series of questions and assignments that we hope will stimulate further reading, writing and discussion both within and outside of the classroom.

Interesting? Maybe. But we know that you don't buy *Batman* to argue about the Cold War; you buy Batman to enjoy the adventures of Batman, and we'd be making a mistake to forget that that fact. We want to discuss serious topics here, but we're also excited and moved by the adventures of these heroes. Comic books are visual, violent, and sexy because they are supposed to be. They are also serious, because they are supposed to be. And they are made to be read, because they are books. In the words of Stan Lee, "'Nuff said."

1

Black Heroes for Hire: Serializing Social Construction in the Comics

The comic industry is going through increasingly radical change. In this chapter, we will consider comic books in the context of social struggles. Comic book authors have aggressively used their heroes to address such issues as racial injustice. We will examine the assumptions behind this approach and reconsider the wisdom of its application. From our perspective, using superheroes to argue for equality is misguided, for in comic books the very idea of the superhero presupposes racial purity and ethnic inequality. Our focus will be on two of Marvel's earliest black heroes, Luke Cage and the Falcon.

Stanley Lieber was the teenage cousin of the wife of Martin Goodman, publisher of Timely Comics. He entered the family business in 1939, one year after the debut of Superman in *Action Comics* #1— a copy of which sold at auction in July 2002 for $46,000. Lieber's first Marvel publication was a two-page filler in *Captain America* #3. He signed the piece "Stan Lee," "because," he said, "I felt someday I'd be writing the Great American Novel and I didn't want to use my real name."

The fact was that in the 1930s and '40s, many Jews changed their names in an effort to ease their entry into the American melting pot. So Lieber's decision to become "Lee" was not only common, it was all but necessary. Nonetheless, when Lee became the creative center of Timely, renamed Marvel Comics in 1961, he moved to enlarge the ethnic dimensions of comics. For example, when designing *Sgt. Fury and His Howling Commandos*, a group of G.I.s fighting the Nazis in the Second World War, he consciously wanted to create a diverse ethnic platoon: "There was a black fella named Gabriel Jones; there's a Jewish soldier named Izzy Cohen; an Italian, Dino

Manelli; and on and on…. There shouldn't have been a way in the world that this book got made."[1] Despite the fact that Gabriel Jones had no "speaking lines" in the issue, and so remained a background character, the move was groundbreaking. Let's recall that American forces during that campaign had no soldiers of color serving with whites. Lee was not only rewriting the Second World War, he was repainting the Red, White and Blue to include the color black. Other black heroes followed, most notably the Black Panther (created 1966), a character who appeared as a member of an ethnically diverse superhero group, The Avengers.

The first black Marvel hero to get his own series was *Luke Cage: Hero For Hire*, developed in 1972. Luke Cage's origin has surprising affinities with those of Captain America, the signal superhero of the Marvel line. In the 1941 debut of *Captain America*, a sickly, blond-haired 4-F recruit, Steve Rogers, volunteers to take a super-soldier serum. It gives him huge muscle mass. He uses his powers to fight the Nazis and, later, to defeat supervillains and common thugs, both in America and around the world. Luke's surroundings are perhaps less grandiose than the front lines in France, but the story is pretty much the same. Instead of being in an army camp, Luke is in jail; he is offered a serum in exchange for a lesser sentence. Luke accepts. He gains super strength, but rather than sitting in a cell, he tears through the walls to freedom and revenge.

A Black Hero or a Black Clown?

Luke's return to society, then, is decidedly hostile. Has American science created yet another supervillain, one with whom Captain America will have to deal? It certainly looks that way when Luke prints up business cards and offers his super-strength services to the highest bidder. This development seems serious, but early on, Luke is framed in comedic terms. In issue #2 (1972; Goodwin/Tuska/Graham), he is in a phone booth, checking his pager service: "This is Cage. Any messages? Client cancelled out 'cause I haven't been able to get together with him yet? Crud! Answerin' service alone ain't makin' it. Gotta get me an office." When two thugs interrupt the call, intent on ridding the world of Luke Cage, the hero's biggest complaint is that he has "[l]ost fifty cents." But his luck soon changes for the better when he meets beautiful Claire Temple, a physician, who catches the obligatory superhero show of bullets bouncing off his chest. When she asks what a superhero like him is doing in a bad neighborhood like this, Luke

1. *Stan Lee's Mutants, Monsters & Marvels*, dir. Scott Zakarin (Columbia Tristar Home Video, 2002). As late as 1981, Gabriel Jones was given no more than a line or two, and that one usually racially derogatory, such as, "Man! This sure beats tootin' a bugle all hollow!" (*Sgt. Fury and His Howling Commandos* #181; Lee/Kirby).

modestly observes that, in New York, "you can't turn around ... without bumpin' an Avenger, or the F.F. [superhero organizations], or something." Astutely, Claire replies that superheroes, who are all white, serve only white areas. "Super-types don't usually move in my circles," she says, "but since you have, let me at least treat your bruises."

Bruises can heal; affording a decent costume is a more pressing concern. In issue #2, Luke searches for a proper superhero outfit, but, as he puts it, he "can't get the bread for most of these vines." He heads to a used clothing shop, where he is offered a costume once used by the Flash: "The original owner," we learn, "got involved in a lawsuit." Even the accessories that Cage buys—a headband and a chain once employed by an escape artist—are "pre-owned." As Luke Cage comments, his act, more comedic than heroic, looks "like a parade going by."[2]

Who Owns the 'Hood?

The scene is unique in the superhero landscape. Batman is rich. Superman has a weekend getaway at the North Pole (the Fortress of Solitude), plus he earns a nice wage as a reporter. Daredevil is a lawyer. Spider-Man, always the good student, thrives on scholarships and makes money as a photographer. Iron Man's alter ego, Tony Stark, is a billionaire. Thor can drink mead at Asgaard anytime. Captain America is on the government payroll. Perhaps even more tellingly, the damage these heroes inflict on their communities presents no special economic worry, for, presumably, their communities are wealthy. Discussing the impact of destruction in an *Iron Man* comic is like Donald Trump discussing the price of a burger. If the Donald wants something he's going to get it. The price is entirely beside the point.

But this is not the case with Luke Cage. His headquarters is no Fortress of Solitude or Bat Cave. Luke rents a shabby room over a movie house that plays nothing but Clint Eastwood movies. As the building manager tells him, "If you're not Hugh Hefner ... there's facilities for livin' back here. Some of 'em even work." Cage agrees to the lease, but only after serious negotiation: "Chop ten bucks a month off the rent." So it is understandable that, when a villain attacks him in his office and Cage dropkicks himself through a wall, he's more worried about the damage to the building

2. Racial matters were to continue to invite comedic handling. In the 1990s, Marvel experimented with turning their green Hulk to grey. One would have suspected that Marvel was attempting to say that nothing, not even The Hulk, is black and white. Instead, Marvel simply turned Hulk into a neo–African American. In issue 358, entitled "Soul Man," The Hulk dresses in a pimp's suit, works as a bouncer for Vegas racketeers, and is only interested in money. See our Chapter 7, "Comics and the Prison System."

Tight on money, Luke Cage goes to a costume shop to get his superhero outfit. (By permission of Marvel Comics.)

than the damage to his health. "I been wantin' to fix the plaster in this spot anyway." The problem is, he's going to wait a long time. His white landlords have made it clear that if there is any damage, Luke will have to foot the bill. Thus, in the context of urban racial conflict, although "property" and "turf" may overlap, they are by no means the same thing. Even if Cage and the "brothers" control the turf, the whites still own the 'hood.

The "turf" motif is demonstrated perhaps best in issue #5 (1972; Englehart/ Tuska/Graham). As the story opens, a fight breaks out in a cinema. On the screen, we see an old western, in which a white man pistol-whips an Indian; in the theater itself, we see a white man bludgeoning a black man. How does Cage impose a sense of reason on this seemingly absurd instance of life imitating art? He beats the white who pounds the black man, but he's powerless to stop the film. Is the comic book arguing that racial violence is learned, and that Hollywood — and indeed, the comics themselves — have much to answer for, or is it implying the historic inevitability of white power and minority oppression?

To explore this double stream of action further, we might begin by considering the movie playing in the theatre — a Clint Eastwood western. Known in the seventies for his outlaw personae, Eastwood explored the edgy role of the vigilante, who is at once a criminal and a hero. This ambivalence is a staple motif in comic books: Batman has an uneasy alliance with the police; Spider-Man and the Punisher are wanted men. But Cage's vigilantism is of an order quite different from those of other crime fighters. Luke is not hunted because he sends criminals to jail by any means necessary. Rather, the police pursue him because he is himself an escaped convict.

Luke Cage, Convict at Large

Luke, we must remember, broke out of jail, and he remains a fugitive. As the series evolves, we learn that Luke was framed for drug trafficking by a boyhood friend who now calls himself "Diamondback." As Cage languished in prison, he spent "night after night, year after year ... just waitin' for it, for a chance to get even." So, in the great American tradition of payback, Luke tracks down his enemy and a showdown ensues. But the violent confrontation is also tinged with some regret: Luke remembers that he and Diamondback were once "kids in Harlem duckin' rival gangs." Still, gang affiliations aside, Luke means business. In the end, Diamondback falls through a skylight, paying the ultimate penalty, not for any of his crimes, but for betraying his childhood buddy.

However, the games of youth violence are somehow less serious for superheroes and villains. Death is only a rare occurrence in the comics, and often dead heroes and villains are resurrected. In a sense, death is merely a show, even for the scripted heroes and villains. Luke knows that Diamondback will return, and Luke will have to kill or capture him yet again.

Hero or Thug for Hire?

That Marvel created a black Everyman for black readers is laudable; that they thought the average black reader would identify only with an ex-gang member and escaped con may be disturbing. Equally troublesome is the nature of Luke's "super" hero lifestyle. Little is super in Luke's life, or even heroic. Even after defeating his archrival, Luke has to hide on a rooftop because the cops, all white, have arrived. He is, after all, still a wanted man. In a confrontation with the white doctor who experimented on him and now wants to turn him over to the authorities, Luke retorts, "The law's just like that experiment of yours. Beautiful ... long as it works. Only for me.... Neither of 'em did! So I lost a hunk'a my life in a Cage — an' only got out by becomin' a freak!"

While Luke complains that science has transformed him into a monster, he doesn't deny that his new powers allow him to make a living. Even his revenge against Diamondback is partially motivated by marketing. Capturing his old friend is an opportunity, Cage believes, "to promote my Hero for Hire routine." Cage's use of the word "routine" indicates the grim,

Luke Cage stops white men from beating black men, but he can't stop the Hollywood movie, which coaches racist behavior. (By permission of Marvel Comics.)

workaday approach of socioeconomic survival in the 'hood. In issue #5 (1972; Englehart/Tuska/Graham), a beautiful woman hires Cage to investigate the death of her husband. Cage agrees to do it free of charge, but when he solves the case, he is forced to pay an informant fifty bucks. The informant demands the money from the grieving widow, who pays Cage. Throwing the money in his face, she says, "If you want money, Mr. Cage, you can have it! But, I think you're a snake!" Cage gives the money to his informant, thinking to himself, " 'Hero for Hire,' huh? What a dandy racket." Cage might make a better living simply working for drug lords.

Indeed, in issue #5, a four-hundred-pound, drug-dealing menace, Black Mariah, scolds him like a surrogate mother, "Dat's yo' weakness, Cage. You got ideals. Only fools die for ideals." Luke doesn't die; instead, he runs from the cops and earns the hatred of his clients, who conclude that he only fights crime when it pays. (Black Mariah's logic is self-evidently similar to that of Bigger Thomas, the villainous hero of Richard Wright's *Native Son* [1940]. Bigger refuses to kowtow to the rich whites he meets and joyfully embraces the role of outlaw and murderer.)

Cage, a black ex-con, pursued by white cops, is prey to Mariah's straightforward proposal. Let's both get rich, she argues, and help each other. However, her argument is also deeply ideological. Why let the whites have all the money and fun? Black Mariah admonishes Cage for picking "on folks lak dat," i.e., the black criminal subculture. He should be on their side. Instead, he seems to serve the white power structure. This point is underlined by a white journalist in issue #5 who dubs Cage the "White Knight" and comments that the idea of a black crime fighter is entertaining to readers "in Indianapolis [who] love choppin' bananas on their corn flakes while readin' about it!"

Luke Learns His Place

We have remarked upon the connection between Luke Cage's career as a crime fighter and the world of entertainment. His vaudevillian costume, his station above a movie theater specializing in Clint Eastwood films—no one recognizes the absurdity of his situation more than Luke Cage. But by issue #7 (Englehart/Tuska/Graham), grim reality overtakes what seems at first like "show biz." Luke learns his place. The story begins when Luke finds a gun in the hands of a demented war vet. Confiscating the gun, Cage explains that veterans, like blacks, should know that guns are dangerous: "Freakin' guns!—And the dudes that sent him over there [to Vietnam] to use 'em! Ain't never gonna be no peace on earth if all the small people keep tryin' to act like big people — and the big people keep tryin' to act like God!"

Cage's acquiescence to social position, of knowing one's place in the

world and not attempting to move beyond it, is an odd ideological position for a man attempting to better himself and his world. Despite this
irony, or perhaps because of it, by the next installment, Cage comes to realize that he will never be a superhero in the "Batman sense." He is a hired
hand. Luckily, he is a hired hand who likes to dish out pain, so his limitations do not preclude compensation. As he mauls a gang of assassins, he
taunts them, too: "you joyboys must groove on pain, to wanna take me on
in my own digs! Or maybe you figure I only pound for profit? Babies, long
before cards got printed, I was lookin' out for number one. 'Sides, I let five
button men take me out, lotta advertisin' goes to waste!" Beating someone
up has nothing to do with justice or freedom; money and return on adver-
tisement dollars are the issue in Cage's world.

Underscoring Cage's separation from the world of white heroes, Cage
rarely fights white villains. Instead, a whole batch of instant black villains
are created for him. These include the aforementioned Diamondback, a black
drug lord with explosive knives, and Black Mariah, a 400-pound black
woman. In addition, Cage battles Mr. Luck, a black man who kills with giant
dice and razor-sharp coins; Big Ben, a menacing black giant with superhuman strength; and Chemistro, a masked black man armed with an acid gun.
The few white villains Cage deals with come from an entirely different cultural world. For instance, in issue #7 (Englehart/Tuska/Graham), Cage
spends Christmas stopping a white madman, Marley, from exploding an
atomic bomb in mid–Manhattan. This villain speaks with an affected British
accent and vocabulary. Indeed, as Luke describes him, he seems more like
a character out of Dickens than Harlem: "[This] cat's like bad peanut brit-
tle — all nuts."[3] Later, Cage refers to him as "Shakespeare," a pejorative that
aptly suggests how foreign this white man is in Harlem. Luke Cage feels
more at home with his criminal brothers. Thus, after defeating Marley, he
hears someone coming down the chimney. It's not Santa, but a black thief.
"I been casin' this joint for weeks, so I could rip it off!" the burglar protests.
Cage catches him easily enough but, instead of turning him in, enjoys Christmas with this burglar from the 'hood.

Of course, this ethic that blacks need to stick together puts racial warriors at loggerheads with the law. However, the law of the ghetto, Cage realizes, moves beyond good and evil. If Luke obeys the law, he breaks solidarity
with his oppressed brothers and sisters; if he persists in violence, he risks
reprisal that is even more violent. This whipsaw effect is central to issue
#14 (Englehart/Graham), in which Big Ben attacks Cage for stealing "his"
woman. Even as they beat each other, they still find time to call each other
"brother"; at the same time, two of Cage's prison friends, also black, break

3. Marley is, of course, a character in Charles Dickens' *A Christmas Carol* (1843).

out of prison and decide, like Cage, to wear costumes. Cage, the escaped con-turned-hired-hood, has set the standard. In both cases, in either seeking personal justice or escaping state-instituted authoritarianism, the black man lives through his fists. Luke Cage's actions suggest that a black man's legitimacy is pegged to violence, not lawfulness.

Still, it would be wrong to think that all *Luke Cage: Hero For Hire* story arcs depend entirely on the theme of black violence. As we have already seen, Cage and Black Mariah understand the value of money. For them, the ghetto is home turf, a cultural fortification, where "equal rights" are subject to the homogenizing process of the American economic system. Cage is *paid* to fight crime and *pays* informants to help him. And he's not the only one. His enemies are similarly motivated. They too are *hired* by yet other criminals (even more powerful — always white — gangsters) to *sell* drugs, or to *steal*, and they, too, *hire* informants. Mr. Lucky, for example, hires one of Luke's own informants, a rapscallion named Flea, to find out where the Hero for Hire is. "Listen, Flea," Mr. Lucky says, "this [information] wins you a $250 credit at any of my casinos, with unlimited bar service — and there is another two-fifty if you tell Cage what I wish you to." Cage cannot blame his own informants for informing on him: "It's still a freakin' good brain, and gray matter collects more than black muscle now!" Against colorblind monetary scales, the concept of "race" is scientifically dubious. Luke understands and embraces the logic of betraying your friend for a quick buck, no matter the moral costs; fealty to green turns all skin color to moral gray.

Black Heroes and Blaxploitation Films

On its cosmetic surface, *Luke Cage: Hero for Hire* suggests the method and tone of the documentary film. That is, each issue focuses on a particular social concern or perceived value of the black community. Contemporary readers responded enthusiastically. One fan wrote:

> I have waited a long time for a superhero who could put it all together; at long last he has arrived! I can really identify with Luke Cage. Not that your other heroes aren't relevant and just fantastic (why, some of my best friends are Spider-Men!) but Luke Cage is someone special to me. He is really the first black superhero in the comics, except the Black Panther, but the Panther is always in his own world of the Wakandas, while Luke is closer to home [fan mail, #5].[4]

4. The sentiment echoes an earlier letter: "For a long time I felt two things were missing from comic magazines: relevancy and black people. Over the last couple of years, relevancy hit the industry with a gigantic impact. I got my first wish, but I never believed I would see my second. However, with LUKE CAGE, you convinced me that not all was lost" (*Luke Cage*, fan mail, issue #3).

We sense here a feeling not only of heightened identification between reader and subject matter, but also one of intimacy, which sounds almost like friendship. Fans support their heroes because their heroes speak to (and for) them.

Not all fans feel like this, of course, and at least one fan registered a faint, if well-meaning, racist rot to the Luke Cage enterprise:

> Comics have made it a habit of drawing everyone who is not white alike. When drawing blacks, you always make them ashen. Also when drawing orientals, the inkers insist on making them yellow or orange. Then there is a group newly arrived to comics, Latins, especially Puerto Ricans, are always made to look exactly like each other. You know, we come in hundreds of different shades, sizes and shapes [Judy Rivas, fan letter in *Luke Cage: Hero for Hire*, issue #5].

The complaint is not only aesthetic ("we don't really look like this"), but social. In fact, blacks, Latins, and "Orientals" are not only different from whites, as a group, but — more importantly, it seems — even more different from each other.

Certainly, there is some justification for this criticism. Marvel's attempts at a black hero were also an attempt at racial profiling, an attempt to reach out to a black comic buyer with a socially engaged product. The concept is ironically skewed, as no one can fully identify with a superhero, who is, by definition, a *super* or unique hero. Nonetheless, black comics were an attempt to do just that: to allow black buyers to see their heroes facing problems as white artists imagined the inner cities to be.

The results were often unintentionally comic. Like the Blaxploitation films of the 1960s and '70s, the world of Luke Cage is full of pimps, hookers, and drug dealers, all of whom are enamored of the most bizarre "Afro" hair styles, bell-bottom jeans, platform shoes, synthetic leopard-skin coats, wide-brimmed hats bedecked with splendiferous ribbon bands, big rings on every finger, gold chains, and bright yellow or burnt orange shirts with no buttons. Luke's language is ungrammatical, punctuated by street thug funk ("lordie-mamma") and borderline racist plantation-speak ("ain't nuttin' to it"); and, even in the pitch of a life-and-death battle, Cage displays a Foghorn Leghorn-style comedic motor-mouth.

Captain America and the Falcon

We noted that Luke's origin, if not his background, was, in many respects, much like that of Marvel's oldest character, Captain America. While the similarities to Captain America's origins are obvious, we should also keep Cap's position as the self-proclaimed "Sentinel of Liberty" in mind. Cap differs from Luke in terms of means and aims: one is interested in freedom, the other in cash; one lives in a mansion, the other in a tenement; one fights sophisticated supervillains, the other beats on inarticulate thugs. Luke Cage bills himself as a "Hero for Hire," but economic circumstances cast him as the "Hood from the 'Hood for Hire." However, Luke's true mirror is not Captain America, but Cap's black partner, the Falcon.

The Falcon and Drugs in Black and White

The Falcon's origins are complex and, like Luke's, are tied to the drug trade. Captain America was captured by his arch-nemesis, the Red Skull, a Nazi he's been fighting since the Second World War. (Cap was frozen in suspended animation for much of the '40s and '50s, a point of importance to which we will return in a later chapter. The Skull's age is simply taken for granted; he seems to be running on pure hate. Don't look for realism everywhere!)[5] In *Captain America* #117 (1969: Lee/Colan), the Skull uses the power of a device called the "Cosmic Cube" to torture Cap. First, he transfers consciousness with Cap, locking him in the body of the Skull, while the Skull uses Cap's body in a long carouse of New York. Meanwhile, Cap, locked within the Skull's body, is marooned on Skull Island and tries to escape assassins at every turn. One of those assassins is a drug dealer named Sam or "Snap." As the story progresses, Cap befriends Sam, teaches him how to fight, and enlists him in his war with the real Red Skull.

Why has the Skull bothered to bring Sam to Skull Island, if Cap can so readily enlist him? The rationale only comes out in a subsequent issue, when the Skull turns Sam, now called the Falcon, on Cap. In fighting to overcome the Nazi's control, Sam "snaps" into his own consciousness and defeats the Skull. Now fully in control of his mind, the Falcon confesses to Cap that he has lead a life of crime. Unlike Luke Cage, however, the Falcon, on Cap's advice, turns himself in. The authorities release him into Cap's custody. Cap continues to train the Falcon, and, together, they fight crime for the next 150 monthly installments. The Falcon's last meaningful story line is in *Captain America* #232 (1979; DeMatteis/Zeck; the Falcon stopped getting co-billing in *Captain America* #222), where his Sam/Snap days come back to haunt him. Put on trial for his past crimes, Sam is found guilty. He won't go to jail, but only because Cap makes him promise that he will give up fighting crime in tights. Sam agrees to drop the costume,

---

5. However, in an alternative universe, the Red Skull passes on his legacy of hate to his son, who looks the same and has his father's name. See *What If* #38 (1983; Margopoulos/Reed/Esposito). For more on Nazis in Marvel comics, see our Chapter 2, "Comic Books, Cold Wars and Desert Storms."

but continues to fight for what he believes in, first becoming a social worker and eventually running (unsuccessfully) for Congress.

The irony is that Captain America, who is supposed to oversee the Falcon's rehabilitation, is himself the product of the drug culture.[6] Remember, Steve Rogers, skin and bone, but blond and blue-eyed, was given a super-soldier serum so that America could finally defeat the Nazis. The experiment was a success, but before the American scientist could make more of the serum, a Nazi assassin killed him and destroyed the lab.

Nevertheless, the Nazi himself must have approved of the American efforts. The ideology is pernicious and unmistakable. The Nazis believed in the superiority of blond-haired, blue-eyed Aryans—Nordic types on whom the Master Race would be constructed. But, in a twist on the Space Race joke, "Our German scientists were better than theirs," the Americans defeat the Nazis with the mirror image of the "perfection" toward which their racial theory aimed. Steve Rogers wraps himself in the insignia of American patriotism, but he looks like a poster boy for the Hitler Youth.[7]

America forwards Hitler's dream to develop the Master Race by a typically American means: the short cut. Representing a nation known for its creativity and utilitarianism as much as for its so-called democratic freedoms, Captain America expresses one variation of the prototypical American Dream: a get-rich-quick scheme for the body. It is no surprise *Captain America* comics often carried Joe Wieder advertisements promising instant muscles from a milkshake. If the Falcon tried to get rich quick by selling drugs, American males, including Captain America, are all too willing to buy steroid-like products to improve their bodies.[8]

Of course, the drugs Sam sold don't offer the same rewards as steroids. Steve Rogers' drug offers tangible and permanent power in this world; Sam's cocaine offers only temporary escape from its stresses and strains. However, in a larger sense, the two forms of drugs work in symbiosis. Steve Rogers' drug allows him to beat up anyone who disagrees with the American agenda, which seems to include fighting inequality abroad and embracing inequality at home. Sam's drug allows the oppressed to adapt to that agenda of discrimination. Steve Rogers' American Dream might sound like an inviting drug, but Sam's cocaine is the only opiate allowed into the criminalized ghettos. This aspect of the American Dream/Nightmare is high-

---

6. Jesse T. Moore analyzes DC Comics' discussion of ghettos and drug culture in *The Green Lantern*. See "The Education of Green Lantern: Culture and Ideology," *The Journal of American Culture* 26.2 (June 2003), 263–78; esp. 268–73.

7. The Germans eventually master the formula as well, creating the man-and-woman team Master Man and Warrior Woman. See *The Invaders* #17 (1977; Thomas/Robbins and Springer).

8. One could say that, long before we had *24 Hour Fitness Centers* on every block, *Captain America* comics were well situated to accommodate American males' desire for masculine enhancement.

lighted in *Captain America* #153–56 (1972; Englehart/Sal Buscema), a complex story arc that involves not one but *two* Captain Americas.

The Two [Captain] Americas

After the Second World War, the first *Captain America* series ended. But in 1964, Marvel Comics brought him back in a cliffhanger of a story, related in *Avengers* #6 (Lee/Kirby). It's 1944 and Captain America faces apparent doom at the hands of Baron Zemo, who has armed a U-2 missile with an atomic warhead. Zemo comes back in *The Avengers* #6 (1965; Lee/Kirby); don't these guys ever die? Tied to the missile is Captain America's original sidekick, the youthful white boy, Bucky Barnes; he is the prototype for Robin: weak and always in need of rescue. The missile launches, but Captain America, using his super-strength thighs, leaps on, desperate to save his chum. The bomb detonates and Bucky dies. Miraculously, Captain America, unconscious but otherwise unharmed, falls into icy waters. His body floats northwards, and he is presumed dead. Twenty years later, the superhero team, The Avengers, finds Captain America preserved in a block of ice and successfully defrosts him.

Although much has happened in the two decades Captain America spent in suspended animation, he readily adjusts to the America of the 1960s. Of course, America had moved on considerably. The 1960s were a period of massive social unrest and the beginning of the end of the American illusion of supreme moral authority. Cap is a throwback, a man who represents a bygone era of racism. Whereas Steve Rogers was a recruit in an army that would not let him serve with blacks, the revived and revamped hero takes a black man as a partner. Never mind for the moment that the Falcon, like Luke Cage, is still stigmatized with a variety of bigotries that leave him a second-class hero, if not citizen. The point is that the Falcon was created not to have blacks identify with him, but to erase the racial injustice of America's past.

It's not just the Second World War which gets a whitewash. In reviving Cap in 1964, the company stated that he had been frozen for twenty years. In point of fact, this was not true: *Captain America* comics continued in the 1950s. This time Cap and his sidekick, Bucky, went around the streets of American inner cities saving white youth from the evils of "Mary Jane"— usually sold by black men — or from the evils of communism, an ideology that nominally embraced desegregation and equality.

The question is, how to reconcile the two Caps?[9] Moreover, if the "real" Cap was frozen in ice during this period, who was the man under the mask

9. In 2002, Marvel made things more complex by again rewriting Cap's past. Now, instead of one Cap replacement, the number was raised to three. See *Captain America* #4 (Brubuker/Epting/ Lark/D'Armara).

in the 1950s? And what happened to this second Cap and Bucky? The problem is solved in *Captain America* #155–6 (1975; Englehart/Sal Busema). In a significant flashback, we learn that after the war, American scientists feverishly worked to recreate the super-soldier serum they had given to Steve Rogers. Marvel's writers, tinkering slightly with the original premise, gave us a Steve Rogers dosed with gamma radiation, a technique that saves the patient from turning into a lunatic. We learn, moreover, that the second Captain America takes not only one shot of the super-soldier serum, but secretly takes a second dose as well. He also shoots up Bucky with the serum; the original Bucky had no super strength other than boyish ingenuity. Neither the new Cap nor the new Bucky take the healing gamma bath. This duo is far stronger and far more aggressive than the original Cap and Bucky — a necessary evil in the ongoing battle against troublemakers who take the Bill of Rights as literal truths. Predictably, they beat up blacks and Jews as well as communists. Finally captured by the authorities, who don't know what to do with them, they are cryogenically frozen until rediscovered in the 1970s. However, whereas the "original" Cap had no trouble fitting into the 1960s, these two are shocked by what they see and go about trying to turn back the racial clock. Meeting the Falcon, Bucky disdainfully calls him a "darkie" and tells him to get "back to the jungle." The Falcon, who has survived in the concrete jungles of American inner cities, will defeat Bucky, with the help of Captain America's girlfriend, the beautiful secret agent Sharon. But the real showdown is between the 1950s Cap and the revamped original. The '50s Cap is stronger, but the '60s Cap does not win simply because he is a better fighter. As he explains, he is the true heir of America's red-white-and-blue freedom, a freedom for all. As the realization dawns in the eyes of the '50s Cap that his world is gone forever, he lunges into a powerful round house that knocks him straight into a monument built to Holocaust survivors.

It all sounds rather moral and uplifting. A more racially tolerant Captain America repudiates his more racist namesake. America, it seems, has moved on. Or has it? Even in this narrative we sense a continued racism: Cap defeats his ersatz 1950s replacement, but it's still white guy against white guy. As for the Falcon, he's left to fight a boy and needs the help of a woman to beat him. Even in this egalitarian world, we can see the implicit injustice. We don't let male boxers into the ring with female fighters or allow boys into the ring with men. Why, then, is the Falcon matched with a child, and why does he need the aid of a woman to beat him?

Captain America and White Power

Admittedly, some readers complained that this 1970s Captain America was nothing but a liberal softie and a wimp:

Captain America continues to fight racist Nazis in 2005. (By permission of Marvel Comics.)

... a new day seems to be dawning! Comics are becoming FUN again!
In Captain America #42 Cap was his old self, and he was kicking commie
butt.
    My only recent complaint is Cap crying at Arlington. Come on! Drop the
"sensitive nineties man" garbage. The guy was born when Calvin Coolidge
was President, and he came of age during the Depression before fighting in
World War II. He shouldn't be portrayed as Phil Donahue in spandex!
[Michael Johnson, fan mail in *Captain America* #47, Nov. 2001].

That real men don't cry is, we suppose, a belief widely held in some
circles, and it is one to which we will return in a later chapter. But what of
the related charge that that Captain America — and, by extension, the Marvel imprint — is politically "liberal"? As we have seen, Marvel did attempt
to reach out to minorities, stressing justice and equality for all. Much of
the equality, however, was apartheid-like, involving separate but equal
heroes trapped by socioeconomic realities in their inner city slums— black
villains who fought black heroes, a black-sized problem for a black-sized
hero.

    Assuming that *Captain America* is the liberal *flag*ship of a company
with a liberal, democratic agenda, it behooves us to ask, just how liberal,
democratic, and egalitarian is Captain America? If Cap is supposed to confront and defeat the darker underside of America's past, he has little long-term effect. Within ten issues of defeating a 1950s Captain America, our
hero is battling his old Nazi enemy, the Red Skull, who now uses American skinheads as recruits. "My whole life," Cap complains, "I've been fighting Nazis. But these are American Nazis. Makes me sick."

    The resourcefulness of the Neo-Nazis to appeal to racist America is the
substance and theme of *Captain America* #264 (1981; DeMatteis/Zeck). In
a storyline very much like the earlier Skull-Cosmic Cube arc, Captain America and the Falcon find themselves caught in a mind control experiment
that causes everyone to believe they are living in the 1940s. For instance,
Steve Rogers finds himself getting a five-cent shoe shine from Sam, who
obligingly tells him, "I sho' am glad to see y'all, today, Massah Roguhs—
you knows you is mah fa-vo-rite cumstomer!"

    As Rogers realizes that something is seriously wrong, a passerby kicks
Sam, shouting: "Out of my way, you black animal!" The nightmare landscape intensifies, with Nazis suddenly appearing on American streets. Steve
and Sam change into their superhero outfits and begin investigating. A
Nazi sees the Falcon and shoots him in the back. Cap reacts with verbal
and physical explosiveness. Cracking the killer's jaw with a jabbing
"WHOOMP!" Cap says, "You animals! You no good stinking animals! You
killed one of the finest men that ever lived! Do you hear me, animals?"
Don't worry; Sam is safe enough. It's all just a dream, after all, but it's Cap's

words more than his actions that concern us here. Cap might be "justified" in seeking revenge for his friend and partner, but his language echoes the Nazi who kicked Sam in the streets. Even in the best of Captain Americas, there is an anti-humanist tendency to see the enemy as subhuman.

Thus, for all his patriotic lip service, Cap's own brand of multiculturalism seems to be distressingly limited. Cap seems fine in walking down a street that has falafel and dim sum; he is equally casual in meeting heroes who wear odd colors or come from different planets or even dimensions. Some of Cap's best friends are robots. As long as they think like Cap, there's no limit to his tolerance. But just how willing is he to allow humans to create their own forms of political systems before branding them "animals"? We're not arguing that Cap should look the other way when injustice presents itself. Nonetheless, Cap's ideas of liberty are at odds with his championing of democracy: The former allows people to set their own course; the latter only allows freedom within set political parameters. When Nazis or commies get in Cap's way, they express anti–American and, thus, inhuman, values.

Small wonder that on at least two occasions, homegrown American hate groups themselves tried to recruit Captain America. At the end of *Captain America* #156, we learn that the '50s Cap and Bucky are refrozen until medical science can cure them of their socially backwards mentality. This scenario presents the American Dream in another guise, politics solved through science. Unsurprisingly, this version of Cap and Bucky is once again defrosted, this time by American Neo-Nazis.[10] Even the revamped, politically-correct Captain America is eventually used as a political pawn of the far right. In *Captain America: Sentinel of Liberty* #8 (1999; Waid/ Hamner/Massengill), the Falcon recalls one of their early encounters with hate groups. It was 1969, the summer of Woodstock, the summer of Love, and in Harlem, the summer of race riots. Breaking up the riots, the Falcon fights side by side with Captain America. But the Falcon notes that there "wasn't a WASP in the bunch [they were fighting] — and don't think my neighbors didn't notice — and didn't judge me by the [white] company I kept."

The Falcon concedes that, from the point of view of the ghetto, he is not Captain America's partner but his "token" sidekick. This perception aids the Neo-Nazi "Sons of the Shield," who find the Falcon's subservience to Captain America in line with their racial cause. Their leader, John Mason,

10. The '50s Bucky, a.k.a. Jack Monroe, is secretly rehabilitated and becomes the hero Nomad. However, Nick Fury still calls him "the crazy one." Further, he's been brainwashed a few times into being a Punisher-type villian called the "Scourge." In this guise, he has killed a few customed villains. On the question of whether this makes figures such as Monroe a villain, see our chapter on comics and the prison system.

explains: "Captain America and the Sons of the Shield are on the same team. We're allies. We both work to show the people how a white America is a strong America.... He [Captain America] stands for the values established by our country's founders—not by immigrants." Although Captain America registers proper indignation at Neo-Nazi tactics, we find him soon after trying to stop an angry black mob from killing the white supremacist. In the ensuing battle, a black man, armed with a sophisticated weapon, shoots the American superhero. Captain America is dead! The Falcon is understandably shocked. But even before he can respond in anger, the Sons of the Shield declare Captain America a martyr to the cause of white supremacy.

Red, White, and ... Black?

With Cap dead, Sam gives up the Falcon costume and puts on a replica of Cap's outfit. A *black* Captain America? From the ghetto, there is only outrage. How dare a black man wear the colors of a white supremacist? But the Falcon holds his ground. "I promise you," he says, "I will not rest until our streets are safe again! America belongs to all people — not just the white supremacist! This is my home — This is your home — This is our home." In effect, he wraps himself in the flag as if to declare himself the protector of all America. But, as we have already suggested, in the ghetto, this perception has its challengers. One, Ajanii, a militant bomber, insists that changing costumes doesn't change the realities of the country's racial divisions: "Yeah, preach it to the Statue of Liberty, Uncle Tom." Even the Falcon concedes that his new costume doesn't fit very well. "Cap," he admits, "protects the country. Falcon protects [only] the 'hood."

Of course, Captain America is not really dead. The white supremacists have staged his death and taken him captive. Now under their mind control, he trains Neo-Nazis in the arts of hand-to-hand combat. Meanwhile, Sam, attired as Captain America, confronts him. This encounter between the two Captain Americas, one white, one black, is brief and violent. Sam breaks the supremacists' hold on Captain America but nevertheless observes that, while the white Captain America enjoys the benefit of the super-soldier serum, he himself is a normal black man. This admission is damaging. Sam has no super strength.[11] He *is* inferior. He *is* and will *never be* more

11. In January 2003, Marvel published *Truth: Red, White and Black* (Morales/Baker) in which we learn that the government first tested the super-soldier formula on unsuspecting black soldiers. The evil Army scientist in the comic baldly declares: "It's necessary to see if our methods apply to the inferior races." In early tests, we see the terrified solders one by one injected. Some balloon and even explode, the laboratory walls splattered with blood. Only one soldier survives the experimentation. As for the other black soldiers spared the ordeal, they are executed to keep

The Falcon becomes the black Captain America but is accepted by neither whites nor blacks. (By permission of Marvel Comics.)

than a sidekick. If Sam believes in his inferiority, then the Sons of the Shield have won their propaganda campaign. As the issue closes, Sam resumes his traditional Falcon apparel and returns to his secondary role of fighting crime in the ghetto. Looking out at Harlem, he proclaims: "I'm back where I belong."[12]

At this point, readers might reasonably infer that, while the Sons of the Shield have lost control of Captain America, the loss is not so great. In

the project secret. Said writer Robert Moralas: "Germany got their eugenics ideas from us. We were way ahead of the curve there. America, England, and a couple of other northern European countries were really into eugenics. Also, along those same lines, one of the really interesting things when you look back at the time period is just how comparatively racist and classist everybody was back then." "Post Mortem — *Truth: Read, White and Black.*" Newsarama.com. http://www. newsarama.com/forums/showthread.php?s= &threadid=6737

12. Implicit racism is also part and parcel of DC Comics' *Green Lantern* series. After Hal Jordan's death (See Chapter 6), ensuing issues were devoted to a series of new Lanterns: a surfer-dude, Kyle Rayner, an African-American from Detroit, John Stewart, and a teenage beauty, Jennie Lynn Hayden (*aka* "Jade"), who dates Kyle. A token appointment, John runs the Corps in American inner cities, but Jade conducts global campaigns—when and if Kyle is off somewhere even more important. We note, however, that in *The Justice League* animated TV series, John gets to fight intergalactic foes as well.

fact, the Neo-Nazis don't need him anymore, because the Falcon is happy to stay among his own people. And who can blame him? Even Captain America must feel more at home in one part of the country than another. The point is that Captain America and the Falcon see America in fundamentally different ways. Cap may believe that all men are created equal, but Neo-Nazi science made him stronger than anyone else; he may argue that everyone has the same freedoms, but he is a government employee who never has to worry about rent, car payments, or paying for damaged property; he may want freedom for all, but to achieve that end he repeatedly emphasizes that might makes right. The Falcon, on the other hand, is closer to Luke Cage. Both Luke and the Falcon recognize that "their" people need more protection, not just from supervillains, but from white authorities as well. Cap may defend existing freedoms, but the Falcon has to fight for ethnic prerogatives that do not yet exist. Of course, one may argue that since Cap and the Falcon routinely work together, the series does demonstrate the harmonious social interaction of racial groups. Yet nothing can be more ludicrous than Captain America and the Falcon fighting side by side for peace in the streets by bashing in the heads of blacks who are protesting a parade of Neo-Nazis.

The Falcon's Short Solo Flight

Even when Marvel's writers were promoting the Falcon, they implied that he was best left in the ghetto. In *Marvel Team-Up* #30 (1974; Conway/Mooney/Colletta), Spider-Man, framed for murder, hides in the one place the police are unlikely to look for him — in the ghetto. Encountering a black gang, Spider-Man promises himself that he won't use his full strength on these weaklings. The Falcon, by contrast must give such fights all he's got. Then again, there are things that the Falcon can do that Spider-Man can't. When Spider-Man questions a black thug, he doesn't get anywhere. But the Falcon has no problem: "Spider-Man, leave it to me. After all ... I speak the language." Exactly what language is this? Some sort of African dialect, or are we to assume some sort of alliance between all blacks? If so, the implication is that the Falcon is friendly with all the criminals in the ghetto, who are, after all, his "brothers."

In 1979, the Falcon returned (*Marvel Premiere* #49; Evanier/Sal Busema) with this fulsome billing: "At last! In his own full-length adventure!" In fact, the fanfare did not quite fit the story, for Sam, who gets invited to an embassy party, spends most of the time defending Captain America from the unpleasantries of the evil Russian Count Rosoff: "A coward is what he [Captain America] is—afraid to face the truth about himself … and the hypocrisy his very costume has come to stand for." As the story unfolds, the Falcon, in over his head, is forced to run to Captain America, who, in a heartbeat, saves the day. The Falcon's own adventure reveals him to be more dependent upon Cap than ever. The tacit suggestion here is that the Falcon, a black hero, will never be truly emancipated.

In 1984, Marvel released a four-issue miniseries called *The Falcon*. Set before both his criminal trial and his run for Congress, we meet the Falcon living in New York, fighting crime in the ghettos, much as Luke did. And like Luke, the Falcon must adjust to the socioeconomic realities of not being a top-tier (read: white) hero. In the first issue (Owsley/Smith/Colletta), the Falcon stops a man in a mechanical suit from destroying a residential tower under construction. Although he defeats his foe, he is unable to capture him. Kane, the white owner of the building, arrives in a Mercedes and complains: "You got any idea how much damage that nut did? You know how much it's gonna cost? And you just let him fly off like it was okay! Couldn't you have clinked him with your batarang or something? I mean, what kind of hero are you anyway? No wonder The Avengers threw you out."

As we will discuss, The Avengers, a loose association of heroes, live by the good will of the wealthy Tony Stark, whose secret identity is Iron Man. There is an East Coast and a West Coast Avengers team. Since Captain America heads the East Coast contingent, the Falcon's affiliation is with that team. But the Falcon was (and is) not an official member of the group. So Kane's remarks are, in fact, incorrect. Still, there is no doubt that The Avengers—with their mansion, sophisticated facilities, high-tech weaponry, and national, international, and galactic reach — are culturally and economically out of the Falcon's league. Moreover, if we were to rank The Avengers by superpowers, only the Black Panther, another black hero, ranks lower than the Falcon. There is one other "weak" associate: Hawkeye, an archer. But even he carries a stunning array of weapons, and has, in fact, even beaten The Hulk (*Avenger Annual* #2, 1968; Roy Thomas/Heck/ Roth/ Colleta).

Nor is Kane the only one who thinks of the Falcon as a second-class hero. In issue #4 (1984; Owsley/Bright/Gustovitch), the Falcon does battle with a notable adversary of Spider-Man: Electro, an energy-hungry villain who drains electrical systems, converting their juice into fiery electric bolts. The Falcon, equipped with only a flying suit and a pet bird, is clearly outclassed. Electro easily sucks the power out of the Falcon's flying suit and then comments derisively: "Falcon, you are truly pathetic, amateurish, sophomoric, ridiculous." Later, when he refers to the Falcon as "boy," the racial slur seems almost superfluous.

If the Falcon is a joke to supervillains, his alter ego, social worker Sam, is just as pathetic to the gang members he counsels. After urging gang members to stop committing crimes, he feels good about his work. But then, at a gang parade in which the brothers show their colors, the police kill a gang member, and the gang turns its back on Sam. Even when Sam returns as the Falcon, they are unfazed. Gang leader Xeon thunders, "My best friend is dead 'cause of you, man. You set us up. You got us to believe in your law 'n'order jive, and then set us up for this…! And now you come flyin' in like Mary Poppins of the ghetto, an' make like nothin's goin' on…! It's over, man. The Legion played it your way. Now we'll play it ours."

To make matters worse, the white cops hold the Falcon in low esteem as well. His only ally is Tork, an undercover cop, and even he complains that the Falcon is soft on crime. "Truth is," he says, "you're so big on forgivin' 'cause you've never forgiven yourself. Remember those days … we called you 'Snap' back then. You used to sell drugs to little darlings just like this [*pointing to gang member*]. Remember? Like lookin' in a mirror, huh, Falc?" By the end of the miniseries, the Falcon does rescue President Reagan from the clutches of The Legion, and he also saves Captain America from Electro. But no matter how much crime the Falcon stops, there is always someone to remind him, and the reader, of the inescapable fact that Sam is an ex-felon.

Like Luke Cage, the Falcon finds himself torn between black and white perceptions of himself. He identifies with his people, who seem to be inclined to criminal behavior, yet he longs to join a white world that defines him as strictly second-class. Even the pace of the miniseries suggests his inferiority. Three and a half issues are devoted to the Falcon's shortcomings, and only half an issue to his resurrection. Xeon, the gang leader, sums his situation up succinctly: "The Legion ain't cooperatin' with Sammy Falcon, the Oreo wonder." The Falcon's reply does not reflect resentment at Xeon's racial slur, but weariness of spirit: "My pride is hurt, and my patience is gone. I'm sick of defending myself."

Hating confrontation is a poor quality for a crime fighter, but it's a foreshadowing of a larger choice in the Falcon's career. As the last panels play out in his miniseries, the Falcon joins Captain America and Tork for an improbable night on the town — just how do you card a superhero anyway? But Sam does more than prefer the company of white men to his brothers: He also prefers their women.

The Falcon Moves Uptown

Sam Wilson never looks back in anger on his black brothers, and his lack of anxiety may well point out that at root he is an opportunist. In the end, he resigns any attempt to improve the conditions of "his people" in favor of improving the condition of himself. His weakness is not just money, or a better apartment, but a sexy blonde. Or, more accurately, what she represents.

The idea that Sam beds women for their symbolic value, not sexual pleasure, is akin to Kurtz in Joseph Conrad's novel *Heart of Darkness* (1899). Kurtz is a highly educated but impoverished European who is engaged to a woman of great beauty, wealth, and high social standing. In part to earn money and her respect, Kurtz goes to Africa, only to discover that at heart he is more savage than the people of the Congo. Like Kurtz's "intended," white women for the Falcon represent more than simply an outlet for sexual gratification; they are markers of social superiority, a sign that one has arrived. But as Kurtz betrays his high-minded ideals for the Congo, so too Sam Wilson, a.k.a. the Falcon, abandons the ghetto for the world of whites, with their endless money and hot blondes.

Sam's resolution again separates him from Luke Cage, who is also a lady's man, but his ladies are black. True, he has a brief flirtation with two white sisters in issue #7, but when Claire, his girlfriend, confronts him, he quickly promises to stop seeing them. Cage might be a man, but he is, as the vernacular has it, "whipped." The Falcon, on the other hand, is whipped by white men, but sleeps with their women. We first meet the blonde, white, and curvaceous Rachel as she falls from the sky. She's parachuting and the Falcon saves her after her chute jams. In issue #4, she comes to his apartment in a low-cut top, promising him a night on the town. Seductively, she notes that her "car is waiting." By flying off with the skydiving girl, who we presume has money—ever meet a skydiver who lives in the Bronx?—the Falcon, it is clear, is abandoning the inner city for middle-class America.

Black and White Clarity

The Falcon's color and class crossover may explain why black fans have never quite embraced him, and why, similarly, white fans continue to hold him at arm's length. Even Marvel Comics has an awkward time explaining Sam's criminal background. In a helpful crib sheet, the editors created a Socratic question and answer session:

LIKE HOW COME EVERYONE CALLS HIMS 'SAM'?
The Falcon's secret identity—that of the social worker Sam Wilson—is public record.

YEAH? WHY?
Due to the well-publicized trial for his past offenses as 'Snap' Wilson, the Falcon's secret identity was revealed.

HUH?
Prior to his becoming the Falcon, Sam was a small-time racketeer who called himself 'Snap' Wilson.

RACKETEER? WHAT'S A RACKETEER?
'Racketeer' is a word they used to use to describe undesirable characters who were running illegal business dealings. Like running numbers. Like drugs. Like 'protection' operations.

YOU MEAN HE WAS A CROOK.
Something like that. (*Marvel Premiere* 49, 1979; Evanier/Sal Busema)

With friends like this, who needs enemies? The uninformed interrogator may begin confused, but he ends the discussion with black and white clarity. His opposite, the informed editors, look for the least offensive word to describe Sam. But if "racketeer" is a word "they used to use," the interrogator understands who the Falcon is, and who Sam was: a crook and a drug dealer. Marvel's superheroes might have their foibles—Tony Stark (Iron Man) is an alcoholic—but a drug dealer, even an ex-drug dealer, is difficult for young readers to embrace; place on top of that his abandonment of his own people, and his token position as Cap's sidekick, and you have all the makings of a loser.

Black Heroes and Minstrel Shows

Had sales warranted, the miniseries *The Falcon* could have been converted into a permanent comic, but with its hero betraying his black fan base, and white readers uninterested in a hero with such limited powers, it died a death of indifference. No one, white or black, cared for the direction of this series. Marvel may have allowed the Falcon to escape the ghetto, but it never again gave the character any independence, never allowed the black hero to take solo flight.

It would allow, however, for the comic book equivalent of a black minstrel show. In January 2001, Marvel brought the Falcon and Cage back and teamed them up with the Black Panther and another superhero named Black Voodoo (*Black Panther* #37; Velluto/Almond). Marvel further debased these black heroes by doing something to Luke and his friends that it had never done with its other heroes: It aged them. Captain America's super serum works to slow the aging process; he will be a handsome, vigorous, virile young male forever. But Luke, who was injected with an identical serum, has gray hair and huffs and puffs after villains, accompanied by the equally decrepit Black Voodoo. Likewise, a gray-haired Falcon soon appears, complaining of an overactive bladder. With their powers fading, these black superheroes find communal solace in their ethnicity. Having defeated an old white man—who, with his comb-over, mustache and glasses, looks suspiciously like their creator, Stan Lee (and why does it take three black heroes to beat one old white man?)—Luke Cage and the Falcon exchange ghetto pleasantries of the shiftless and unemployed:

LUKE: Sammy, you the man.
FALCON: Nah, you.
LUKE: You.

Despite their mature bodies and mannish language, it's clear that Marvel never allowed its black heroes the dignity of retirement, or even the glory of a real job.

A New Falcon or the Same Old Snap?

The Falcon returns to the fore in the mini-series *Captain America and the Falcon* #8 (2004; Priest/DiVito/Kolish). This time our star-spangled hero actually sides with the Colombian farmers growing coca plants that feed the American addicts back home. As the story progresses, we learn that the Navy is in partnership with the Colombian drug cartel. The Navy is helping Rivas, a Colombian drug lord, get his product onto American shores in exchange for intelligence on terrorism. Unlike most *Captain America and the Falcon* stories, the Falcon—inexplicably young again—is a valuable asset here, since he used to be a drug dealer. But, mysteriously, he seems to be out for himself. When he storms into Rivas' drug depot, he meets a young dealer, Tommy, who says: "You and my dad was tight back in the day, Snap. I give respect, but...." The Falcon cuts him off: "Respect. Is that what I've inspired? This is the last thing your dad wanted for you, Tommy. The very last.... This ... mess [the drug cartel] ... I helped create it." But he's apparently not as interested in cleaning it up as he is in reasserting his criminal role: He steals $300 grand from the cartel.

Let's put the theft aside for a moment. After all, it's drug money. And who knows? At this point, he might be giving it to the Colombian government. What about Tommy calling the Falcon "Snap"? Despite wearing the Falcon costume, Tommy, and nearly everyone, seems to see right through it. J. Jonah Jameson calls him "Two Gun Wilson" and "Dirty Sam," and wants to know when he's going to get a check for all the damage he's caused over the years to the *Daily Bugle*. Cap stands right next to the Falcon, but Jameson remains deferential and polite to the white hero. An issue later (#9/Priest/Bennett/Jadson), a soldier is rescued by the Falcon. Or is it Snap Wilson? The Falcon is not in uniform; he has a goatee, wears dark shades, and presides over a gang of black youths, whom he refers to as "My folk. Mi familia." This is his gang, and their dress (gold chains, baggy pants, dog tags, prison tattoos) suggests the urban rhythms of inner-city violence. As the issue goes on, the Falcon explains that he isn't like the white heroes, who are restricted by "moral codes. Love me them moral codes." Whether government agents or white heroes live or die no longer "means zip to me." Snap, it seems, is back. Cap can't believe what's going on. But the Falcon replies that he's had enough of Cap acting like he's Snap's father: "So ... Is this a big spanking or a little spanking?"

The Falcon has a point. Just how long does he have to be Captain America's Robin? He's a grown man. If he wants to commit crimes, well, he's an adult and will take responsibility for his own actions. By issue # 10 (Priest/Bennett/Jadson), the Falcon and his gang are moving up from simple drug dealing. They begin to extort a congressman, also in the employ of Rivas. In exchange for his safety, he'll now pay $10,000 a month to the Falcon's gang. By issue #11 (Priest/Bennett/Jadson), government agents are now asking Cap whether we're seeing "the guy he truly is?" Cap refuses to believe it, but, given the overwhelming evidence, he seems naïve. The Falcon is no hero.

Sam Wilson, a.k.a. the Falcon, unlike Marvel's white heroes, he is allowed to age rather ungracefully and comically. (By permission of Marvel Comics.)

Coda: A New Luke Cage?

In 1992, Marvel tried once more to get Luke Cage right (*Cage* #1–4; Azzarello/Crbam/

Villarrubia). Getting it right for Marvel was to turn their first independent America black hero into a thug. In terms of artwork, Richard Corben, famed for his sexually explicit underground art, was brought on board to give Luke a more sensual appeal. Corben restored Cage's youth but stripped him of any pretense of costume. Instead, Luke wears jeans, which he leaves unbuttoned, and a sweat suit top, which he leaves unzipped. He spends most of his time listening to his Walkman and drinking beer or having casual sex with strippers. He still does the occasional job for the unfortunate mother whose daughter was caught by a stray bullet, but most of the time he's employed by the Italian Mafia, local drug runners, or both. For fun, or to prove he still can, he beats on local teenage gangbangers and scams new ways to "make cake an' retire." Even his backstory of having landed in jail as a result of being framed by his childhood friend has been rewritten. In a flashback, we now learn that Luke really was a drug dealer — a petty one, but a drug dealer nonetheless.

Gone are Luke's wisecracks, which at least suggested a quick mind. Instead, we are presented with a grim and grimy Cage. His opening lines tell us all we need to know. "Shit happens. Everyday, in every city, on every corner. Shit muthafuckin' happens…. But if you've got Bank…? I'm your toilet paper, baby." If, in Luke's view, the world is a toilet, it is by no means a small one. This is a Cage who sees no sense in leaving the ghetto, not because there's still crime to be fought on his home turf, but because, in his eyes, there is nothing other than the ghetto. The world is dog-eat-dog, and, in the muted tones of Jose Villarrubia's colors, there is no end to the urban sprawl, gangs, drunks, and whores. Shakespeare's Coriolanus says that there is a world elsewhere, a world of possibilities. This black hero lacks Coriloanus' imaginative capacity. This rewrite does not correct blaxploitation; it merely updates it.

THINKING, DEBATING, WRITING

1. Was the Falcon betraying his people by temporarily adopting Captain America's flag-colored uniform? Can a black man be a representative of white America?

2. Think of an example in which an individual's racial background affected his or her legal status. What are your feelings about this example?

3. In your city or town, are police officers paid too little, too much, or about right?

4. Initiate a conversation with a police officer and write an essay, or make a brief statement in class, explaining how that interview altered or confirmed the opinion you have of law enforcement professionals.

5. What role, if any, did black men and women play in the victory of the Allies in World War II?

6. Are there people in the world whom you regard as "subhuman"? What makes us human?

7. Do some research on blackface and minstrel acts and compare the portrayal of color to the heroes of these comics.

8. Captain America complains, "I've been fighting Nazis my whole life. But these are American Nazis. Makes me sick." Find out of there are any American Nazi movement or on other hate groups in your state.

9. Compare American race relations in the 1950s to those of today.

10. We wrote, "Marvel may have allowed the Falcon to escape the ghetto, but it never again gave the character any independence, never allowed the black hero to take solo flight." What would Marvel have to do to establish the Falcon's real independence?

2

Comic Books, Cold Wars, and Desert Storms

As the superpowers of America and the Soviet Union grappled for world domination, comic writers turned their attention to superheroes with super powers pitted against supervillains with global ambitions. DC Comics, home to Superman and Batman, revamped its hero Green Lantern to reflect (with growing unease) America's policy of détente. Marvel Comics, on the other hand, created The Fantastic Four, who waged unceasing war against Dr. Doom and his robot armies of the East. With the fall of the Soviet Union, the United States had to adapt to a new world and new challenges, and so too did the comics.

The original Green Lantern appeared in the July 1940 issue of *All American* #16. The hero was Alan Scott, test pilot, born in Metropolis— the same town Superman would later use as his base. When Alan comes across a luminescent meteorite, he begins to hear voices; they order him to fashion a ring from the astral material, which will give him super speed and super strength. In effect, the ring will make Alan Scott's role as fighter pilot unnecessary. He will not longer have to pilot a weapon. Wearing the ring, he is a weapon.

The Lantern then uses his powers (and his poetry) to stop bank robbers, pickpockets, and the occasional space invasion:

In brightest day, in Darkest night,
No evil shall escape my sight,
Beware the power — Green Lantern's Light!

Alan Scott's idealism and aggressive assertion of right and wrong fit the times perfectly. America had just entered the Second World War, was at work on atomic weapons, and saw itself as a beacon of freedom.

The conviction that America should lead the world, by domination if necessary, is one outcome of World War II. Not only was she victorious in her war against Germany, Italy, and Japan, but America's industry was untouched by the saturation bombing of such cities as London, Hamburg, and Berlin, not to mention Hiroshima and Nagasaki. Factories in the United States were operating at full capacity and needed only to be retooled to turn out automobiles, refrigerators, televisions and other items to meet the demand for consumer goods. Even unused material from the war gave rise to Army-Navy surplus stores. With the largest economy on earth, the most powerful military force in history, and sole possession of the atomic bomb, the United States, less than a century after a civil war that threatened her very existence, now exercised unparalleled global influence. The comics began to craft a hero reflective of America's global power, an American who was an all-seeing guardian, careful to judge and quick to punish.

That golden age of American power came to an abrupt end in 1949, when the Soviets exploded an atomic device. American governmental policy rapidly shifted to reflect this severe challenge to the uniquely American sense of righteousness and inevitability. There were now two superpowers, and between them, two competing worldviews of what history would deem right and inevitable. Soon, other countries—England (1952), France (1960), and China (1964)[1]—joined the nuclear club, further complicating what had once seemed a univocal voice of reason and propriety. By the late 1960s, the mood in America had changed. She was no longer as confident about the future course of democracy. A bloody war in Korea, called a "police action," had been followed by a bloodier war in Viet Nam. Both were chastening adventures that divided the country. People began to say that World War II was, and would remain, the nation's "last singing war." Still, despite saber-rattling in Europe and in Asia, the United States avoided direct conflict with the Soviet Union and (as it was then called) Red China.

Maintaining the Peace: Intergalactic Détente

In 1959, Alan Scott was replaced by Hal Jordan. It wasn't just the hero's name that was changed. The ring's origins and powers were also re-adjusted to reflect a new mission of intergalactic peace. In this new version, the ring came from an alien, Abin Sur, who had crash-landed on Earth. As he lay dying, Abin Sur sought a proper successor to take his place in the Green Lantern Corps, an intergalactic police force. Jordan swore to maintain peace and to fight evil in all its forms, alien as well as terrestrial. But fighting for

1. Today, the nuclear club includes also Argentina, Brazil, India, Israel, Pakistan, South Africa, and North Korea.

justice, the Lantern quickly learned, was often at odds with maintaining the peace. It can be no coincidence that *Green Lantern*'s writers came to this opinion at the height of the Cold War.

As the Cold War escalated, the world was unofficially carved up. Russia took control of Eastern Europe and exercised influence in much of Latin and South America; the United States maintained alliances with Western Europe and also allied itself with Japan and Australia.[2] China and the United States carved up Southeast Asia. The Arab and Persian nations sided with the Soviets, and Israel with the United States. Reflective of these policies, by the mid 1960s, the Green Lantern Corps, which had held a "zero tolerance" policy toward evil, lowered its standards. It would now fight for the more modest goals of order and tranquility. This meant that, tactically, the Corps accepted that autocrats and tyrants could rule some planets. Just as the Corps looked the other way to maintain the peace, the U.S. installed petty dictators in Iran, the Philippines, and much of South America. The alternative for both the world and the comics was unthinkable: nuclear war and global holocaust.

The Comics and the Cold War

It seems obvious that the comics were following American policy here. World order, however, did not mean an absence of political struggle. Through the '70s and '80s, the United States and the Soviet Union avoided direct confrontation. Accordingly, the two superpowers fought a good part of the Cold War by proxy, arming countries believed to be amenable to their causes, in particular the emerging nations of Africa. In the Congo, for instance, the Soviets sent military advisors and hardware, while its client nation, Cuba, supplied troops. The United States countered by arming rebels, and by looking the other way when South Africa and other countries friendly to the West committed human rights violations against their own peoples. Both sides had a stake in the outcome of African political struggles. Not only did the continent possess vast mineral resources, but it also straddled the rich oil fields of the Middle East and the Western democracies.

The comics of the era made their own political observations and

2. After the Second World War, Winston Churchill negotiated what became known as the 1944 "Percentages" agreement, by which America and Russia agreed to remain neutral in the former Yugoslavia, Bulgaria, and Greece. The agreement meant little: Russia instituted puppet regimes in both Yugoslavia and Bulgaria. Greece was a thornier problem. In 1944, the communists in Greece won the popular vote; the British installed troops to make sure the nation did not come under Russian control. On March 12, 1947, Russia invaded anyway. America did not go to war, but started a process called the "Truman Doctrine," which limited the further spread of communism.

pledged their own allegiances. For example, Julius Schwartz, a writer and editor for DC Comics, relates how the original "good guy" Green Lantern Guardians were all supposed to look like Israeli President David Ben-Gurion.[3] In the Marvel world, the Russian-American proxy wars were revamped in *Astonishing Tales* #6–7 (1971, Larry Lieber/George Tuska), in which the eastern armies of Dr. Doom invade the Black Panther's kingdom of Wakanda in search of vibranium, a metal with enormous strategic value.

Order and Dictatorships

During the administrations of Presidents Ronald Reagan and George H.W. Bush, the White House showed itself willing to confront its enemies. Again, the comic book registered the change in attitude. The aforementioned *Green Lantern* series was further modified. Although the Green Lantern Corps still might look the other way from time to time, in the 1980s, it was more willing to overthrow evil rulers. The shift was subtle, but nonetheless important. Moral considerations could be set aside, but they could no longer be completely ignored.

This new outlook, with its overarching attitude of a restored sense of purpose, remained in place until the first Gulf War, which began in 1990 when Iraqi strongman Saddam Hussein invaded oil-rich Kuwait. America's President Bush responded by putting together a coalition of nations to drive out the Iraqis and restore Kuwait's independence. Before that conflict was over, allied tanks rolled to within sixty miles of Baghdad. But Hussein stayed in power until, under George W. Bush, the Americans returned in 2003 with an international coalition to topple the dictator.

Like other dictators in the region, Hussein had been armed and supported, to a minor extent, by America. Why had she supported him? She knew of his use of torture, of his hatred of ethnic minorities, but the politics of that oil-rich region have never been simple, much less stable. Suffice it to say that the world economy relies on petroleum, but not every industrial nation has enough oil to meet its real or imagined needs. As a major oil exporter, Iraq was a player in the geopolitics of the region. In addition to oil, America had also to deal with Iran, which had been run by another American-supported dictator, the Shah.[4] When the Shah was overthrown by his own people and replaced by Islamic fundamentalists, the United

3. Julius Schwartz, *Man of Two Worlds: My Life in Science Fiction and Comics* (New York: Harper Entertainment, 2000), 77.
4. DC Comics did make a nodding glance to the overthrow of Iran's Shah, which took place in 1979. In *Superman and Supergirl* #28 (1980; Wein/Starlin and Tanghal), the villain Mongul rules his world with a tyrannical hand, until religious fanatics oust him.

States lent military aid to Saddam to counter the threat of Iran. A war soon developed between Iraq and Iran, and the United States, weighing Saddam against the Iranians, chose the lesser of two evils, siding with Saddam over Iran's Ayatollah Khomeini. American policy was (and, perhaps, still is) guided by the hard logic of *realpolitik*. Even when Saddam used U.S.–made weapons against the defenseless Kurds and other Iraqi dissents, America looked the other way. American interests were sustained, as long as fundamentalism was checked and the oil barrels kept rolling.

It is in this context of *realpolitik* that we return to the trend in comic books of the period. In a six-part mini-series entitled *Green Lantern: Emerald Dawn* (1991; Giffin/Jones/Bright/Tanghal), we meet a frustrated Green Lantern Corps, whose members are anything but thrilled with Hal Jordan. In a troubled galaxy, he exhibits a naïve high-mindedness, which, if encouraged, will only increase the danger of war. What Jordan needs is the check of a savvier Lantern, to show him how to create and to sustain peace. The Corps selects Sinestro as his instructor, and with good reason: Sinestro has the most peaceful, well-ordered sector in the galaxy. Sinestro explains the secret of his success: "Your only obligation is to your duty as a Green Lantern. The only concern is order."

Hal agrees to visit Sinestro's world and finds it remarkably peaceful — too peaceful. The streets are clean, the walls covered in ubiquitous posters of Sinestro. Loyal subjects call him "father"; he calls them "children." Sinestro is a tyrant, but he really does seem to believe that his subjects love him. When rebellion breaks out, he's dumbfounded: "They couldn't rise against me! I had them too well trained!" Hal replies: "Trained? What is this, a planet of seals? Those are human beings down there, or at least sentient beings." Predictably, Sinestro disagrees. He insists that the rebellion must be put down at once, preferably with brutal force: "The people need to be [re]tamed! They need to be broken." The rebels themselves have a visceral reaction to Sinestro's totalitarianism: "Orderly! Orderly! How the word has burned in our ears! How it has weighed down our spirits. I will never be oppressed by it again!"

Perhaps such rebellions are more informed by anger than by logic. Fans of Shakespeare's *Coriolanus* will recall Menenius' confidence that the mob cannot defeat the will of Rome's government. They might as well strike against the will of heaven. Yet, as Rome learns, one ignores the complaints of rioters in the street at considerable expense to the state. In the end, the citizens have their way. Likewise, in the present case, the uprising succeeds, and the Corps removes Sinestro. But, as in the Shakespearean scenario, the outcome is anything but simple, and the victory for the galaxy is dubious.

Incredibly, this uprising does nothing to dissuade the Corps from maintaining the *status quo*. As far as the Corps is concerned, Sinestro simply went too far: Yes, people need order, but Sinestro forgot that they also need at least the illusion of freedom. The confrontation ends when the Corps recruits the rebel leader, who will, through a local intermediary, now maintain order. In the process, Hal learns a lesson not intended by Sinestro's mentoring. Even though oppressed by a dictator, a population will not embrace its alien liberators. They insist on the semblance of liberty, and that illusion is enhanced by local rule, administered by people the locals consider their natural leaders.

The Lives of Millions Versus the Good of Billions

Eventually, hypocritical enforcement of its own rules leads to the Corps' downfall. When Hal's home, Coast City (a thinly veiled version of Los Angeles), is decimated by terrorist attack, he uses the power of the ring to turn back time.[5] The city is saved. The Corps, arguing that such a shift in the space-time continuum would entail negative consequences, is not pleased and demands that Hal Jordan let the people of Coast City die.

Obviously, this policy has its current, mundane equivalent. Would it be right to annihilate a foreign city to save the life of one American? Presumably not, if you're not an American. But if you are an American and you read the last question, we bet you at least considered the option. After all, even "just" American wars—the defeat of the Nazis in World War II, for example—cannot be fought without hard choices and great suffering.

Hal rejects the orders of the Corps, but not on moral grounds. His thinking is purely nationalist. So what if entire planets full of green aliens have to die so that citizens of Coast City can survive? After all, Coast City is filled with red-blooded Americans, not foreign-speaking aliens. He is a guardian of all life, yes, but a guardian of human life first and foremost. He has only one course of action. If the Corps is stopping him from saving American lives, then the Corps is the enemy.

His attack is swift. Arriving on the home world of the Green Lantern Corps, Hal steals its emerald power. The Corps fights back, but to no avail. The Green Lantern slaughters them to a man ... or rather, to a creature.[6]

Hal becomes his own Sinestro, establishing an order in which America comes first. But is it fair to see him as a villain like Sinestro? Fan

5. Green Lantern's attempt to reconstitute Coast City is chronicled in *Green Lantern* #48 (1994; Marz/Willingham/Tanghal).

6. This new, politically interventionist Green Lantern was a hit with older audiences and won industry accolades. Younger readers, however, wanted escapism in their comics. Sales fell and the concept was abandoned. Schwartz, 131.

websites regularly debate the point. Some see him as a hero, others as a traitor. The majority of fans—judging by the website registrations, all American — regularly rate Hal Jordan as their favorite holder of the ring. There is even one website dedicated to bringing him back, or at least in having the reconstituted Corps remember him with honor.[7] (Hal died in 1987, saving the earth from a solar meltdown.) These websites tell us something, we think, about the way fans see themselves and their country in the face of current dangers. Hal caused the death of thousands of Corps members and, indirectly, affected the lives of billions on an equal number of worlds. But he made these choices to save humanity, and perhaps more to the point, American lives.

This American focus is fitting. Not only are comic books largely an American invention, but, we should remember, nearly all of its superheroes were either born or live within the contiguous forty-eight states. Even Spider-Man, perhaps the most internationally revered superhero, seldom goes beyond the boroughs of New York City. Moreover, not only are these superheroes American, but their villainous adversaries are often foreigners.

Doctor Victor von Doom, Communism, and Time Travel

As noted, Stan Lee, a descendant of Jewish immigrants, created a stable of heroes, including Spiderman, Daredevil, and The Fantastic Four. These heroes all cope with serious physical or social problems: Spiderman can't get a date; The Fantastic Four's Thing is ugly; Daredevil is blind; and so on. However, Lee also created supervillains who were often equally flawed and, given their circumstances, even sympathetic. Victor von Doom, one of his most popular creations, is a case in point. The son of a Gypsy healer and witch, a youthful Victor watched as the authorities in his homeland of Latveria ethnically cleansed Gypsies and other minorities. Somehow, Victor survives, but he neither forgives nor forgets his oppressors. Raised by a man named Boris, Victor comes upon a box left to him by his father. It is filled with magical artifacts. From these remnants, Victor learns the lost Gypsy arts, which he combines with the science taught in state-run schools. He is such a good student that he earns a scholarship to America's prestigious Empire State University in New York, where, with the help of a talented faculty, he begins to experiment with time travel. It is here, in

7. That's the wonderful thing about the comics: wait long enough and every fantasy comes true. In December 2004, DC Comics began a six-issue mini-series designed to rehabilitate Hal Jordan. See our Chapter 6, "9-11 and the Man Without Fear."

America, that Dr. Doom, as he is now known, first meets the brilliant young
Reed Richards. They become fast friends and share the secrets of each other's
work.

When Richards takes a look at Dr. Doom's time machine, he alerts him
to a flaw in the design. Doom dismisses him as stupid and jealous, but, predictably, the machine explodes on its first trial run. Badly scarred from

Doom travels to the future and alternative dimensions to ensure the life, if not
liberty, of his homeland. In each time and dimension, he finds just one enemy: the
American superhero group, The Fantastic Four: (*clockwise*) Sue Richards, John Storm
or the Human Torch, Ben Grimm, also known as The Thing, and their leader, the
scientist Reed Richards. (By permission of Marvel Comics.)

burns suffered in the explosion, Dr. Doom blames Richards, accusing him of having sabotaged his work. Expelled from the university, Doom travels to Tibet, where he furthers his study of science and magic, eventually earning the title of "Master." Meanwhile, when word reaches him that ethnic cleansing in his country has begun anew, Doom takes the initiative. Fashioning a suit of armor, he returns to Latveria, where he quickly overthrows the monarchy and installs himself as absolute ruler. Putting a halt to ethnic cleansing, Doom establishes a nation of peace, if not prosperity, enforced by a stern dictatorship. Anyone who disagrees with his rule is rounded up, enslaved, or executed. America objects, but Doom, always the clever student, has robot armies and nuclear warheads. Weighing the lives of its citizens first, America backs down. Meanwhile, Doom continues his research with time travel.

Why Time Travel?

Stan Lee's script depicts an ideological war not far removed from the actual conflicts of the 1960s. While the West was primarily interested in technology, the East focused on ideology. It is true that the Soviets were first in space, but it is also true that they did not hold that edge for long. Political purges were part of the very structure of communism, and they extended into the realms of literature, art, and even science. These ideological crackdowns were based on belief in a linear history, in which capitalism would inevitably be replaced by the next logical development, namely communism, which would pave the way to a socialist utopia. This scenario inspires Doom's purely humanitarian interest in time travel.[8] A time machine would allow Doom to "fast-forward" history to an epoch after communism had inevitably defeated capitalism. The world would be spared the negative aspects of history's dialectical march: repression, mass arrests, executions, war.

Without the ability to fast-forward, however, Dr. Doom's utopia is very much a work in progress, and a bleak one at that. Everyone in his country must wear traditional livery and till the land, while he, as lord of the manor, fulfills his role as master and stern teacher. Since all that he does is for the people's ultimate good, Dr. Doom's rule is justified in his own mind. That the Latverian people resent this cruel tyranny, which is enforced through surveillance and mistrust, only underscores why Dr. Doom must adhere to the most unrelenting administrative measures.

8. In *Captain America* 16-20 (2003; Gobbons/Weeks/Paler), we learn that the Nazis were also experimenting with time travel. Perhaps the point of the story is to further ally communism with fascism.

Capitalism and a Culture of Invention

Early *Fantastic-Four* stories generally centered on the theme of Doom as thief. Repeatedly, we learn that the "good" Reed Richards invents and profits, while the "evil" Doom steals and falters. But the question remains: What choice does Dr. Doom have? He can't compete with American technology, which seems bent on destroying him. His only option, in order to fulfill his historical destiny, is to steal American (or alien) technology and turn it against the West. This pattern is repeated in numerous issues. We see it in *The Fantastic Four* #57–60 (1966–1967; Lee/Kirby), a sequence in which Doom steals the capabilities of the Silver Surfer, a peace-loving but powerful alien marooned on earth.[9] Doom uses the alien's power to set up a worldwide authoritarian regime. Unfortunately for him, the Americans destroy Doom's new power and re-establish the status quo. Similarly, in *Avengers* #156 (1977; Shooter), Dr. Doom steals an American cell stimulator, but the Vision, an android, destroys it. In an animated TV episode of *The Fantastic Four* entitled "And a Blind Man Shall Lead" (1995), Doom steals one of their primary weapons, the Fantast-i-car. This pattern is repeated in various issues. Doom steals from, or sets out to destroy, Richard's Baxter Building headquarters, the heart and soul of the inventor's intrusive technology.[10]

Doom does not limit his operations to thefts of inventions. When necessary, he stoops to common kidnapping. In *Thor* #183 (1970; Lee/John Buscema), a brilliant Latverian scientist is abducted and barely escapes Doom's country. Likewise, in *Incredible Hulk* #143–4 (1971; Thomas/ Ayers), Doom provides sanctuary to Dr. Banner at his embassy before transporting him to Latveria, where he means to harness Banner's scientific skills to produce weapons of mass destruction. Dr. Banner, of course, is also The Incredible Hulk, who loses his temper and tears the place to pieces. Similarly, in *Sub-Mariner* #20 (1969, Roy Thomas/John Buscema), Doom takes Prince Namor, Lord of Atlantis, prisoner in the Latverian Embassy. Unlike his other forays, this attempt ends in a spectacular success: Once Namor hears Doom out, he's happy to form an alliance with him.

Doom's International Alliance Against America

On the face of it, Namor, a.k.a. the Sub-Mariner, has much to gain in the partnership. The Submariner's history is filled with plenty of good

---

9. Doom is, we learn, a great surfer. Hang Ten evil master! Doom will attempt to harness the Surfer's power again in *The Fantastic Four* #156 (Mar., 1975 Len Wein/Rich Buckler), but we digress from the action-packed narrative.

10. Doom is not the only one stealing technology: In *Super-Villain Team-Up* #12 (Mantlo/ Hall/Perlin), the Red Skull steals Doom's technology. Message: Doom, a fascist, is bad, but Skull, a Nazi, is worse.

reasons to hate Americans. Namor is the son of Atlantis's Princess Fen and an American ship's captain, Leonard McKenzie. In the 1920s, McKenzie was hired by the evil industrialist Paul Destine to look for a lost underwater kingdom. Suspecting Paul Destine's motives, McKenzie decides to sabotage the mission. Stealing a small boat, he abandons Destine, only to be trapped by the ice floes caused by the explosions that he has set off, explosions that heavily damage the lost city of Atlantis. The underwater city's King Thakorr sends his mer-daughter, Fen, to investigate. The result of that assignment is just as unforeseen as the explosions themselves: The princess is captured, then falls in love with and marries her captor, McKenzie. Soon after, she leaves the human and returns to Atlantis, pregnant with Namor. Fifteen years pass before Namor catches his first glimpse of a human being. It's 1939, and King Thakorr, fearing another attack, orders his half-human grandson, Namor, to attack New York. However, shortly after he issues that order, Nazi troops attack Atlantis. So, instead of declaring war on New York, Namor signs on with a group of Western heroes, called the Invaders (later, the All-Winners Squad) to fight the Nazis.

After the war, Paul Destine returns to his oceanographic studies. By now, he is experimenting with a device that causes earthquakes, one of which destroys most of Atlantis. Namor is now king, but he hasn't forgotten Destine, whom he has tracked to New York. Namor is only a man... well, half a man, but even without his army backing him, Namor is still formidable. At peak capacity, he can lift 85 tons; he can fly for several hours at speeds of up to 60 miles per hour; and he's bullet-proof.

It may look as if Destine, at least by himself, is outclassed and outgunned. But in the interim, Destine has designed a new weapon, a ray gun, which wipes out Namor's memory. Namor, the Sub-Mariner, King of Atlantis, becomes a homeless drunk, just another victim of what President Dwight Eisenhower called America's "military-industrial complex."

Namor As American Indian

Like the hunting and gathering cultures of the Americas, Namor's way of life gives way to Western values. Alcohol takes the place of the old Atlantean ways. Eventually, Namor is rediscovered in a homeless shelter and dropped in to New York harbor. The forced immersion restores most of Namor's memories and he happily swims home, only to discover that Atlantis has been virtually destroyed by American pollution. An industrialist has been dumping toxins into the sea, which renders his people little more than zombies. In this context, these toxins appear to symbolize alcohol. We further suggest that Namor's plight mirrors those of the Indians and Eskimos, indigenous peoples thrown off their lands, hunters forced to become farmers and, plied with alcohol, thereafter dismissed as drunks. The angry prince builds a glass dome to protect his people from further toxins and awaits the day when science will enable him to cure them.[11]

Since Namor sees the West as the source of his woes, it is understandable that he turns to Dr. Doom for help. Namor and Doom agree in principle on many key issues: America uses her military and economic might recklessly; her culture is an abhorrent toxin, which enthralls with alcohol and vapid commercialism. Doom first proposes an alliance with Namor in *The Fantastic Four* #6 (1961; Lee/Kirby), but each side betrays the other — Doom is only using Namor as a diversion, and Namor, in love with the Invisible Girl, can't bear to destroy civilization. Nonetheless, as time passes, Doom and Namor grow to know and to trust each other. Marvel even made much of the negotiations between the two monarchs: In *Giant Size Super-Villain Team-Up* #1 (1975; Thomas/Sexowsky), Doom proposes an alliance with Namor and displays his new android army. But when it becomes clear that Doom is again merely using Prince Namor, the budding alliance is rent asunder. In *Super-Villain Team-Up* #2 (1975; Isabella/Tuska), Namor is taken prisoner by his most vicious enemies, Attuma the Barbarian and Tiger Shark. Doom, monitoring his capture, feels an odd affinity with Namor and decides to intervene: "Our way of life being as it is, Namor will sooner or later face grave peril — peril he will perhaps be unable to overcome alone. And when that proud prince faces his hour of deadliest peril — he shall face it — with Doom at his side!" In *Super-Villain Team-Up* #3 (1975; Shooter/Evans), Doom helps Namor defeat his foes; in *Super-Villain Team-Up* #4 (1976; Mantlo/Trimpe) Doom and Namor fight over differing ethics, but make up an issue later in *Super-Villain Team-Up* #5 (1976; Englehart/Trimpe), when Namor reaffirms his alliance with Doom.

In *Sub-Mariner* #47–48 (1972; Conway/Colan), Doom rescues Namor from yet another amnesiac stupor, and convinces him to become an ally in a war against the evil army of AIM — an army that, like its rival Hydra, is privately funded, American, and intent on taking over the world. With Doom's magic and science and Namor's control of the seas, they can, perhaps, even defeat America's most evil force: The Fantastic Four.

11. In a variation of this theme, the super group Guardians of the Galaxy, led by an American ex-astronaut, spread American values of freedom in the multiethnic future. In issue #56 (1995; Gallagher/West), they engage in a battle with Ripjack, an alien who steals valuable chemicals. It turns out they were meant as an antitoxin for a virus that destroys Ripjack's race. Surveying the copses of his extinguished race, Ripjack blames the Guardians and their adherence to their property-protecting principles: "Your over-zealous vigilantism delayed me! You Guardians bear the responsibility for this holocaust! Gaze upon what you have done!"

The Fantastic Four and the Threat
of the Global Market

To understand the importance Doom places on a defeat of The Fantastic Four, we must return to Reed Richards. We remember that Dr. Doom's experiments left him a misshapen monster. By comparison, Reed Richards is a veritable poster boy for free enterprise. As a billionaire industrialist, Reed Richards is able also to fund his own space program and to place a manned rocket in orbit. Unfortunately, the pod is bombarded by gamma rays, which have strange effects on everyone on board. Richards is turned into a rubber man. The rays transform his girlfriend (later his wife), blonde beauty Sue Storm, into the Invisible Woman. She is also endowed with psychokinetic powers. Her brother Johnny becomes the Human Torch. The pilot, gruff Ben Grimm, is hideously covered in a skin with the texture and hardness of rock, and so is impervious to most weapons. He adopts the name "The Thing." Now renamed "The Fantastic Four," Reed and his cohorts use his fortune to turn his company's headquarters, the Baxter Building, into an intelligence tower, from which his people monitor conflicts around the world and intervene when their services are needed — namely, when America's, or Reed's, interests are threatened.

Reed Richards' global reach and his fantastic wealth are not the issue. From Doom's perspective, Richards is America's *de facto* military, protecting a corporate environment on a mission of ethnic cleansing not unlike that practiced upon his Gypsy brothers and sisters. True, their methods differ. The United States doesn't round people up and shoot them. Instead, she sells people blue jeans, rap music, pornography, and cocaine. This new, urban blitzkrieg annihilates indigenous cultures, wiping away centuries of tradition and loyalty, all in the beguiling name of freedom.

From Dr. Doom's point of view, the world has to choose between mindless capitalism on the one hand, and a Doom-led world order on the other, an order, aimed at ending hunger and poverty and preserving native tradition. Thus, in *The Fantastic Four* #87 (1969; Lee/Kirby), Doom acts to prevent the destruction of serious and nationally important artwork. From our twenty-first-century vantage, the message is clear. Marvel was arguing that without Doom, Latveria would go the way of Canada, an American satellite state, complete with McDonald's, Madonna, Eminem, pornography, AIDS, drugs, and cultural decline.

One need only look at Reed's right-hand man, Ben Grimm, pilot of the doomed space mission, to see the price of Americanization. Grimm is a barbarian. Covered in but not masked by concrete, he prefers beer and burgers, and he neither understands nor tolerates anyone with different tastes. One could say that he gives the "ugly American" a bad name, in that he is ignorant and proud of it.[12] Compare Ben Grimm to Doom himself: The American is a superficial, cultural clod; the Latverian is a polymath, a statesman, a scientist, and a wizard. Doom speaks several languages and has studied in Tibet; Grimm barely speaks any language and thinks God's green earth ends in the outfield of Yankee Stadium. If we're throwing a party, or going to a lecture, an art exhibit, or a museum, we're taking Doom. We'll save Grimm for taking out the trash or knocking down the occasional wall.

Is Doom a Flawed Hero?

Doom fans (yes, he has fans) tend to emphasize his archaic and aristocratic language as proof of his intellectual superiority. He has a right to rule because he is both ambitious and sensitive to injustice. As this typical Doom monologue indicates, this critical judgment may be right on target: "All the world has turned against me. Again. Is this what I received in return for offering them a planet ... at peace? A peace to be overseen by the benevolence of Doom?" (*Doom: The Emperor Returns* #1, 2002; Dixon/Manco.)

Sympathizing with Doom, Marvel's writers turned good and evil into subjective political terms. Marvel thereby allowed its readers— some of whom were children, but the vast majority of whom were of high school and college age — to see that from another vantage, America's foreign policy was economically selfish and an obstacle to world peace. In so doing, it undertook an ideological program that was in many ways antithetical to the McCarthy brand of anticommunist fervor running through the country.

Early on, this ideological campaign was waged by giving Doom the power to switch minds with others. As Doom took over a superhero's body (another form of kidnapping), readers were encouraged to see the world through Doom's eyes, while having the continued inner monologue of Doom's perspective. Taking the body of Reed Richards, Doom walks down the streets of New York, watching Americans poison themselves on pop culture, drink and drugs. Doom cannot help but long for the day when America will be as peaceful and orderly as his homeland. Also while in Richards' body, Doom mates with Sue Richards to produce Valeria von Doom (*a.k.a.* Marvel Girl). Doom's ability to cuckold Richards may seem like an evil act; no doubt, as far as Richards was concerned, it was. Nevertheless, Sue's own version of the events suggests that Doom is in many ways a romantic, Byronic figure, a sensitive artist misunderstood by the world. Hero and

---

12. As if to emphasize the superficiality of contemporary American values, The Thing is so ugly he needs to find a blind girlfriend, but he makes sure that she is a fox.

villain, as Sue quickly learns, are largely matters of perspective. Even Reed Richards comes to the same conclusion: Trapped in Doom's armor, he begins to take on the villain's personality. Perhaps there is no such thing as a villain? Perhaps Doom is merely fighting for what he believes in.

It's clear that many comic book readers admired Doom, but Marvel came to see the value inherent in keeping Doom a despot. In *Astonishing Tales* #4 (1971; Lieber/Wood), the Red Skull and his Nazi exiles seize Latveria while Doom is on vacation in Monte Carlo. He gives up this temporary western decadence to defeat his enemies by using a shrinking ray. But the Red Skull will again seize control of Latveria. In *Super-Villain Team-Up* #10–12 (1977; Mantlo/Hall), Captain America storms the Latverian embassy to confront Doom. He fears that the ironclad dictator has formed yet another alliance, this time with the Red Skull! The Skull has been fomenting revolution by promising the citizenry of Latveria American–style democracy. With Doom's overthrow, however, the Skull reveals his true Nazi self. Yes, he will offer them democracy, the same sort of democracy Hitler gave to Germany after he won the popular vote.

To Captain America's surprise, he learns that Doom knows nothing about the Skull's latest coup of Latveria. Meanwhile, Namor returns to his kingdom to find that Doom's work crews have been wrecking the place. Namor defeats them and wonders why Doom would have backed out of their alliance so soon. He decides to pay him a visit.

As Captain America and Doom race to Latveria, more surprises are in store. The Skull has somehow accessed Doom's defense computers. Doom's jet is shot down by missiles he designed for his own protection. It looks like the Skull will win, but then the Latverians take arms against their new leader. At one point, the American hero, Shroud, counsels the rebels to show some restraint. The rebel leader replies, "Never! You cannot know how the monster [The Red Skull] tormented us—toying with us like rats in a maze! Offering us false freedoms so that our subjugation might be all the more bitter!" The Skull laughs at these peasants and their call for greater democratic freedoms: "The past is gone! Soon all men shall raise their hands to a New Order! A Fourth Reich!"

In the following issue (1977; Mantlo/Hall), the Skull and Namor have a talk. As the Skull explains, it was not he, but Doom, who ordered the demolition of Atlantis. He proposes an alliance: Latveria and Atlantis against America and her allies. Such a war is now winnable because the Skull holds Doom's greatest weapon, the Hypno-Ray—designed to turn all human minds into putty—putty to be shaped by the hands of Doom. Now this weapon has fallen into the hands of a Nazi.

As any life-long reader of Marvel Comics knows, Nazis are always the worst villains in the Marvel Universe. In fact, Hitler's ageless cronies seem to be everywhere: Red Skull and his team of evil agents, Baron Zemo, Baron von Strucker, and the brilliant but mad Armin Zola, a.k.a. the Bio-Fanatic. And then there is the one villain even the Skull and Zola bow to: the Hate Monger, who made his first appearance in *Fantastic Four* #21 (1963; Lee/Kirby). In *Super-Villain Team Up* #17 (1980; Gillis/Jones and Patterson), the Hate Monger allies himself with the aforementioned Red Skull and the Bio-Fanatic to recreate the all-powerful Cosmic Cube. As part of the process, the Bio-Fanatic uses Jewish slaves as bio-computers. They will all die, but, as the Skull notes, the Nazis "have an adequate stock of replacement parts."

When the Israeli secret agent Rachel leads a Shin Bet brigade — the Israeli equivalent of the Green Berets — against the villains' stronghold, she and her team are taken captive. Escaping, she alerts S.H.I.E.L.D., who launches an invasion of this secret Nazi island. As the paratroops begin their assault, the Hate Monger rushes to Zola's lab. Yes, the Cube is ready:

> ZOLA: ... Herr Hate Monger! What do you want?
> HATE MONGER (*peeling off his mask*): Do not call me by that stupid pseudonym! You know who I am! Now and forever, I am Adolph Hitler!

No worries concerning Hitler's age: Armin Zola has perfected a technique that allows Hitler to transfer from one specially-prepared body to another, almost at will. In 1977, Hitler was unleashed as "Nazi X", an android/genetic creation with the brain of Adolf Hitler and face of Captain America (*Captain America* #211–212; Kirby). Now reunited with the Skull, it seems that Hitler will triumph at last! But the world is saved by the Red Skull, who, jealous of his master's power, traps Hitler within the Cosmic Cube. It will not be Hitler who rules the world, but the Red Skull! So, in the Marvel Universe at least, we shouldn't see Nazism as an anachronism. In fact, its scientists are cutting-edge and its followers are always scheming to control the world. Now, with the Red Skull's control of the Cosmic Cube and Doom's Hypno-Ray, that dream is about to become a reality.

Doom and Captain America survive the plane crash and make their way to the capitol. Along their way, Doom espies one of his old retainers, Boris, now in chains. When Doom swears revenge, Captain America is surprised: He never expected Doom to actually care for his own people. Faced with a world controlled by Doom or the Skull, Captain America's choice is clear: He'll take his chances with Doom. The Shroud, who has been aiding the rebels, is shocked. Confronting his hero, he says:

> SHROUD: I — I read about you all my life — Idolized you! My one dream was to be more like Captain America ... but — you're siding with Doom?
> CAPTAIN AMERICA: Try to understand! There was no choice!

When the Skull is finally defeated, Captain America destroys the Hypno-Ray, but leaves Doom in charge of Latveria. Like the Shroud, Captain America does not remain deaf to the Latverian rebels, who long for democracy. His hope is that in time Doom will give his people more freedom. While this thinking seems naïve, Doom has satisfied Captain America in one important regard: Doom wants the best for his people. Perhaps being ruled by Doom isn't so bad after all?

Doom and the New World (Dis)Order

If Doom was being recast as a hero, how to explain away his many crimes, his kidnappings, his sneak attacks? As the Soviet Union endured a rapid succession of leaders (Mikhail Suslov, Andrei Gromyko, Yuri Andropov, and Konstantin Chernenko), Marvel followed suit by introducing a series of false Dooms, each mitigating in turn the offenses of the original character. The suggestion was that since there were many Dooms, the false Dooms were responsible, wholly or in part, for the so-called aggressive actions of this peace-loving dictator.

Marvel also introduced a series of Doom stories built around the motif of time travel, in several of which Doom is the supreme ruler of a counter-earth; but each time, in each world, he is defeated by capitalism. In one scenario, *Doom 2099*, our hero (There! We said it!) improves his time machine and leads rebellions against the corporate world order.[13] Then, when Doom returns to the contemporary world, he again finds Latveria torn by ethnic conflict. Believing that he has no choice, Doom turns for help to the rich Americans, who send The Avengers. These specialists in counterinsurgency dismantle the conspiracy, and Doom easily ends the political challenge.

If Marvel was suggesting that the West should bolster the fading Soviets in the same way that The Avengers bolstered Doom, then Marvel Comics certainly envisioned a darker future for the former Eastern Bloc nations than has come to pass. Nonetheless, in many ways their anticipation of things to come proved accurate, at least in terms of the geopolitical changes at work from the 1960s to the 1990s. We could argue, for instance, that the first Gulf War exhibited Marvel's geopolitical savvy, if not, indeed, prescience. Several years later, during a broadcast of "This

---

13. Other Marvel characters have used Doom's machine: In *Marvel Team-Up* #41 (1976; Bill Mantlo/Sal Buscema), Spider-Man and the Scarlet Witch are drawn by Doom's time platform to 1692 Salem to face the witch trials. The story concludes in *Marvel Team-Up* #42 (1976; Mantlo/Buscema), when Doom rescues them. In *Marvel Team-Up* #45 (1976; Mantlo/Buscema), Spider-Man accidentally falls into Doom's time platform and lands in the year 2019. To his astonishment, he discovers the world is controlled by Doom.

Week with Sam Donaldson and Cokie Roberts," then–Defense Secretary William Cohen was referred to as "Dr. Doom" when he stated that "we" had enough VX nerve gas "to kill every man, woman, and child on the face of the earth" (*Newsweek*, 8 December 1997). A correction of his misstatement was quickly made. Saddam, not Cohen, would be assigned the role of Dr. Doom.

The Re-Emergence of Ethnic Cleansing and Holy War

It is probably not too much of a stretch to ask television viewers to see Saddam Hussein as the moral equivalent of Dr. Doom. The assumption would be that, given the demands of packaging in the medium, many viewers probably perceived the run-up to the first Gulf War, and the war itself, in episodic installments, much like the story arcs in comic books. But Doom was also involved in discussions other wars and military interventions, including America's current War on Terror. The first President Bush sent troops to Somalia to stop ethnic cleansing there; President Clinton sent air strikes into Bosnia to try to stop, or at least slow, ethnic cleansing in the Balkans. In the context of this interventionist policy, we might consider another Marvel story arc, involving Doom and ethnic cleansing. In *Iron Man* #409 (2003; Grell/Davis/Riggs), a cult in the European nation of Slovakia has returned to the ancient worship of Thor, God of Thunder. Thor, a member of The Avengers, responds when the Slovakian dictatorship, armed with Doom's weaponry, attempts to stamp out the cult. Thor's involvement threatens to bring war to the entire region, so Iron Man, who knows that Thor's worshippers are being arrested and executed, is dispatched to placate his friend. Naturally, Iron Man is not happy with any form of persecution, but he takes the hard-line approach, typical of Cold War politics, counseling Thor that it is better to tolerate a few massacres than to provoke nuclear war, which Slovakia threatens. At a subsequent private summit, Iron Man and Dr. Doom, both clad in metal suits, map out the boundaries of a new "iron" curtain:

> IRON MAN: Bothered by a few religious fanatics or worried about World War III breaking out in your backyard?

Doom, it seems, is ready to play at trade-offs. Ethnic cleansing is better than having American troops near his borders:

> DOOM: There are those parties ... the United States, for instance ... who might use this opportunity to impose their ideas of democracy on people who have no need for such foolishness ... and others willing to push the world over

the brink of war for their own ideals. If that were to happen... in my back-yard, as it were ... I would be forced to take a hand in the matter. And I assure you, I am not constrained by collateral damage.

That Doom, once the persecuted Gypsy, now looks the other way when eth-nic cleansing occurs in his "own backyard" is a profound change in course. But the bombshell is in his use of the term "collateral damage," made famous by one particular American experience of terrorism, recounted in this news report:

> On April 19th, 1995, a fertilizer bomb blew up the Alfred P. Murrah Federal Building in Oklahoma City, Oklahoma. By the time the dust settled, 168 peo-ple — 19 of them children — were dead.
> Within weeks, a decorated veteran of the Gulf War named Timothy McVeigh had been arrested. After being convicted of the act, he defiantly justified it as retaliation for the U.S. government's actions at Waco and Ruby Ridge. In a famously chilling quote, he described the deaths of all those women and children as "collateral damage."

The point here is that Dr. Doom proceeds on the critical assumption, shared by terrorists, that everything and everyone are legitimate targets of war. It seems to us reasonable to suppose that this tactical assumption affects the way we perceive Dr. Doom. When portrayed as a Cold War tyrant, Doom posed a threat to all Americans, but he was no terrorist. He aimed his fury, not at women and children, but at The Fantastic Four, a quasi-military organ-ization with ties to the government. Now, the situation is different: Doom resorts to terror tactics, aiming not at superheroes (who represent the mili-tary forces of the West), but at unarmed women and children. Iron Man goes along with him and fights Thor, who is shocked by the Faustian deal his for-mer ally has struck. But such are the fortunes of politics and war: Without lifting his iron glove, or dropping a single bomb, Doom wins the war.

Superheroes and Anti-War Protestors: Hey, They Buy Comics Too!

Thus far, we have described the ways in which DC and Marvel repre-sented American foreign policy before, during, and after the Cold War. Comics played an important role in the education of young readers, most of them male, many of them ready to enter the army. For those actually interested in military service, comic books offered (and offer) an easy intro-duction to the logic of political and military conflict. We must add to this advantage that comics offer an attractive view of war. Very rarely does any-one die. And we should not forget that the picture we get is one, like the recruitment poster "Uncle Sam Wants You!," of glorified masculinity. But, we would ask, what of the conscientious objector, the flower child, the peacenik? How does the comic book treat those — some would say "feminized" — naysayers who want to make love, not war?

DC Comics all but abandoned this audience. True, its long-running series, *Star Spangled War Stories*, often depicted the gruesome aspects of war. In issue #168 (1973; Kubert), for instance, we meet a hideously scarred grunt, known only as the "Unknown Soldier," who removes his bandages so that the others may see the true face of war. As the soldiers stare at him, horrified, he warns: "It's not fighting and dying gloriously for Baker Company [that's important].... It's not a game." But, by and large, that series was dedicated to portraying all soldiers, regardless of national allegiance, as brothers in arms. For example, in issue #165 (1972; Kerbert), a Nazi risks his freedom, and perhaps his life, to testify on behalf of an American soldier accused of deserting his post. Once cleared, the American helps the Nazi return to his native German soil. Likewise, in issue #190 (1974, Robbins/Sparling), an American soldier stops a Japanese kamikaze pilot from killing himself. They are marooned on an island and work together as comrades until rescued. The American can only reflect admiringly that "In the end, I guess every man has to be true to his own tradition.... But at least for a moment, there was understanding between two enemies ... it's not much ... but it's something." Whether American, German, or Japanese, these soldiers think of themselves as playing a deadly game, but playing it by strict and honorable rules.

Thor and Green Party

If DC championed the seasoned older man, hardened by experience, as the true soldier, Marvel was decidedly contrarian. Echoing the message of The Who's anthem, "My Generation," Marvel Comics registered a mistrust of authority, especially of authority accompanied by age. Consider: The most illustrious Marvel superheroes are striplings. Spider-Man is a college student; Daredevil a young attorney with an inclination to take on corporate giants. There are exceptions to Marvel's "under-thirty" tendency. Nick Fury and Reed Richards are graying professionals, the former a military man answering to the President, the latter a scientist. But, by and large, our point holds. Marvel's heroes are young and hip, mindful of the danger of being too cozy with "the Man." Marvel's heroes bear witness to a growing theme in popular culture that the law simply doesn't work, or if it does, it works only to serve the interests of the rich and powerful.

Ironically, mankind's greatest champion is not even a man, but the

Norse god, Thor. Like Spiderman and Daredevil, the God of Thunder has an alter ego, Donald Blake, a crippled doctor. When he smashes his stick to the ground, he is transformed into the eternally young, longhaired prince of Asgard, the mythological land of Norse gods. In the 1960s and '70s, Thor routinely waged war against his upstart half-brother Loki, or his insane but extremely powerful father Odin. And yet he was, by nature, a peacekeeper.

We should not, therefore, be surprised that in the 1990s Marvel turned the God of Thunder into an antiwar activist who distrusts America, the postmodern reincarnation of Odin, the All-Father. In the Marvel mini-series, *The Ultimates* (2001; Miller/Hitch/Currie), we find Thor camping under the stars. Nick Fury and Iron Man want him to sign on with The Avengers. But Thor is more interested in a different kind of resistance:

> FURY: I thought you were here to save the world.
> THOR: Oh, I am here to save the world, General Fury. Save it from people like you.

In a later chapter, we return to the question of the danger posed by the likes of Fury. For now, it is enough to say that Thor refuses to recognize America's enemies as *his* enemies. Nor is Thor sympathetic to Dr. Doom, although, as a nearly forgotten god, he does have a concern for minority rights. If he were active in politics today, Thor might join with the Green Party, or with the anti-globalism rioters that congregate at IMF meetings:

> THOR: Go back to your paymasters and tell them that the Son of Odin is not interested in working for a military industrial complex who engineers wars and murders innocents. Your talk might be of supervillains now, but it is only a matter of time before you are sent to kill for oil or free trade.

The God of Thunder perceives danger in terms of global function, and so targets his ire at what American military agents and industries do. This is not to say that he thinks Americans are dangerous; he knows that Americans themselves are good, noble, and generous. He has fought alongside Captain America and is on good terms with Iron Man and the other Avengers. Thor is motivated to action when the planet is in peril, and he directs that action without prejudice against the source of that peril. When New York is attacked, Thor is there to defend. But he is nobody's lackey. He will never turn his back on his worshippers, nor abandon his commitment to a peaceful earth.

Thor and the Second Gulf War

Is America to be trusted without the Soviets to keep them honest? That's Thor's basic concern. It's also one shared by key members of The

Avengers. In *Avengers* #57 (2002; Johns/Dwyer/Remender), Captain America and the Falcon discuss the rebuilding of "the World Trade area"—that is, the twin towers destroyed on 9-11. The Falcon's everyday persona, Sam Wilson, will be overseeing the urban planning. But rebuilding New York soon becomes a minor headache when a new danger presents itself. Washington D.C. is literally being enveloped in a black void. The President, Congress, the Senate, the Pentagon — are all seemingly lost in a chasm in reality. And it's not just Washington. The phenomenon is repeating itself all over the world: Moscow, Paris, Madrid, Beijing. The world will soon be leaderless.

At an emergency session of the U.N., Secretary General Kofi Annan calls on The Avengers to maintain world stability and to counter this new dark menace. Led by Captain America, the group seems up to the challenge. But soon, not everyone is so happy with an American leading the group. First, when it comes to nuclear weapons, America may be the most powerful country on earth, but when it comes to superpowers, Captain America is among the weakest of The Avengers. Why should he lead? Second, Captain America's very name suggests that he will put American interests first. Indeed, he has a rapport with Henry Gyrich, a member of the President's inner circle. As Gyrich sees it, the current crisis may work to America's advantage; as he points out, even Iraq trusts The Avengers.

But there are others who do not share that confidence. For one, there is Doctor Doom, who has somehow escaped the black void. When Doom contacts The Avengers with key information to unravel the mystery of the black void, they treat him as an enemy. They soon learn that Doom is working with the Black Panther, against the expressed interests of Captain America and other U.S.–based Avengers.

Why would he do so? To start with, the Black Panther is, like Doom, a sovereign of his own nation. As such, he isn't very happy with The Avengers'—and America's—new global power. Cap and Iron Man, both Americans, are shocked by the Panther's new pact. But they shouldn't be. After all, The Panther can't count on The Avengers to help him.

And that goes for much of the world. When the world's money reserves run dry, billionaire Tony Stark promises to use his capital to stabilize world markets. Addressing the U.N., Tony presents what looks like a fair-enough offer: "Let's talk business." But is this an offer anyone can refuse? After all, why should the world have to do "business" with America? What does it mean to do business? If he's talking about loans, then Tony is about to make the entire world his personal I.O.U. And doesn't Cap's dislike of Doom suggest that these "aid" packages will be extended to "friends" only? America is not just helping the world, but helping itself.

Small wonder that Thor soon leaves the group, as does Namor, who comes to see little difference between dealing with The Avengers and his former ally, Victor von Doom.

By *Avengers* #77 (2004; Austin/Coipel/Lanning), what is left of the team, now consisting solely of Americans, moves with impunity throughout much of the world. An amalgam of supervillains are surprised to find The Avengers in London. "What," asks the Wrecker, "are the Avengers doing in England? You're American heroes." American heroes for American crimes, English heroes for English crimes, presumably Iraqi heroes for Iraqi crimes — the idea is mired in isolationism.[14] But since September 11, the rules have changed. Moreover, the American heroes expect their enemies to understand this new paradigm: "Dude," replies Hawkeye, "turn on the news once in a while. We're international now." Nonetheless, the American heroes are well aware that many Europeans are hostile to them. In the same issue, when Hawkeye meets a young fan of The Avengers, he is surprised: "It's hard to tell how people feel about Americans these days." Apropos of Captain America, the toddler's sister replies: "Most people wouldn't give two shillings for him." Such a response suggests, at least from the point of view of Marvel's writers, that America's interventions in Afghanistan and Iraq have won few friends and have perhaps irrevocably strained relations with countries who were once steadfast allies.

A more developed and thoughtful assessment of America's recent policy of intervention appears in *Thor* #556 (2002; Jurgens/Bennett/Jadson). Here, upset by man's inability to rule with justice and decency, the Thunder God decides he has had enough. He orders his army of Norse gods to take control, first of New York, and then of the planet. Hearing the prayers of sufferers in the death camps of Kalanya — presumably based on the camps in Rwanda where genocide was then taking place — Thor brings huge numbers of refugees to New York, a city now under his direct protection. When asked what right he has to intervene in the actions of sovereign governments, he replies: " 'Tis my policy to recognize the governing body of any sovereign land. However, D'Andaa [the ruler of Kalanya] was unquestionably a tyrant and a thug, who took power by force of arms. Not a true ruler ... but a subjector." Now, even liberal interventionists are alarmed:

ACTIVIST: You ... overthrew his government?
THOR: As I would a common street thug. D'Andaa hath caused more misery than any thousand criminals combined.

14. The media have not embraced the idea of American intervention abroad whole-heartedly. Leonard Maltin and Joyce Kulhawik's syndicated "Hot Ticket" reviewed *Spiderman II* and Michael Moore's *Fahrenheit 9/11*. Connecting the two films, Kulhawik asked: "Who's the greatest villain of them all: the Green Goblin, Dr. Octopus, or George W. Bush?" The show aired June 19, 2004.

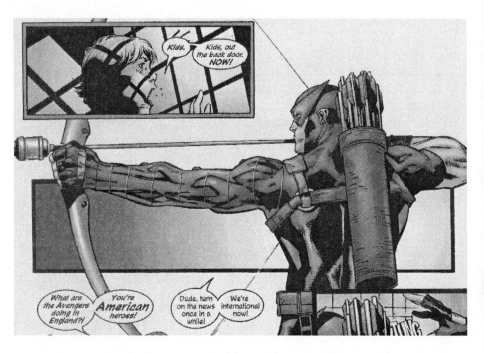

Hawkeye explaining that America's right to fight terror allows it to strike wherever it wishes. (By permission of Marvel Comics.)

> ACTIVIST: And... you get to decide all that?
> THOR: Evil cannot be protected by office, title or uniform. Justice must ever be served.... A map's borders must not silence the cries of the suffering. Not when they need salvation.

Of course, not everyone agrees with this brand of "salvation," a religious term that we use advisedly. In *Thor* #557 (2002; Jurgens/Raney/Hanna), when Thor and his Norse-god companions make short work of Arab armies, he becomes a symbol of American adventurism. Addressing the U.N., Thor understands that some governments are upset with him. After all, he has stolen their thunder. But he has been even-handed, and since he is more powerful than they are, they might as well accept his changes. And it's not all bad. He has freed slaves from death camps, alleviated world hunger, given humans a magical crystal to supply power to their industries, and stopped countries from producing chemical weapons which they swore they did not possess.

This interventionist policy tacitly supports the latest war in Iraq, which was undertaken, in large part, because of perceptions, justified or not, based on intelligence, informed or faulty, that Saddam Hussein possessed weapons of mass destruction (WMDs). As hindsight now instructs us, it is doubt-

Thor and his fellow gods have conquered the earth and forced peace upon everyone, whether they want it or not. The outcome is disastrous for both mortals and gods. (By permission of Marvel Comics.)

ful that such weapons existed in Iraq, at least at the time coalition forces, led by U. S. Marines, invaded. Doubtless there will be controversy over this matter, with military and academic careers on the line, for decades to come.

Thor and the New Reign of Terror

Arab militants in Thor's world don't want this "Infidel" controlling their holy lands and are ready to martyr themselves to the cause of resisting him. Nor are Christians less steadfast in this regard. Even the Pope demands that Christians resist this upstart Thor-sect, which, by its very existence, questions the supremacy of the Judeo-Christian God. Thus, in *Thor* #566 (2003; Jurgens/Medina/Vlasco), a priest explains the Vatican's position:

> PRIEST: You offer the masses simple solutions to complex problems, dazzle them with seeming miracles. It is an affront to God and his word.
> THOR: Do your God and I not preach the same doctrine? That the strong must protect the weak? That life is to be cherished above all else?
> PRIEST: None may place himself on a par with the Lord.

Upset that so many are now worshipping Thor, who is, after all, a god, the Christians firebomb newly-built Thor churches; Thor's faithful respond in kind. The violence escalates. A Christian videotapes his suicide confession before blowing up one of Thor's magical power plants.

Asgard as America: Under Attack

Governments around the globe plan even more ambitious attacks. Allying herself with an old enemy (Dr. Doom), America sends military transports to Thor's base of Asgard, a floating city, which is now suspended over New York, blowing it to bits. Asgard falls from the sky and smashes into New York, reducing both to cinders. Meanwhile, Thor is lured to a deserted island for a conference with a representative of the Pope. The envoy blows himself up with a thermonuclear bomb, a martyr to the Christian cause, willing to sacrifice himself if he can take the false-god Thor with him. The envoy from Rome never learned what every comic book fan takes for granted: not even a nuclear blast can kill a god. Of course, Thor survives; the envoy's self-immolation only infuriates him (*Thor* #568, 2003; Jurgens/Mandrake). Soon after (#570, 2003; Jurgens/Eaton/Smith), we see the consequences of this misguided act.

By the year 2020, Thor, still in control of the earth, no longer depends on justice and good will to govern, but on the operations of a global police state, which executes or imprisons anyone who disobeys, or even questions, Thor's wisdom. After the destruction of Asgard and New York, Thor explains, "I have pledged my life to making sure such a thing never — ever happens again."

How does this narrative register in reference to current events? We suggest that Thor is intended to mirror President George W. Bush. Both aspire to extend the values implicit in their beliefs and practices into other countries and cultures. For instance, Thor explains: "I would have expected all humanity to feel the same way. But even after New York's demise and the fall of Asgard, the [military and terrorist] attacks did not stop. Since then, many other attempts have been made to remove me." At this point, a mere human speaks up, daring to explain matters to the most powerful force on earth: "The people are afraid of you! They want their freedom!" Yet, even after popular uprisings throughout the world, Thor still believes that the common man is on his side. He responds: "They [the peoples of the earth] have their freedom. What those who oppose me truly fear is their inability to control the world's economy and governments."

Again, Marvel suggests comparison with the contemporary political landscape. The second Bush administration appears to disregard demonstrations against American policy, some of them reaching dimensions comparable with those experienced during the Vietnam War. Classical historians may argue that a more compelling parallel can be found in the writings of the ancient Greek historian, Herodotus, who chronicled the ill-fated Greek invasion of Persia, which comprised present-day Iraq and Iran. As the Greek King readied his forces, an old and wise commander cautioned him against the invasion. As he explained, the Greeks were about to attack people who owned nothing of value. There was little to gain and much to lose, for if the Greeks failed, the Persians, seeing how wealthy the Greeks were, would certainly attack. Similarly, with the armies of the world now poised against him, Thor no longer thinks he can better the earth. He hopes only to strengthen the things that remain.

As time passes (by issue #574, "Paradise Lost," 2004; Jurgens/Eaton/ Koblish), Thor's high-minded ideals are laid waste. Anticipating the activities at Abu-Graib Prison, torture and indefinite detention become routine. Thor's government remains in power only because he has abandoned the day-to-day administration of the empire to Loki, his half-brother and former enemy. As long as peace is maintained, Thor pays no attention to Loki's methods.

But — and this is crucial — Thor's concept of peace is no longer linked to freedom. In a scenario eerily prescient of the events in Iraq, Loki rules the conquered territories with an iron hand, arresting, torturing or killing anyone who questions the legitimacy of his rule. When Thor's son Magni comes of age, he assists his Uncle Loki. As the rebels are mowed down, the Prince of Asgard, horrified, intervenes, and begs the rebels to surrender: "Your rebellion is over. Not only will you never again persecute those who follow us—you will accept our ways without protest." But victory is not that easy. One revolutionary opens his coat to reveal a TNT vest: "We reject you! And we'll gladly die if we can take you with us!" The Prince is unhurt by the subsequent explosion but is nonetheless surprised: "I had ... I had no idea ... they hated us so." His uncle shrugs, "These humans are all insane. Don't rationalize anything they do. They're animals. We need to be disciplined with them. It's all they understand."

Magni knows that Loki's answers do not really explain the way things are. He knows who's really at fault. Thor began his war wanting to protect the freedom of his worshippers. Thor still wants peace on earth, but makes no distinction between peace and obedience. He wants to end war, a war to re-establish his church, but the only weapon in his arsenal to achieve that end is a *jihad* against all non-believers.

THINKING, DEBATING, WRITING

1. We suggest that fans probably want Dr. Doom to remain a villain. Write an essay defending his belief system.

2. In your area of the country, does the legal system work? Do the citizens respect the courts? What names and what court cases, or what events with legal implications, come to mind when people talk about the justice system?

3. Is there freedom of religion in your school and in your neighborhood? On what part of the Constitution of the United States does that freedom, if it exists, rest?

4. Read about history of the first Gulf War. What was the rationale for keeping Saddam in power?

5. Look at the Cold War in relation to the Green Lantern series. Were the Green Lantern Corps right to trying to maintain order? Is war worth fighting if millions are going to die? If not, under what principles would you be willing to put lives, even planets, on the line?

6. Thor wants the best for all. What is Marvel trying to say about freedom and human potential? Compare achievements in totalitarian regimes against our own system to measure the success of each political system.

7. Look into the sixties and the birth of youth culture. Why did Pete Townsend, in the song "My Generation," hope that he died before he got

old? How does American youth culture differ from the values of other cultures?

8. Who, in your view, is today's Dr. Doom, and why?

9. Do you know anyone who has served in the military? Interview that person and ask if his or her values have changed since enlisting. What values changed or did not change, and why?

10. If the Middle East nations were producers of oranges rather than oil, would America be as willing to go to war there, or are there more humanitarian principles at stake? Take a side in this debate and write a detailed essay, using recent events as a backdrop.

3

Spider-Man and
Corporate Responsibility

The largest-grossing movie of 2002 was Spider-Man, *an adaptation of the Marvel comic. The gross take on the film exceeded $800 million, a tacit approval of the movie's primary message: "With great power comes great responsibility." The appeal of Spider-Man's message was in some ways bolstered by the events that formed a backdrop to the movie. The year of the film's release was marked by corporate irresponsibility, falling stock prices, and the debacles at three huge firms: Arthur Andersen, Enron, and WorldCom.*

As the movie *Spider-Man* begins, we meet Peter Parker, an overachiever, in love with Mary Jane Watson, a redhead suffering from an inferiority complex. Degraded by her brutal father and unappreciated by a succession of rich but brainless boyfriends, she has yet to notice the boy next door, the gee-whiz goodnik, Peter. This is a basic inversion of the knight-in-shining-armor story: here, the knight is a squire, and the shining knights in their fast cars are really covered in moral manure.

That manure takes its physical form in money. When Peter decides to win Mary Jane, he sets out to buy a sports car, which he thinks will impress her. He has reason to think she will be vulnerable to this approach: Her present boyfriend, the muscular Flash, drives a Porsche Boxer.

Looking for quick cash, Peter sees an ad in a newspaper. If he survives three minutes in the ring with the wrestler known as "Bone-Crusher," he'll get $3000, enough for a used Fiat *Spider*. Thus, Parker's first goal is economic: He wants to use his new powers as Spider-Man to earn money for a nice car. If Parker believes that money can buy him the girl of his dreams, it's clear that even before he becomes Spider-Man, capitalism has enmeshed Parker with a common marketing technique: fast car equals hot girl. He beats Bone-Crusher and awaits his pay-off. Predictably, the manager rips him off: Parker is promised $3000 to survive three minutes in the ring, but he beats his opponent in *less* than three minutes. On this legal loophole, the slick manager refuses to pay Parker more than fifty dollars.

Peter accuses the manager of paying him less than he's worth, but the manager has little interest in discussing ethics. "How is that my problem?" he asks. This attitude seems unfair, but really it's Capitalism 101 according to Marx, who says an employer must steal from his employee. The difference in the value of his work versus what he is paid is the profit.[1] If a worker is paid what he is worth, the profit disappears. Profit is based upon giving the worker less than he deserves. Parker's loss is the manager's gain.

After leaving the wrestling manager's office, Parker broods over his hard-knock lesson. As he waits for the elevator, he sees a thug hold up the manager and speed off with the day's profits. To Parker, there is some justice: The manager stole from Peter, now another criminal steals from the manager. All is fair in capitalism, even in its debased forms. Parker lets the thief escape with the money. When the manager asks Parker why he didn't intervene, Parker replies in kind: "How is that my problem?" Parker is right, of course, at least according to the rules of capitalism. If every man is out for himself and profit is legal stealing, who is Parker to get in the way of the circulation of capital?

The robbery leaves Peter with a sense of satisfaction, but also with a vague sense of unease. Is Peter Parker as culpable as the manager? The dilemma is real and long-running, an echo of the film's prologue, in which Peter asks with some unease, "Who am I?" Given what we have just seen, the answer seems to be not merely Spider-Man, but a victim of capitalism.

Evidence for this point of view quickly mounts. Parker, we recall, was bitten by a radioactive bug that escaped from a top-security lab. The lead scientist is told that there is a missing spider, but is the lab shut down until the dangerous and expensive experiment can be accounted for? No. Instead, she blithely blames someone else for not following protocol. "Oh," she says, "the boys in the lab must have taken him for tests." Meanwhile, the spider spins its webs and threatens imminent poisonings.

With respect to the power of corporations to shape or ruin human lives, we shouldn't forget that Peter's Uncle Ben, with whom Peter lives, is the victim of corporate downsizing. Despite being with the firm for over twenty years, he is laid off, with little savings and less hope. Alone in the

---

1. On the idea that corporations are criminal organizations, when an unnamed investor decides to fund the supergroup The Thunderbolts, the superhero Songbird chirps that "White collar crime must be paying very well" (*The Thunderbolts: Reassembled* #1 2005; Nicieza/ Grummett/Erskine). As it turns out, she's right. The group's moneyman is actually a Nazi.

kitchen, Uncle Ben wonders what will become of him, now that he is unemployed and unemployable.

We can see the connection between Peter Parker's home situation and his first experience in the economic rat race. What do bosses owe their employees, and what do employees owe their bosses? Or, even more broadly, what do any of us owe to each other? We may accept the biblical notion that we should "love our neighbors as ourselves," but, in the complex world in which we live, who are our neighbors? Working nine to five, the average worker may spend more time on the factory floor with other workers than he does with his family. Doesn't he owe his fellow workers, and the bosses who pay his salary, some loyalty? Any yet those bosses may be people he has never met, strangers who serve on the company's board of directors.

In the case of Uncle Ben, the company recognizes that it owes him something, since it awards him two weeks' severance pay. Obviously, Peter Parker thinks the company owes Uncle Ben much more. But Peter has problems of his own. Mr. Jameson, the newspaper magnate, is willing to pay almost any price for a picture of Spider-Man. Yet when Peter offers him the picture, Jameson pays only a small flat fee for Peter's photographic gold. If Peter feels ripped off, that's not Jameson's problem.[2]

Predatory business practices don't just victimize Peter Parker. Norman Osborn, CEO of Osborn Enterprises, makes his money by dabbling with DNA strands in an effort to create more efficient soldiers. The test serum has some serious flaws; for instance, one subject was transformed into a homicidal maniac, an antisocial variant of the super soldier. Told that the formula should be taken "offline" for further testing, Osborn worries that this delay will affect his profits. He has shareholders who want profits now, and if the product has dangerous side effects, well, how is that his problem? Let the buyer beware.

Osborn's villainous persona, the Green Goblin, is a perfect spokesman for his predatory style of capitalism. To "gobble" suggests ravenous hunger — in this case, Osborn's hunger for more money and more power. Yet from a business standpoint, Osborn is only trying to grow his company aggressively. He is a good, indeed model, businessman, in the sense that he is trying to survive and expand in a highly competitive environment.

Returning to Peter Parker's situations when Ben is killed by the thief Peter might have stopped, the question "How is that my problem?" is finally answered. Whereas capitalism has taught Peter to think of every man for himself, the death of his uncle teaches him that we are all linked. What

---

2. We note that in the sequel, *Spider-Man II*, Peter negotiates with Jameson, demands payment in advance, and even uses the term: "Take it or leave it." Peter is slowly learning the rules of capitalism, and Rule #1 is supply and demand. Since only he can supply what Jameson demands, he gets to name his own price.

affects one eventually affects all. It's like a spider web: We're all caught in it, and we can't pretend that, when the capitalist feeds, we don't feel the tremor of the monster moving along the web.

For some fans, this issue may be reminiscent of Kafka's *The Metamorphosis*, a famous short story about Gregor, a man who wakes up one morning to discover that he has turned into a giant insect. Kafka's invertebrate figure captures Gregor's sense of helplessness. He feels powerless both at home and at work. In the *Spider-Man* series, the corporate world inflicts suffering, but Peter is no spineless insect. Rather, he is a superhero who affirms the value of the "insects" or "little guys" of the world. Peter Parker's powers must be aimed at the predators of his world; he must intervene for the good of all. If he were to do otherwise, if he were to exploit his power for his own profit, he would be no better than the exploiters and thieves, corporate and otherwise, who have destroyed his family.

Daredevil and the Kingpin

Many *Spider-man* stories are framed around the man in the street, rather than the mogul in the executive penthouse. Like a labor union leader, Spider-Man is often seen as fighting for the ordinary worker or the socially downtrodden. This is brought home forcefully in *Spider-Man* #9 (April 1991), in which a small-town representative asks Spider-Man to fight a robber-baron named Windigo, who is terrorizing the citizenry. Spider-Man, who has never met Windigo, agrees because he thinks hard-working folks deserve a chance to escape a life of brutality. The anti-corporate message here is clear. Big companies steal. Moreover, the aforementioned anti-corporate theme is part and parcel of what constitutes a supervillain in the Marvel Universe. Spider-Man's enemies include Electro, a foe who sucks up power from all electrical sources — Enron's illegal price spikes in tights. His greatest enemy, however, is the corporate overlord, Kingpin, whose empire stretches from his executive suite above the city to the catacombs of the criminal underworld. Kingpin debuted in the 1966 *Spider-Man* animated TV series, as the head of an ersatz-pharmaceuticals firm, who forces fake drugs on legitimate pharmacists, who in turn sell them to unwary customers filling prescriptions. When Aunt May finds that the pills she is taking make her more ill, Spider-Man steps in. But when Spider-Man is too busy to watch the Kingpin, Daredevil takes up the fight.

Daredevil's "radioactive" origins are similar to Spider-Man's. His father was a boxer who, when his jab began to fade, made a living working as an enforcer for the mob. Later, his son, Matt Murdock, sees a little old lady walking across the street. A truck is about to hit her. Throwing his body in front of the truck, he saves the woman. The truck is carrying radioactive material, some of which spatters onto Matt's eyes. He is blinded, but, as he recovers in the hospital, he learns that he has also gained extraordinarily heightened abilities. He can hear a heartbeat, the sound of a bullet, even the falling of dust. Soon after, Matt's father is murdered by his former employers. Matt vows that when he is old enough, he will avenge his father. As Matt grows up, he comes to realize that his fight will entail more than simply donning a cape. Going to law school, he vows to protect the poor and the innocent. Unafraid of mobsters and their top-dollar lawyers, Murdock fearlessly fights crime both in the courts and in the alleys. He is truly "The Man Without Fear."

The Kingpin is a perfect foil for lawyer Matt Murdock and his crime-fighting persona, Daredevil, because his villainies do not rely solely on brute force. For instance, in the *Daredevil* graphic novel, *Born Again* (1987; Miller/Mazzucchelli), the Kingpin employs the very mechanisms that have made decades of economic expansion possible: computers. As the story begins, we find the Kingpin of Crime surveying his city empire and plotting to kill Daredevil, but not by a weapon from the usual arsenal used by supervillains. Rather than targeting Daredevil with a guided missile or super-ray, the Kingpin aims to conquer him by capturing control of cyberspace. He is encouraged in this endeavor by having learned Daredevil's true identity, the redoubtable lawyer for the poor, Matt Murdock. There is no need now to send assassins, or at least not ordinary ones. Instead, the Kingpin of Crime will use computers to strip Murdock's bank account. He will then tamper with the lawyer's bank statements, so that the banks will think he has fallen behind on his mortgage and the IRS will nail him for back taxes. Matt Murdock's life will wind down into just one more tale of identity theft:

> He [The Kingpin] has gathered the warring gangs of the city, organized them into an army — no, a business, so efficient and so profitable that the city's economy depends on the thieves, extortionists, and murderers at his command. He is the Kingpin — and Matthew Murdock has become the blight of his days. As Daredevil, Murdock had cost him little, but hounded him, annoyed him, as a fly would. Now, with all the joy of a malicious child, the Kingpin tortures the fly.

What, we might wonder, does the Kingpin have against Daredevil? The answer is simple: Justice is bad for business. Addressing board members of his corporation, the Kingpin declares: "Crime is on the rise and therefore, so are our profits." Is the Kingpin a bad guy? Certainly Daredevil thinks so, but as the Kingpin explains to a member of an elite American military unit, trade unionists and lawyers like Matt Murdock are the *true* villains:

> I am under constant scrutiny by the police. I am, in the strictest sense of the law, a criminal. I know this startles you, but, as I said — so much has

changed. America's enemies have grown so strong that our boys die in Asian jungles—and our people will not honor them... and it tortures me that the noble concept of free enterprise — the crowning triumph of our forefathers— has been murdered by endless, corrosive legislation. To simply keep some shadow of that dream alive, I must ... break the law.... We who ... decide such things have formed a proud trinity — of state — and military — and business. We must have unity—against the infection of the American spirit. There are those who say that unity is conspiracy—that America is evil. I am not a villain, my son, I am a corporation in the conglomerate that is America.

The Kingpin claims, with some justification, that the business of America is crime. Lawyers and unions have turned the country upside down, so that the spirit of free enterprise has been criminalized. By turning on Murdock and those like him, the Kingpin claims to be fighting the good fight to restore the true American spirit.

Intellectual Capitalism

From the perspective of comic-book writers, seeing the computer as the ultimate weapon makes perfect sense. In a world where the primacy—even the usefulness—of print is rapidly being replaced by megabytes and gigahertz, it is not surprising that cyber-space is demonized in print culture, including comic books. And yet the creators of Daredevil and Spider-Man do not seem to be saying that technology is, in and of itself, evil. A pen and ledger can be just as deadly. In *Daredevil* #323 (Chichester/McDaniel), Daredevil must face the *Kusariagma*, a criminal combine of Asians bent on taking over the world. Its newest recruit is Harry "TNT" Kenroy, a general in the U.S. Army, who promises them weapons. They disdain his offer as both inconsequential and outdated: "There is all the time we need to exploit the world around. Our plans are not just for today—but for the future." The world is to be conquered, not by murder and mayhem, but by business mergers and political connections. In *Spider-Man 2099* #28 (1995; David/St. Pierre), an army of businessmen offers the same challenge. Meeting a bunch of lawyers, Spider-Man reflects: "They look absurd, laughable in their power suits and ties.... Yet of all the loonies I've encountered, they're the most cold-blooded ... whatever souls they may once have had ... sucked away by the corporate mentality."

Dr. Freeze, Poison Ivy and Anti-Industrialist Practices

Villainous corporations are at the heart of the DC Universe as well. In the Joel Schumacher film *Batman & Robin* (1997), we meet Dr. Victor Fries

Spider-Man's greatest foe, Kingpin, has no unusual powers. He's just a CEO with lots of money and no scruples. (By permission of Marvel Comics.)

(Arnold Schwarzenegger), who is fighting the corporate profiteers of the health care system. Dr. Fries becomes a criminal in an attempt to save his wife Nora. Like many who look for answers in cutting-edge technology, Dr. Fries turns to cryogenics, hoping to freeze his wife until his research cures her. Unfortunately, Fries accidentally falls into a vat of cryogenic fluid. He survives but finds that he must now keep his own body temperature below the freezing point. Thus, Dr. Fries becomes Mr. Freeze, armed with a weapon that instantly glaciates his adversaries. Mr. Freeze's desire to save his wife doesn't make him, by itself, an enemy of Batman; it's his thievery that does so. But at heart, Mr. Freeze isn't a criminal: he's the victim of a poor HMO plan.

It might seem odd that Freeze doesn't simply ask Bruce Wayne, noted philanthropist, for the money to save his wife. Freeze's disgust with capitalist practices make such a request impossible. His very body suggests a preferred return to ice age simplicity. By contrast, his ally Poison Ivy (Uma Thurman) wants the earth to return to an Arcadian wonderland. She is a "Greenpeacer" *par excellence*, who wants to destroy the meat-based economy of McDonald's and other so-called eco-terrorist corporations.

Batman Beyond: Capitalism Gone Mad

Ivy's dream comes to withered fruit, at least as envisioned in the successful animated series *Batman Beyond*, launched with the two-hour movie, *Rebirth* (1999). Set in the near future, the story unfolds in a steel and glass Gotham; trees, parks, greenery of any kind, are a thing of the past. The movie centers on the rise of Derrick Powers, a corporate villain who takes control of Wayne Enterprises in a stock takeover. Wayne is powerless to stop Powers from turning the company into a high-tech weapons manufacturer. Thus, the same technology that allowed Bruce Wayne to design and build the Batmobile and other gadgets is now perverted by big business in the name of easy profits.

The new Batman is Terry McGinnis, whose father is killed by Powers upon discovering Powers' illegal but profitable plans to sell a DNA nerve gas that eats away skin like locusts on corn. McGinnis seeks Wayne's assistance; Wayne tells him to go to the cops. Instead, he steals Batman's suit, thereby committing a crime in order to avenge a crime. Using a radio transceiver, Wayne warns him to return the suit: "That suit is not yours, you have no right..." This argument does not ring true. Wayne it seems, should be on Terry's side. They have much in common, since both Terry's and Wayne's parents were murdered. If Wayne can take vengeance in a bat suit, why shouldn't Terry be able to do the same?

Wayne's surprisingly legalistic case is based on the concept of private property, not an odd position for a man who has had his business stolen from him. Terry's position is that he has a moral right to the bat suit because, he believes, combating murder cancels out all other crimes. He tells Wayne, "Someone had to do something; you sure weren't going to..." Even Wayne must admit that Terry has a point — after all, how many warehouses has Batman broken into in the course of his career? That being said, Terry's can-do logic, his willingness to square corners, is not radically different from Powers' pragmatic rationale for making and selling nerve gas. If there's business to be made, a businessman should make it. This makes Terry, were it not for his personal vendetta, a natural heir apparent for Powers, the "let's make a deal" profiteer.

As the movie draws to an end, Powers is exposed to his own DNA nerve gas and is almost completely destroyed. Doctors work feverishly to save him, but all they can do is render him a translucent wraith, symbolic of both his all-consuming greed and superficial ambitions. But Powers' defeat is hardly Terry's victory. Even after Wayne hires Terry to be his personal assistant — i.e., to be the new Batman — Powers still controls the city. Wayne is forced to return to his useless existence, one more dusty and forlorn antique taking up space in Wayne Manor.

Superman and Lex Luthor

Money and business are also the cankered apples that poison Smallville, home to Clark Kent, a.k.a. Superman. The caped crusader's greatest nemesis is not a costumed villain, but his bald, boyhood friend Lex Luthor, business genius and CEO of the weapons-for-profit manufacturer, Lex Corp. Superman/Clark Kent's relationship with Lex is perhaps unique in that they have known each other since childhood. Both grew up in Smallville, but on opposite sides of the economic tracks. Clark's parents were lower-middle-class farmers, part of the old world of Jeffersonian independence. Lex comes from new money: His father is the president of Lex Corp, a company his son will one day transform into a multinational conglomerate. Despite their differences, Lex and Clark go to the same high school and become fast friends and competitors for girls and for the admiration of their peers.

Friendship aside, Lex and Clark are competitors first and foremost. This raises a basic question that is central to capitalism: Can people treat each other as equals when they are economically unequal? Friendship itself is not dependent upon money; it is a relationship in which one privileges another over those outside one's friendship circle. You generally treat your friends better than your enemies. But privileging someone over another creates the problems of capitalism — i.e., inequality and exclusivity — in a social context. Not *everyone* can be Clark's *best* friend; Lex will not invite *everyone* to his expensive parties. Lex and Clark's friendship, then, presents a *prima facie* conflict. In a world where Lex can apologize to Clark by buying him a car, it's difficult for Clark to express his friendship in equal terms. This is, surprisingly, more of an issue for Lex than it is for Clark. Lex is never sure whether girls like him for his personality, charm, and sex appeal, or for his ever-ready checkbook. Thus, Lex envies no one so much as his friend Clark, who, though comparatively poor, is rich with friends who care about him. Money has ruined Lex's ability to trust others or to value himself.

But Clark has issues as well. How can he have friends and serve everyone equally? Can a hero have friends or lovers? If he does, don't those very relationships get in the way of his serving the public? These questions were answered in the movie *Superman* (1978), in which Lois dies in an earthquake, but, putting his love of Lois before all the world, Superman literally turns back time to save her. Yet Superman doesn't accomplish this feat to save anyone other than the woman he loves. The cost of having friends, it seems, is to be unfair to the innocent.

The Punisher Movie

A variation on the same theme is found in the 2004 movie *The Punisher*, starring Tom Jane as Frank Castle. Within minutes of the opening credits, we meet Frank's fetching wife and adoring son, as well as his extended family, all vacationing in a tropical island paradise. His marriage is rock-solid; his son and in-laws are happy and healthy. Too bad they're about to be remorselessly gunned down by John Travolta's hired thugs. Frank Castle, though beaten, shot, and tossed off a pier, survives to return to New York. And, although no one can find him, he buys (and presumably somehow gets license plates for) a jalopy he then transforms into his personal armored-assault vehicle.

While customizing his new ride and gathering information on his enemies, Frank lives in a rundown tenement where he is pretty much adopted by the tenants—a grab-bag of B-movie character types: the fat-friendly guy — John Pinette/think John Candy — the pathetic loser — Ben Foster/think David Spade without the humor — and the babe who doesn't know she's a babe — Rebecca Romijn Stamos/think Rebecca Romijn Stamos. Our *femme dejour*, Jonnie by name, is friendly, unassuming, single, and has been beaten by her past boyfriends. Despite what would undoubtedly make her reluctant to ever date any man on the planet, she senses in Frank a soft spot in that midriff of rock-hard muscles. Instead of taking her up on her casual but clear invitation, the monastic Frank keeps to himself, looks at pictures of his dead wife and son, and plans for the task at hand — not rebuilding his life, but punishing those who destroyed it.

John Travolta's character, Howard Saint, feels the same way. After all, he only goes after Frank's family because Frank, an FBI agent, killed his son during a raid. What makes Frank better than his nemesis is open to serious debate, since they are both vengeful family men. The main difference is one of purity. Frank has gone through a ritual cleansing process, one in which everything he had was taken from him. He was immersed in water and reborn as this vengeful animus, the Punisher. His power is maintained by cutting himself off from all pleasures. He eats just enough to maintain his strength, drinks alcohol to numb his emotions. There is no pleasure in being the Punisher. As Travolta's character rightly suggests, "He misses his family. He wants to die. Let's help him."

On the other hand, Howard Saint still has, despite the loss of his son, much to live for. He's rich; he enjoys nightclubs and the media spotlight. He has close friends, another son he is grooming in the family business, and above all, a wife he adores. And it is this weakness for his wife that is his undoing. When Howard Saint thinks his best friend is sleeping with his wife, his jealousy is enough to destroy his own empire.

As the movie unfolds, it looks like the Punisher is being similarly weakened. Reluctant at first, Frank is drawn out by his neighbors, particularly the attractive Jonnie. He has short but increasingly revealing conversations. He discusses the death of his wife, the loss of his son, his thirst for revenge. When someone knocks at the door, he thinks it's one of the neighbors, who have become his friends, and thinks nothing of opening the door. Unfortunately, his unexpected guest is a huge Russian assassin of amazing ferocity, and a lengthy brawl follows.

By the closing credits, the Punisher has a cool million, no enemies left to kill, and his new family of neighbors ready to take the place of the one taken from him. Instead, what does he do? He gives away the money and walks away from his new family, including Jonnie. We learn by voice-over that although the Punisher has punished all his personal enemies, he's now on a crusade to punish all evildoers. When Jonnie asks where he is going, they have the following exchange:

> FRANK: I have work to do. Read the paper. You'll understand.
> JOANIE: What section?
> FRANK: Obituaries.

These new targets will be people Frank does not know personally. Nothing personal, as the gangsters say, it's just business. But Frank is not trying to replace Howard Saint as a mob boss. Instead, having finished personal "business," Frank is opening the equivalent of a non-profit. The "company" will now torture, maim and kill on the public's behalf. Frank can't do his "work" if he has a wife and kids or even friends. The road he walks, he walks alone.

Spider-Man II: "Am I not supposed to have what I want? What I need?"

Spider-Man II also explores this fundamental problem of the hero's human relationships but comes to a far different resolution. As the movie develops, we see that being Spider-Man has its downside. Peter can save the world, but he's not very good at saving himself. He works as a pizza delivery boy, but since he's always stopping along the way to fight crime, his deliveries are late, and he is fired. He owes back rent, and his landlord, understandably, thinks little of him; his poor Aunt May is getting poorer by the day, and the bank is about to foreclose on her house. Peter's failing school, again because he's spending all his time fighting crime. His former best friend, Harry Osborn, hates him because he thinks Peter has betrayed him by befriending Spider-Man, who killed Harry's father Norman Osborn, a.k.a. the Green Goblin. His love life... What love life? Because he swore to keep Mary Jane out of harm's way, he refuses to confess his love to her and is helpless to stop her dating other men. She even accepts the hand of one suitor in marriage. Dejected, Peter asks, "Am I not supposed to have what I want? What I need?" What does Peter need? Money, certainly. But does he need a love life or even friends?

Rousseau, Dumas and the Value of a Man

The problem of altruism and friendship is not new. In his novel *Emile*, Jean-Jacques Rousseau sets out his ideal educational plan for the creation of an intellectually and morally self-sufficient superman. Having been raised without attachment to people or property, Emile, at age fifteen, has remained free from all passions. He is an example of the truly natural man, man as man was meant to be, free from society and from capitalistic tendencies such as greed.

While this ideal man is free, he is still, paradoxically, connected to society: "At bottom, since all the commitments of society are reciprocal in nature, it is impossible to put oneself outside the law without renouncing its advantages, and no one owes anything to someone who claims to owe nothing to anyone."[3] In essence, Rousseau rejects the theory that people are linked only by fear and greed. To Rousseau, the ideal man's—the superman's—respect for law or the rights of men is indivisible from his personal independence.

Likewise, in Alexandre Dumas' play, *Kean* (1832), we meet the English actor, Edmund Kean, loved by all of London. His best friend is the Prince of Wales, with whom he competes for the love of the Countess Koefield. All of London is intrigued by the friendship of the Prince and the actor, but few believe that they are truly equals. Most believe that the Prince keeps Kean like a pet or a performing clown for the entertainment of his *real* friends, the rich aristocrats. In truth, the Prince does measure his friendship with Kean in economic terms. When Kean shows his displeasure with the Prince, the latter whines, "Isn't my purse always at your service? Isn't my palace open to [you] at all hours?"[4] However, Kean weighs the Prince's actions, not his purse. Kean *allows* the friendship; he does not *court* it.

At the end of both these works, however, the illusion of equality bursts. Emile re-enters the world of class and money and even has to come up with sufficient and practical funds to marry and live in Paris; Kean may think he's the equal of the Prince of Wales, but he still has to work for a living, and when he calls out the Prince for betraying a promise not to chase after Kean's girl, he learns very quickly the limits and values of their "equal" friendship. The Prince does not apologize. Instead, he turns his back on his friend and, further, makes it impossible for Kean to make a living in France. Kean is barred from performing and, having no other livelihood, has to move to America.

Spider-Man's Solution

Spider-Man may delve into the occasional book of poetry, but philosophical writers such as Rousseau, at least as of *Spider-Man II*, have yet to make his reading list. What is his solution to the problem of prioritizing money, friendship, love, and fighting for everyone? For a time, it seems the answer is no longer necessary. Spider-Man begins to lose his powers, which conveniently allows him to resume a normal and selfish life without having to deal with the moral issues of abandoning the people of New York.

It's not all bad. Although crime rates soar, the city is well enough. It's not like Spider-Man disappeared one day and the sky fell the next. Indeed,

3. Jean-Jacques Rousseau, *On the Social Contract; Discourse on the Origin of Inequality; Discourse on Political Economy*, trans. and ed. Donald A Cress; introduction by Peter Gay (Indianapolis: Hackett, 1983), 169.
4. Alexandre Dumas, *Edmund Kean: Or, The Genius and the Libertine* (London: G. Vickers, E. Appleyard, William Strange, 1847), 132.

Spider-Man comes to trust the ability of the city to deal with its own problems. Instead of rushing after police cruisers on their way to a crime scene, he lets the cops get on with their work. After all, it's what they're trained — and paid — to do. His powers gradually return, and Spider-Man learns to trust others, even to the point of revealing his identity to a trainload of passengers he has just saved. They all swear to a pact of secrecy; they owe him one.

The message of trust is reiterated in a later encounter with Mary Jane, who also learns of Peter's secret. She wants to help him to be happy: "Can't someone save *your* life?" This payment of emotional debt suggests that capitalism is being replaced by moral obligation. If the hero is to save society, he must also trust that those worth saving would do the same for him. Thus, we see Aunt May whacking "Doc Ock" (Dr. Octopus, the villain of the piece) on the head with her umbrella, and Mary Jane at least attempting the same, as all as a train car full of people telling the villain that if he wants Spider-Man, he'll have to go through them first.

All well and good; certainly Peter Parker is happier than Frank Castle. But we know the hollowness of this fiction. In reality, no one would keep Peter's secret. They'd tell their friends, or, when faced with a bill in arrears, they'd spill their story to the tabloids. After all, moral obligation doesn't pay the rent. As Spider-Man himself demonstrates, it's easy to say you will be heroic always, but even heroes need some time off.

Money, Power, and Reality TV

In *Silver Surfer* #41 (1990; Starlin/Lim), the title hero, having lost his ability to sail on his surfboard through the stars, is stranded on a planet that requires a hefty departure fee. Stripped by this environment of his superpowers and desperately in need of money, the Surfer discovers that he has few marketable skills. Even menial labor presents a challenge. He does have one resource he can sell: his dreams, which can be broadcast on interplanetary reality TV. But exposing his innermost thoughts to the public is humiliating, worse than any physical punishment the Surfer has ever known. "They have taken everything from me," he says, "[M]y privacy, my dignity, my inner self."

In developing this theme, we think, Marvel was ahead of the times. Within a decade, Jerry Springer and other talk-show hosts were encouraging people to expose their darkest secrets on national television. So-called Reality TV went even further. Popular series such as *Survivor*, *Big Brother*, *The Bachelor*, *Who Wants to Marry My Dad?*, *Love or Money*, *Blind Date* and *Elim-i-date* all encourage "ordinary" people to act in extraordinary ways

in the hope of "staying in the game" or "on the island." Even more flam-
boyantly, internet web-cams offer sites where viewers can watch people
urinate, defecate, and fornicate. Even "true crime" has developed on hundreds of channels available 24/7 (*Judge Judy*, *America's Most Wanted*). In
shows such as *American Idol*, "stars"—perhaps "celebrities" is a more accurate term—are born, not because they are good, but because they are "on
TV."

Some would say that presenting oneself as a vehicle for entertainment
is very much in keeping with an age of instant communication—of computers, digital cameras, and 24-hour news—and with a world in which it
may seem that anyone may be under surveillance at any time, anywhere.
As essayist Cintra Wilson observes:

> The good old way of getting famous was to be very good at something
> artistic, and have everybody fall in love with you for it. That doesn't really
> work now, because, as many critics have pointed out, nobody is very inter-
> ested in art for its own sake anymore; now one only does 'art' as a necessary
> part of the equation, the means to the end of getting famous, so one can get
> plastic surgery and go to parties in order to lick and be licked upon by
> famous people like puppies in a basket.[5]

What if Doctor Doom had read Wilson's book? In the film *The Fantastic
Four* (2005), Victor von Doom understands the world of finance, but he is
a hopeless neophyte when it comes to "spin." The media speaks the language of American youth. It is Doom's failure to understand the American
youth culture, more than the combined might of the Fantastic Four, that
brings about his downfall.

Recasting Victor von Doom as the CEO of a major corporation may
seem like a betrayal of the original character, but, after the fall of the Soviet
Union, Marvel increasingly portrayed him as a capitalist. In *Namor: The
Sub-Mariner* #31 (1992; Byrne/Lee/Miggins), Doom's fishing fleet has to pay
exorbitant docking fees because his kingdom is landlocked. Resourceful
entrepreneur that he is, Doom acts on the principle that one must pay dearly
for what one does not have. So he builds a super-fleet with which he is able
to monopolize the worldwide fishing industry, thus reversing the situation.
His plan is to force everyone to pay exorbitant fees for his catch. This angers
Fen, a princess of Atlantis, who notes that with all the over-fishing and pollution, Atlantis is already on the brink of destruction. Victor von Doom's
monopoly will finish them. But Doom remains unmoved. In capitalism, the
weak die off: "It matters not at all to me... If a few million freaks perish on
the sacrificial altar of my plan."

---

5. Cintra Wilson, *A Massive Swelling: Celebrity Re-Examined as a Grotesque, Crippling Disease
and Other Cultural Revelations* (New York: Penguin, 2000), xvi–xvii.

In the 2005 *The Fantastic Four* movie, Doom's predatory monopoly seems ill-equipped to deal with a world in which the rules appear to have changed. As the film opens, Reed Richards (Ioan Gruffudd) approaches his old friend Victor von Doom (Julian McMahon) with an offer of a partnership in a potentially very profitable space probe. If Doom will allow Richards and his three associates to use his company's space shuttle and orbital station to track a passing cosmic storm, Reed will share the profits of that research. The cosmic storm should permit researchers to relive the moment of maximum change in the Earth's gene pool. In effect, the speed of evolution could be increased exponentially.

Victor von Doom sees this venture as a chance to make seventy-five percent of the profit on this genomic experiment, and to cement his relationship with the lovely Susan Storm (Jessica Alba), one of the four astronauts with whom he will be taking the trip. Though the profit split unfairly favors von Doom, Richard and his friends go along. After all, as Ben Grimm (Michael Chiklis) says, "What could go wrong?" His view is that the four astronauts, who venture only their lives, have nothing important to lose. By contrast, Doom, the investor, owns both the rocket and the space station. And, in fact, just about everything that can go wrong goes wrong, and the project's failure costs Victor his company.

Why? Because the media turn Victor von Doom into a victim of bad publicity. The world views him and the others as freaks because their DNA has, as a result of the cosmic storm, undergone incredibly rapid change. But the film is at pains to establish that, despite their physical alterations, The Fantastic Four — plus one (Doom) — remain very much the same people they were prior to their takeoff.

It is the media that determines who is the good guy and who is the bad. In an effort at damage control, Doom orders his secretary to book him on the Larry King Show. But The Fantastic Four steal the media spotlight, and Doom's company pays the price of public doubt. His IPO fails, and his investors foreclose on the company.

There is something of the 1939's *The Wizard of Oz* about what this foursome learn from their new powers. Reed, the intellectual, must learn to stretch his emotions; Johnny Storm, already a firebrand, has to learn when to turn on and off his adrenaline; Ben, The Thing, must learn that outer beauty is not "The (only) Thing"; and Sue, the most beautiful of the group, learns that she gains power by becoming invisible. But what does Doom learn or gain from the cosmic radiation? Superficially, he becomes a lightning rod for his own resentment, but intellectually and emotionally, he's as ossified as his armor. Doom's lack of intellectual flexibility is obvious. At the start of the film, he desires the world as a bauble; at the end, he's old-world junk.

Doom might have avoided his fate had he only taken a page from upstart Johnny (Chris Evans), who, being a bit younger, seems to understand intuitively that the media determine the flow of money, fame, and power. Johnny gives the team its name and logo and markets the team's "differences" to a toy company, a move that parodies the product tie-ins and endorsements of Marvel Enterprises. For even before *The Fantastic Four* opened, toy images of The Thing were hyped on television and available for sale in toy stores.

There are upsides and downsides to media attention. Sue hates the visibility that her invisibility earns her, and Ben, the powerful stone human, is like the Frankenstein monster, famous but also feared. In any case, thanks to Johnny, The Fantastic Four are celebrities, and therefore, unlike Doom's company, commercially viable. They make a fortune just by exploiting their "otherness." In contrast, Doom holds on to his old-fashioned privacy, hiding his physical metamorphosis as if it were a company secret. He tells his doctor, just before killing him, that "there are millions of dollars involved." This is both justifiable homicide and justifiable secrecy, in Doom's view.

At the same time, Johnny is selling Reed and the others as a reality show, taking pains to make their "private" discussions as public as possible. Johnny is not just an exhibitionist. He is a cutting-edge American entrepreneur, willing and able to profit from his personal abnormality. He lives his life as a form of drama, with himself as the lead. He is always photographed with his arms around good-looking women with no names. He is, both literally and figuratively, "hot"—a postmodern Hugh Hefner.

Victor von Doom is the villain of this piece, but he is surely not unique. He is not the only person who wants enough money to be able to cut ethical corners; even Richards will allow Doom to risk everything and is willing to make off with twenty-five percent of the proceeds. Nor is Doom alone in his pursuit of power. Consider the bankers who, until the project fails, fund the experiment. Doom's problem is that he cannot see that money is no longer the only financial asset, and that fame is a form of currency. Reed Richards, another failed businessman, objects to Johnny's marketing ploys: "We're scientists, not celebrities." But Johnny knows better. Media attention creates fame, and fame *is* power. Compared to Johnny and his ability to market himself and the team, Victor's own attempts at self-aggrandizement are comical. He has a thirty-foot statue of himself placed in front of his office building, but what is that compared to network TV coverage? Doom is a symbol of an "Old World" industrial economy, in which things are manufactured. Johnny in an integral part of a world of advertising, in which one sells, first and foremost, oneself. After that, the "tie-in" transactions follow as a matter of course. One's own image is the template from which ridiculously expensive replicas are made, boxed, and shipped from China.

Unable to cope with the media spotlight, a bankrupt Doom is told that he should go back to his homeland, Latveria. This advice is not an incidental expression of xenophobia, but a characterization of the limits of Victor's economic vision. We must remember that Victor von Doom is an interloper, a foreigner, who sought to tangle with the "big boys" of Wall Street. America is the largest economy in the world; Latveria is not even a minor international player. In their dismissal of Doom's appeal for continued support, the bankers make clear that, to them, Victor will always be a marginal player. This motif of minimizing Doom is a recurring theme in the film. At the opening, Doom imagines himself to be the divine expression of capitalism, a granite statute thirty feet tall. At the close, Doom is a tin man, packed in a cargo hold, the proportions of which suggest his insignificance to the global economy. He is far less important than the toys that Johnny means to mass-produce, toys that will segue into various forms of family entertainment involving The Fantastic Four, including television, DVD, and video games. Johnny and Doom are, in the final analysis, both playing the capitalistic game — but one game has outmoded the other. Doom is playing Monopoly; Johnny has a Gameboy.

Marvel and the Media

Johnny Storm's media savvy may be in part modeled on Marvel's ideological leader, Stan Lee, who has always had a keen eye for the consumer of his product. In an interview conducted with Kevin Smith, Lee discussed the creation of *The Fantastic Four*:

> My publisher had been playing golf with the publisher of DC Comics, which in those days was called National Comics. The publisher of National Comics said to him, "Boy, I've got this book, *The Justice League*, and it's a team of superheroes and it's selling real well." So my publisher... came to me, he said, "Hey, let's do a team" comic.[6]

Comic-book executives, schmoozing over a golf game, creating heroes that will sell.... Clearly, market forces were (and are) the reason behind many of Marvel's most interesting titles.

What is perhaps more interesting is Lee's admission that he was in a war of sorts with DC Comics, his main competitor. In a 1992 column of "Stan's Soapbox"—a monthly column Stan Lee wrote on all things Marvel — was suggesting that competition between Marvel and DC was good for the industry:

6. *Stan Lee's Mutants, Monsters & Marvels*, dir. Scott Zakarin (Columbia Tristar Home Video, 2002).

Hi Heroes!

It's time to correct a mistaken notion! We often get letters from loyal Marvelites gloating over the fact that some of our books may be outselling the competition, and wishing us well in our mission to conquer the comicbook world by defeating our rivals!

And therein lies the mistake! The last thing we want to do is conquer anything or defeat anyone. Sure, we have competitors, but just between us, most of them are friends of ours....

That's why we truly wish our competitors the best of luck. The better they get, the better we have to be. That's what competition is all about; that's what keeps each of us on our toes....

So here's to every hard-working hero at every comicbook company throughout the land! Let's never stop trying to top each other, we owe it to the most important gang of all — our readers!

Excelsior!

The fact that he had to explain suggests that most readers saw the competition between Marvel and DC as anything but friendly or healthy. There is some truth to this suggestion. Whether encouraged by the companies themselves or not, most comic book fans still see themselves as either in the Marvel camp or the DC camp. It's common to overhear someone in a comic book shop say to another, "Did you read the new *Batman*?" "No, I'm a Marvel guy." Even when artist/writer and fan favorite John Byrne left Marvel to work for DC, few fans defected with him.[7] This comic-book version of the Coke and Pepsi rivalry seems to have developed on its own and is probably due to readers' political and ideological sympathies. Of the two companies, Marvel, particularly in the 1960s, was ideologically more liberal and was more aggressively tackling social themes. While the two companies are relatively similar on many topics nowadays, loyalties remain. *Justice League* readers don't generally read *The Avengers*, although both titles concern groups of superheroes. *Captain America* readers don't generally read *Superman*, though the costumes of both of these all-American heroes are based upon the colors of the American flag. There have been attempts at crossover stories (a fight between Batman and The Hulk, or Stan Lee trying his hand at a *Superman* story, etc.), but fans have generally shunned these crossover stories, which are almost always dull.

Stan Lee Needs Matt Murdock

If, in fact, fans thought there was a corporate war of sorts going on in the comics, they were right. It was a civil war and it was going on the board-

---

7. However, as we suggest in our conclusion, if these readers were dissatisfied with Byrne's replacement, they may have shifted their consumer loyalties to another title in the Marvel line.

room of Marvel. There were no heroes, plenty of villains, and — for comic readers, writers and artists— plenty of victims.

In 2002, Dan Raviv published a study of Marvel's corporate culture entitled *Comic Wars: How Two Tycoons Battled Over the Marvel Comics Empire — and Both Lost.* In it, Raviv, a national correspondent for CBS news, recounts a Wall Street story of greed. The narrative concerns the battle for control of the company waged by Ronald Perelman and Carl Icahn. Neither was a comic book fan. For them, Marvel's characters served as the perfect vehicles for product placement. The idea may have been sound, but the venture itself failed. In 1997, Marvel Enterprises went into bankruptcy, taking investors (including one of the authors of this book) "to the cleaners."[8]

Although both Icahn and Perelman departed Marvel for greener corporate pastures, their policies eventually bore commercial fruit. The recent Marvel catalogue has everything from collector Spider-Man pens to Punisher bathrobes and Daredevil lunch boxes; Internet pop-ups remind us that Spider-Man now hawks cell phones. Every time we walk into a convenience store, we see our heroes reduced to corporate pitchmen: Captain America on bottled water flasks, The Hulk on rubber footballs and cookie jars, and so forth. And let's not forget the box office. It seems that every year we are bombarded by summer offerings of yet more Marvel heroes. Just since 2002, we can count the following blockbusters: *Spider-Man, Spider-Man II, The Hulk, X-Men, X-Men II, The Punisher, Blade, Blade II* — with receipts tallying in excess of two billion dollars.

Stan Lee and Marvel

But when we think of Marvel, particularly under the stewardship of Lee, we don't really think of a huge company. As the above reference "Stan's Soapbox" demonstrated, Lee wrote colorful and personal letters to us, his fans, and he encouraged a friendly camaraderie by using folksy names. He called himself "Smilin' Stan," and somehow over the years he made us feel that we were cool insiders, part of the Marvel Universe. His co-workers apparently felt the same way. Present Marvel editor Joe Quesada confessed in a documentary found in the *Daredevil* DVD that "Stan is a mutant — he makes you feel you're the most special person in the room."

Stan even approved of his friend Jack Kirby's drawing him as a comic book superhero! In *What If* # 11(1978; Kirby/Royer and Wray), Stan Lee,

8. Perelman also owns a controlling share of Panavision, which makes the film projectors for over 80 percent of the movie houses in the U.S. On January 28, 2003, the front page of *The Los Angeles Times* business section reported that Panavision was in "shaky condition" due to Perelman's corporate borrowings.

Jack Kirby and two other colleagues from the company find themselves transformed into The Fantastic Four. By day, they fight crime; by night, they write, draw, ink and color their adventures. Sales, as you might expect, soar. Stan (or Mr. Fantastic) uses his crime-fighting experiences to drive the commercial sales of his comic books, which are now read as newspapers! Yes, it was just one issue of life playfully imitating art. Yet even outside the fantasy of this *What If* issue, we can say that since Stan created Spider-Man and The Fantastic Four, he must share in their virtues. Though no longer running the company he built, we can still affirm that Stan was a superhero on a super-team called Marvel. His superpower was to craft superhero stories; Jack's was to draw them. Together, they worked to make the world a better place.

These virtuous images of Lee, were, of course, either self-constructed or approved by him. And we're certainly not going to argue that the single most creative and revered man in the comic book industry is a fraud. But even Stan Lee could not live up to the hype of being a superhero. Perhaps we were naïve, but we used to think that Stan Lee hated what had become of his company, but it turns out he was, and is, at least as economically motivated as the board members who replaced him.

Granted, Stan Lee was no Kingpin, though for a time it seemed he might become as wealthy as the crime boss. In 1998, he established Stan Lee Media from the ashes of a bankrupt Marvel Enterprises. Under his guidance, the company quickly earned praise for its innovation in online animation. Stan Lee Media developed a loyal audience for its new characters and attracted high-profile clients such as the Backstreet Boys for its animation services. With dot-com money lining its pockets, the company hired away talent from major studios like Disney and attracted animators looking for the creative freedom and the chance to work with the legendary Stan Lee. In 2000, soon after launching its stanlee.net website, Stan Lee Media's market capitalization was worth well over $300 million, about a third more than the value of the old Marvel Enterprises.

Like a character in one of his own *Daredevil* stories, Lee soon found himself embroiled in a spate of legal problems, ranging from insider trading to political bribery. Meanwhile, Stan Lee's business partner Peter Paul, an ex-cocaine dealer and racketeer who had spent three years in federal prison, was indicted for contributing $2 million to Hillary Clinton's Senate campaign in exchange for her endorsement of Stan Lee's receiving the American Medal of Freedom. Although Hillary Clinton was elected, Stan Lee was not awarded the medal. One can imagine Stan Lee complaining that this was unfair and Hillary replying, "How is that my problem?"

Stan Lee's stockholders would soon be complaining of unfair, and indeed illegal, practices. As with many Internet-related companies, Stan

Lee Media's perceived success did not accurately reflect conditions behind the scenes. With only just over $1 million in revenue, the company within one year spent $20 million. When the company folded, there was an outburst of protest from shareholders, who argued that the company's financial books had been cooked. The courts agreed. In 2000, a federal grand jury indicted Paul and three other company officers for allegedly bilking investors out of $25 million. Stan himself was never implicated or charged. But some of the victims of the bankruptcy, including one of the two authors of this book, may have asked: Where is Matt Murdock when we need him? The story isn't over. On February 2, 2005, Stan Lee complained to *60 Minutes II* that Marvel had attempted to cheat him of his cut of the *Spider-Man* movie and merchandizing profits. He sued and won. If the inevitable appeal is denied, Stan Lee stands to collect tens of millions of dollars.

Time Warner, the New Lex Luthor Enterprises?

Things are no less complicated at DC Comics, which is now owned by Warner Brothers, whose studios make the *Batman* movies and the animated series. Warner also owns Bugs Bunny, *Mad Magazine, People Magazine, Sports Illustrated, The Matrix* and *Harry Potter* films, and produces a large portion of the stuff we watch on TV, including *Gilmore Girls, Friends, Babylon 5, ER, The Drew Carey Show, Cold Case, The Ellen DeGeneres Show, George Lopez, Everwood,* and *The West Wing.* You only watch cable? No problem. Warner Brothers owns WB Network, CNN, HBO (which owns *Sex in the City* and the *Sopranos*), TNT, the Cartoon Network, and the TBS Superstation. Don't watch TV but like DVDs? Warner owns Castle Rock, Turner Entertainment, the classic MGM library, select titles from RKO, HBO Home Video, New Line Home Video, Redbus Films (in the UK) and BBC Video (in North America). It operates the Warner Stores, and it owns Rhino Records and Warner Brothers Records, which owns the rights to Madonna, Black Sabbath, Linkin Park, Alanis Morissette, Janet Jackson, Papa Roach, Snoop Dogg, Ashlee Simpson, and Lindsay Lohan. It owns AOL, the Internet behemoth with more than 25 million subscribers. And AOL owns Netscape, Road Runner Cable, Mapquest, Compuserve, and Moviefone.

In short, Time Warner is a corporation that in size and reach resembles those mega-evil corporations portrayed in the comic books. In addition, Warner has no qualms about leasing out any of its character for a quick buck. Take, for example, Jerry Seinfeld's recent American Express commercials, featuring Superman revamped as a New York consumer, who is hostage to his dry cleaner and dreams of buying surround-sound stereos for his Fortress of Solitude.

Comic Book Writers of the World Unite!

That fact is that Marvel and DC are now huge corporations. Well, that's the price of success. But there are signs of dissatisfaction among writers for both companies. In *Captain America* Vol. 3 #1-7 (2002; Garney/Waicek), Captain America is horrified to learn that Hollywood has made his life into a movie and has co-branded a slew of consumer tie-ins: Captain America T-shirts, masks, toys, video games. Cap registers concern, observing that "Captain America isn't a business venture."[9] But he can't stop the endorsement machine: Thinly disguised versions of *Access Hollywood* and *Extra* run stories on whether or not it is true that Captain America was once the bass player for the rock band Fleetwood Mac, and whether, in his spare time, Cap had not in fact invented Snapple. Cap is disgusted by it all, suggestive that perhaps Cap's writers are dissatisfied with the Fortune 500 status of Marvel Enterprises Incorporated. There may be duplicity at work here. After all, comic book writers and artists have always been aware that they help produce a commercial product. They are paid for their work. But there is a difference between the cottage industry that was Marvel and the huge company it has become, with its theme park rides and restaurants—fries served by Quicksilver and kept piping hot by the Human Torch. As Captain America says, he's been "catapulted from symbol to product icon."

There seems to be a similar and perhaps more obvious dissatisfaction among DC writers. In *Wonder Woman* #7 (1987; Perez/Patterson), Wonder Woman employs a publicists to get her message of peace out. This Diana, Princess of the Amazons, becomes the comic book version of Lady Diana, former Princess of Wales. And like the late Lady Di, she is exploited by the media. Her face adorns the covers of *Time, Life, National Geographic* and *People.* Worse, her agent exploits her face and figure, selling T-shirts, action figures, and costumes—one of which is purchased and used by a stripper!

Echoing the theme of turning superheroes into eye candy, in *JSA All Stars* #4 (Johns/Goyer/McKone/Faucher/Robinson/Harris), the former Star Spangled Kid gives his uniform to his curvaceous stepdaughter. He tell her that the camera loves a pretty girl, then adds: "I'm going to make a fortune on ebay sellin' the Star Spangled Kid's underwear!" Likewise, in *The Thunderbolts: Reassembled* #1 (2005; Nicieza/Grummett/Erskine), Captain Marvel suggests that one of the better-looking members of the group be propped up in front of the cameras. The media crafts heroes, and Captain Marvel knows that deeds are not enough — photo ops are also necessary.

9. This is not the first time a Captain America movie has been made in the Marvel Universe itself. Audiences flocked to see a documentary of the hero in *Captain America and the Falcon* #179 (1974; Englehart/Buscema/Colletta).

If such sly attacks bite the hand that feeds them, these writers are playing a dangerous game. In 1992, Marvel and DC published almost 250 titles a month. Today, that number has been cut by more than half. The result is that fans have been forced to read titles they may not normally support, and half the comic industry has been laid off. The half that are working don't dare ask for more money. After all, when there is a surplus in the labor pool — when supply exceeds demand — you never ask for a raise. Someone willing to do the work for less money is always waiting in the wings. Meanwhile, comic book prices continue to skyrocket — from $1.25 in 1992 to $3.99 in 2005. Graphic novels have gone from $5 to $15 or even $25. This is no longer a medium geared to kids, unless they are very rich kids. Then again, perhaps only the rich can afford to be idealistic.

I Gave at the Office

The perceived failure of capitalism to address the wants and needs of the many is perhaps no fault of its own. After all, the business of business is to make money, not to run a charitable trust (though in fact a great many corporations fund philanthropic foundations). Unprofitable handouts are what government is popularly perceived to be for. No one expects the government offices that mail out the unemployment checks to turn a profit. Nor do we expect the departments of water and power, sanitation, etc., to make money. Foreign policy mavens don't generate ready money, nor does the military. All these government departments run at a loss. That, in theory, is what taxes pay for: things that can't be run profitably.

But what if government and its officials are run like a business? Today, we have political parties raising hundreds of millions of dollars for campaigns; we have politicians who promise the world and then give us almost nothing they promised. We even *expect* a bad return on our investment. When a politician actually delivers on a substantial promise, we're shocked.

Here too the comics have incisive commentary to offer. In *Batman Dark Detective: Vote For Me* #1 (2005; Englehart/Rogers/Austin), we meet a rich Bruce Wayne, admired not just in America but around the world for his charitable donations. Bruce states that he believes "a man with money has to give back." So far so good. This might be a *Batman* comic, but we're in Spider-Man's world of social obligation. A man who profits from the efforts of his workers owes them something more than money. And a conglomerate like Wayne Enterprises, therefore, owes the entire world because it garners profits from the entire world. But such obligations are corporate, not political. Indeed, as the story progresses, it seems that politicians, always asking for a handout, don't follow this golden rule of obligation. Instead, Gotham's newest gubernatorial candidate, the Joker, doesn't ask for money but demands it: "Vote for me or I Kill You!" If the Joker were a run-of-the-mill politician, we'd think he was joking. But, unlike other politicians, the Joker takes his promises seriously.

Yes, this is a comic book, and no one would in reality ever vote for this madman, but the larger point shouldn't be missed here. No one would want to vote for the Joker, but at least he keeps his promises. If we vote for politicians who don't do what they say they will, then we give ourselves permission to be equally negligent. Making a contribution to a candidate who does what he promises is literally to pass the buck, abdicating our responsibility to help each other.

In the last decade, the public has been inundated with news of insider trading, illegal accounting methods, and stock fraud. Perhaps it is natural to demonize privileged people who seem to make millions at the expense of less privileged folks. And maybe it's easy to say that, if we lose our jobs or our 401(k)s, then someone is to blame and should be punished, or sued, or run out of business, and that we, the small investor-consumers, should be compensated. Doesn't the Constitution say something about our "right" to "the pursuit of happiness"? We ordinary folks must at least *seem* to be happy, or we will... What? Sue a company full of lawyers? Put on a mask and beat someone up?

These stories suggest that we can't rely on big business or big government to help us or our neighbors. Nor can we turn to violence as a solution. When someone we know gets laid off, when someone is robbed, when someone is defrauded, we should do more than shrug our shoulders and say, "How is that my problem?" Profits rise and fall, corporations come and go, but people, as individuals and as members of a community, need to help each other.

Spider-Man director Sam Raimi described the character this way:

> Peter is on a journey toward responsibility... and he's wrestling with all the sacrifices we all have to make to be responsible. He's learning what the cost of being responsible is... We all want to do good for each other, and the stories of heroes—I think that's their worth—remind us that's right. That "I too want to risk something to help others, to have this wonderful feeling about myself just like I do for this character [Spider-Man] I identify with when he does the right thing." That's why we like these stories. They show us the way.[10]

As Spider-Man learns, the rewards of being a hero are great, even if the pay stinks.

10. Fred Scheur, "Spider's Man," *Los Angeles Times*, June 27, 2004, E1, E4.

THINKING, DEBATING, WRITING

1. We have argued that a hero can't have friends. But can a hero understand the value of human life if she or he is detached from human society? Discuss the problem with a doctor or firefighter and present your findings to the class or to your friends.

2. A company pays its workers by the hour. Does it owe its employees anything more than a wage? Interview your parents or friends on this point and write an essay either defending the existing corporate structure, or suggest reasons why those companies owe workers more than just a paycheck.

3. We suggest that profit is akin to stealing. Defend capitalism from this charge.

4. We have argued that money gets in the way of friendship. Given that we will always have friends with more or less money than ourselves, can we ever know if this supposition is true or not? Weigh your own friendships and write an essay in which you state your criteria for friendship and the reasons why friendships fail.

5. What do you think of comic heroes selling things? What about athletes? Do such practices undermine your sense of the "pitchman's" worth? Write an open letter to a company that exploits one of your heroes, explaining why the company is or is not devaluing your favorite icon.

6. We suggested that the Spider-Man's foe Kingpin is much like any other CEO. Study the recent fall of WorldCom or Enron and discuss the crimes committed by these CEOs and how these companies affected people across the country.

7. Compare the selfish acts of Igor in Kafka's *The Metamorphosis* with the selfless acts of Peter Parker.

8. We have argued that Mary Jane is, in Peter's eyes, more than just a girl; she is a psychological prize that will make him feel more powerful, manlier, more in control of his world. Looking at the *Spider-Man* films, write an essay in which the tables are turned. After all, doesn't she pick and choose, like a shopper, the men she wants?

9. The Kingpin argues that there is too much red tape in business; Thomas Hobbes argues that governmental regulation benefits consumers. Looking at the recent antitrust case against Microsoft, take a side in this debate.

10. The Silver Surfer complains, "They have taken everything from me.... [M]y privacy, my dignity, my inner self." Interview a private detective or a computer consultant and determine how invasive is the Internet. You might, for example, do a Google search on your parents or friends and see what you can find.

4

The Comic Book Code
and American F-agg

If comic book readers are young, innocent, and open to suggestions, it stands to reason they need to be protected from images and ideas that might warp their minds. Yet comic book writers and artists have dealt with homosexuality, inter-racial marriage, and the AIDS epidemic. For many liberals, the comics may be a useful tool for sex education; most social conservatives, however, are less likely to see the benefits of super-hero sex.

Fredric Wertham's *Seduction of the Innocent* (1954) was among the most discussed books of the 1950s because it dealt centrally with a growing threat to America's youth: comic books! Wertham's major concern with comic books was that they exposed children to casual sex, including such deviant behavior as sadomasochism and homosexuality.

In his seventh chapter (entitled "I Want to Be a Sex Maniac!"), Wertham presents case after case in which "normal" children become perverts because of repeated exposure to the comic book superhero *Superman*:

> In one such drawing [from one of his patients], a girl is tied nude to a post. A handkerchief is stuffed in her mouth. On the floor are her discarded panties. In front of her is a boy heating some torture instruments over a fire. On his chest is the S of the superman [181].

The more Wertham studied the comics, the more he worried. Comic books famously represented the heroic actions of powerful men, but they also depicted these heroes enjoying situations of intense sadomasochism[1]:

> A nineteen-year-old boy told me about his high-heel fantasies: "You are the first one I tell it to. I think of girls twisting their heels on my chest and face."

---

1. This theme reportedly meets its most pernicious form in the popular Japanese comic *Rapeman*. We've never read an issue but, as we understand it, it's about a guy who rapes women to teach them that the phallus rules.

His first complete sexual stimulation had come from masochistic scenes in comic books at the age of about ten or eleven [182].

A twelve-year-old sex delinquent told me, "In the comic books sometimes the men threaten the girls. They beat them with their hands. They tie them around to a chair and then they beat them. When I read such a book I get sexually excited. They don't get me excited all the time, only when they tie them up" [183].

Wertham argued that we couldn't view these reactions as the isolated behavior of a few sick children. The notoriously repetitive nature of the comics themselves were pounding sick images into young minds. Seeing the same heroes undergo the same adventures month after month turned situations into set pieces, and so, by dint of familiarity, children learned the mechanisms of deviant sex.[2] Thus, reading *Superman* leads children to dream of S&M; reading about Batman and Robin turns them gay. Here is Wertham characterizing the way in which the handsome, rich bachelor, Bruce Wayne, cleaves to the all-male company of his butler, Alfred, and young ward, Dick Grayson (a.k.a. Robin):

> It is like a wish dream of two homosexuals living together. Sometimes they are shown on a couch, Bruce reclining and Dick sitting next to him, jacket off, collar open, and his hand on his friend's arm....
>
> Robin is a handsome ephebic boy, usually shown in his uniform with bare legs. He is buoyant with energy and devoted to nothing on earth or in interplanetary space so much as to Bruce Wayne. He often stands with his legs spread, the genital region discreetly evident [191].

Censorship and the Comics Code

Frightened by the findings in Dr. Fredric Wertham's book, *Seduction of the Innocent*, the U.S. Senate began to study "the comic book menace."[3] The industry, sensing that a McCarthy-like witch hunt was about to ensue, imposed a stringent code of self-regulation. The comics agreed that they could feature violence, but not death; no sex or titillation of any kind; tight costumes, but no genitalia; muscles might bulge, but nothing else.

DC Comics, publishers of *Batman*, tacitly agreed that something was wrong with their product and gave Robin a girlfriend. This only reinforced

---

2. The debate concerning what children learn through repetition is far from over. As the AP reported July 6, 2004, the same concerns are now being expressed about video-game violence. See "Lawmakers Attack Violent Video Games," http://story.news.yahoo.com/news?tmpl=story& cid=528&ncid=528&e=8&u=/ap/20040706/ap_on_hi_te/video_game_violence_1

3. See Dwight Decker, "Fredric Wertham — Anti-Comics Crusader Who Turned Advocate," *The Art Bin.* http://art-bin.com/art/awertham.html.

Wertham's argument. If Robin's relationship with Batman wasn't pederastic, why fix what was not originally broken? In a related quirk, DC fans were once polled as to whether Robin should be killed. Overwhelmingly, male fans voted to kill the kid. But doesn't the poll itself hint that even among straight readers of the comics, there is something tempting about the Boy Wonder?[4] Andy Medhurst undertakes a similarly "probing" homosocial investigation of Batman and Robin, arguing that heterosexual comic readers were afraid that Batman was gay, and that Robin had to be removed to reaffirm Batman's manhood.[5]

Batman and Robin and Family Values

The "problem" of Batman's sexual proclivities also recurs in Joel Schumacher's movie, *Batman and Robin* (1997). Schumacher handles the so-called homosocial contents of the material in ways that suggest an adherence to "family values." Not only is the film rated PG, but also the motives of the Dynamic Duo are pure, almost to the point of piety. Robin (Chris O'Donnell) copes with problems endemic to adolescence as he struggles for an independent role in crime fighting. He fits right into the typical family moviegoers' notion of a "normal" household. The tension here comes from the teenager's "normal" unwillingness to tolerate the heretofore customary conditions of the father/son relationship. Unsurprisingly, Batman (George Clooney) thinks of that household — the three of them, including the Wayne dynasty's old retainer, Alfred Pennyworth (Michael Gough)— as a "family." This "family values" motif is reinforced when Alfred Pennyworth's niece, Barbara Wilson (Alicia Silverstone), shows up and is adopted into the superhero household as Batgirl. Yet even in this family unit, we see glimmers of Wertham's sexual "dysfunction." Robin falls for the sexy Poison Ivy, affirming his heterosexuality, but Batman *doesn't* fall for her, suggesting that he's not completely straight. This notion is strengthened by Wayne's affirming gaze when Robin first appears in tight leather. "Nice

4. In reaction to Wertham, we might also look at *Mad Magazine's Captain Klutz*, which first appeared in 1967. His costume is clearly an amalgam of both the Marvel and DC universe: Captain America's mask with Batman's cape and utility belt. As the name suggests, Captain Klutz is a comedic character. The thrust of the comedy is sexual. His appearance alone is a clue to the bawdy nature of the humor: a nose the size and shape of a monstrously distended phallus; his pants, infantile diapers. Yes, it's all good fun, but within each joke is a kernel of Wertham's perspective: Klutz is an example of what comics can do for you. They fill your head with puerile fantasies that confuse the victim, ultimately displacing his true, healthy personality with masturbatory fantasies.

5. See his essay, "Batman, Deviance, and Camp," in *The Many Lives of the Batman: Critical Approaches to a Superhero and his Media*, eds. Roberta E. Pearson and William Uricchio (New York: Routledge, 1991), 149–64.

outfit," Batman coos. And, following Wertham, there is still no maternal force in Wayne manor. It is Uncle, not Aunt, Pennyworth who attends to these two attractive men, who have been living together under the watchful eye of this older, presumably unmarried gentleman's gentleman.

The First Super-Sexual Hero: American Flagg

So sex remained off the rack until a new company, First Comics, recruited *Batman* artist and writer Howie Chaykin, who demanded that his new book be free to violate all aspects of the comics code. First, wanting to live up to its name, agreed; and in July of 1983, *American Flagg* appeared.

Chaykin presumed his readers had a solid grounding in comic book lore. Even the title of his comic makes this point. The history of American comic books is replete with flag-draped characters such as Captain America. Yet the hero of *American Flagg* wears no part of the flag on his person. In fact, he looks very little like the "average" superhero. He has no actual costume, no cosmic or mechanical powers; he is just an average ... American?[6] No, he isn't even that. Born and bred on Mars, Reuben Flagg immigrates to America when his film career falters.

The idea of an immigrant becoming an American hero is not, in and of itself, unusual. Superman was an immigrant, having come from another planet, and you can't get more alien than that! He is the son of Jor-El, but raised by John and Martha Kent, who teach the boy how to speak English, milk cows, and love his country. The country that Clark Kent loves, with its rural idyllic pastures and clean vertical cities, its dashing, generous millionaires, well-meaning citizens, and always-honest politicians, captures the idealism of the post–Word War II era in America, when anything was possible except failure.

The America in which Reuben lives captures its mirror opposite. After a nuclear war, which Russia wins, American commercial interests relocate on Mars. America itself is left to a variety of multicultural desperadoes who are continually attempting to take back the planet from the Russians and their allies (and sometime rivals), the Brazilians. The problem is that the reactionaries are often too busy killing each other to band together effectively against the Russians. The Jewish Offense Brigadiers are often at

6. Following *American Flagg*, Marvel introduced *Nomad*, a *Captain America* spin-off, in which the hero has no costume. In issue #11 (1993; Nicieza/Mays/Eliopoulos/Herdling/Defalco), Nomad captures a killer by posing as a transvestite. He notes that wearing women's gear is not a huge difference from wearing the standard superhero's spandex outfit, although the high heels wreak havoc with his arches. In *Daredevil* #324 (1994; Chichester/McDaniel/Oakley) a gun-toting maniac bursts in upon Daredevil, proclaiming, "Name's John Barrett, S.H.I.E.L.D. cyborg, and a real man's man! You don't see me runnin' around in tights now, do ya?"

odds with the American Survivalist Labor Committee, who hate the black-only Committee for a New Brazilia. American interests eventually regain control of parts of the former United States. However, they are not interested in reviving lost freedoms; their main concern is reawakening consumerism. In place of Congress, the Mars Corporation sets up an administrative center called the "Mall," where its citizens shop, shop, shop. To keep consumerism high, the "Plex"—as the government calls itself—pumps its citizens full of drugs and porn. The biggest star on Earth makes his films on Mars. His name? Reuben Flagg. When Reuben tires of making porn, he decides that law enforcement might be more his thing. So he applies to the Plex, which sends him to what used to be Chicago. Eventually, he becomes mayor of the city.[7]

Hail the Hulk

While First Comics was violating the comics code by having a porn star sleep with beautiful women in every issue, Marvel remained comparatively staid. The company openly dealt with the Cold War, but when it came to sex, it could only approach the issue metaphorically. One of the prime vehicles for this discussion was its popular title *The Incredible Hulk*. The origins of The Hulk go back to the standard Marvel ploy of the military-industrial complex gone awry. This time, we have the scientist, mild-mannered Bruce Banner, in love with Betty, the daughter of General Ross.

Ross hates Banner, whom he considers to be a venal egghead, but Banner, eager to please the man he hopes is his future father-in-law, presses on with his genetic research into replicating the lost super-soldier serum (discussed in our chapter on black superheroes). Afraid that he will lose his Betty to one of those beefy soldiers, Banner injects himself with the serum, with disastrous results. He is transformed into an eight-foot, 400-pound, green-skinned imbecile with a dangerous temper. At heart, The Hulk isn't all that different from a good-natured child who wouldn't hurt a butterfly unless angered. But The Hulk is angered repeatedly—by a military that wants to capture him, by villains who want to control him, and by Banner, who works to suppress him.

Banner blames The Hulk for ruining and re-ruining his life. A typical Hulk story goes something like this: Banner, on the lam because The Hulk

7. Reuben's transformation is clearly meant to ridicule an America fascinated with image. At the time *Flagg* was written, the actor Ronald Reagan was finishing his second term as President. Reagan, who had made a film in which he co-starred with a chimpanzee (*Bedtime for Bonzo*), is slightly reformed in Flagg, who is assisted by a talking *pussy*-cat named Raul.

is hunted, walks into a town and finds work. He uses the money to buy lab equipment so that he can find an antidote for The Hulk serum in his blood. But then someone steps on his foot, or puts a new friend in danger, and out comes The Hulk. Crash goes the lab and, afterwards, anything that stands in The Hulk's way. Banner then awakens, usually on the side of the road, and sees that The Hulk has destroyed yet another town. Banner walks to the next town and the story repeats itself.

Banner has no idea what The Hulk does when he transforms into the creature, but interestingly, the converse is not true. When The Hulk appears, he seems to know exactly what has happened to Banner while he's been away. The Hulk is never really dormant in Banner. He's like a silent giant, watching everything that happens to him. For example, in the miniseries *The Ultimates* (2001; Miller/Hitch/Currie), Banner is fearful that Betty is going to leave him for another, more successful scientist. Turning into The Hulk, the monster grabs this rival, Hank Pym, and says: "You always make Banner look like an idiot in front of Betty, Pym ... that's why Hulk's gonna tear off your head."

Despite The Hulk's best intentions, in issue #372 (1990; David/Keown/McLeod), Banner finds himself once more in ripped clothes and left without money on the outskirts of some nondescript town. Holding his head, he mutters to himself, "I'm sick of being kicked and shoved around and treated like dirt! I've had it! I want Betty! And you [the Hulk] won't stop me! So get out of my way!" As if on cue, The Hulk again takes possession of Banner's body.

In this sense, The Hulk is a comic book version of Robert Louis Stevenson's *The Strange Case of Dr. Jekyll and Mr. Hyde*. We all know the story, thanks to those great old black-and-white horror movies. The well-respected doctor sneaks off to his lab to gulp down his test-tube of chemical goodies; the test tube falls crashing to the floor, the doctor grabs at his throat, his hands grow hairy, his spine curls, he loosens his collar and, *presto*, Hyde appears. While the good doctor is away, Hyde comes out to play: he gambles, steals, kills, and indulges in all the vices denied to Jekyll. Similarly, Banner goes away while The Hulk storms around smashing things. Then Banner comes back to see the consequences, which he invariably blames on The Hulk. Banner is always the victim, even if The Hulk is, by nature, both innocent and untouchable. Hail The Hulk! No one is going to give this bad boy a parking ticket, raise his taxes, or cut him off on the freeway. These stories give us a vicarious thrill of vengeance. If we, the Banners of the world, can't get justice, the hidden Hulk within us will find a way to smash our enemies, leaving us, like Banner, seemingly innocent of the consequences.

Yet there is one way in which The Hulk is not, and never will be, like Mr. Hyde. Mr. Hyde — in the movies, at least — has sex; The Hulk does not.

The Hulk may be an adult from the waist up, and from the thighs down. But, in the pelvic region, he remains a child. The growth hormones in the super-soldier serum affect his muscles, but radically suppress his libido. If this is so, why is The Hulk so attracted to Betty?

The Hulk Just Wants a Hug

Sigmund Freud argued that because humans derive their first feelings of pleasure at their mothers' breasts, they therefore secretly desire to return to that site of physical comfort. Later physical pleasures, such as sex, are measured against that first moment of pleasure. Hence, according to Freud, men seek women who remind them of their mothers. Freudianism further holds that male crime and creativity are different ways of dealing with this incestuous drive. Because we can't have sex with our mothers—or can't have sex with the women who remind us of our mothers—we divert our libidos into channels, sometimes creative, sometimes destructive.

Whether such a perception is scientifically tenable or not, this paradigm fits the Banner/Hulk dichotomy rather well. In the Ang Lee film *The Hulk* (2003), we learn that when Bruce was only an infant, his father killed his mother in a domestic quarrel. Since that quarrel was about *him*, the child suppresses the memory, along with the emotional storm accompanying that dreadful event. This bottleneck of feeling within him explains why, when he meets Betty, he's unable to connect with her. An inner sense of foreboding plagues Banner; he senses the monster within, born not when he was exposed to gamma radiation, but when he watched his mother being murdered by his father. When he meets Betty he transfers his yearning for his lost mother onto his girlfriend, but finds himself unable to act on his emotions, to express his love for Betty. From a Freudian perspective, a declaration of love would be a confession of his competitive war with his father over the love of his mother.

It seems clear that Banner needs The Hulk for more than attacking his future father-in-law's tanks. Indeed, his most important function is to deal with sexual frustration. The Hulk allows him to express his love for Betty, but only as a child expresses his love for his mother. Put another way, when Banner is The Hulk, he can go anywhere he wants, but he doesn't go to Vegas; instead, he heads to Sesame Street. Perhaps The Hulk is like King Kong, who treats Fay Wray like a doll. The idea of sex would never occur to The Hulk. Mentally, he's a child who will never age. As The Hulk, Banner has discovered a serum not just for strength, but for immortality. The price is a Faustian trade-off. The Hulk becomes the emotional voice of Banner's life, while Banner, the brains, is locked out of The Hulk's tender moments with Betty.

Such an analysis allows us to understand why, again and again, The Hulk kidnaps Betty. He loves her, and he sees even Bruce Banner as a rival. Despite his physical prowess, The Hulk cannot express his feelings for Betty. We might infer that he doesn't want to have sex with her. This is not to deny that The Hulk wants Betty's affection, but it must be expressed only in hugs and kisses.

Beauty and the Green Beast

Without his rage, Banner's relationship with Betty would be all but impossible, because she likes demonstrative men. In some part of her, at least in the Ang Lee film, Betty wants to be picked up and cared for by a powerful man, whose physical strength she can see and feel and rely upon. She wants to look up to a man, or as some might say, to be mastered.

If we take Betty's inclination toward strong men in the crudest way, as the totality of her sexual interest, what she wants is The Hulk to be "The Hunk." But one's impulses do not determine the totality of one's desires. It seems just as clear that Betty also has feelings for Bruce Banner, mild, well-behaved, sublimated-libido scientist that he is.

To Banner, being The Hulk is a test of love: "I wanted to see you because I had to find out why you loved me, or if you did...." Betty doesn't buy the story. She suggests that he uses his Hulk-rage as a way of avoiding commitment: "You never would [commit] because of what's inside you" (*The Ultimates* #1). In fact, it may well be Banner's fear of commitment that is the real concern. As the story continues, Banner discovers the antidote to The Hulk syndrome, only to realize that he misses the uproar and the violence of The Hulk's episodes. Perhaps most of all, Banner misses the thrill of The Hulk's masculinity. As Banner admits to Betty, "The honest-to-God truth of the matter is that I just missed being big."

Banner's inability to feel comfortable, much less sexy, in his own skin is not unique. The Thing also faces related issues of beauty and self-esteem. Ben Grimm often has to choose between being handsome and weak or ugly and strong. In the animated TV episode of *The Fantastic Four* entitled "And a Blind Man Shall Lead Them" (1995), Doctor Doom attacks The Fantastic Four with a nuclear bomb. Although they survive, they lose their powers, and Ben regains his normal appearance. Accustomed to being covered in orange concrete, Ben is thrilled: "I just went from a chump to a hunk." Soon after, Ben visits the zoo, where he sees a mother and child looking at the orangutans: "Mommy, mommy, look at that big ugly orange thing." Ben shares his thoughts with the primate behind the bars: "Buddy, I know just how you feel." His girlfriend, Alicia, is blind, and so is indifferent to physical appearances. "Sometimes we blind people can see more clearly than those with sight," she says. But Ben can see, and when he turns into The Thing again, he finds that his self-esteem is so low that sex with Alicia is impossible.

The Vision and the Mechanics of Sex

Reed Richards is married to the voluptuous Invisible Woman. They even have a child, but their sex life is attenuated by the fact that her voluptuousness cannot be seen. Wertham's reign over the comics was so complete that heroin was a less taboo subject than intercourse.[8] Thus, in 1971, Marvel Comics dared to show Peter Parker's friend Harry suffering from heroin addiction, but the scene was only a page long, and the problem referred to obliquely, and Peter's concern for his friend briefly overshadowed his strong, though prudish, attraction for Mary Jane.[9] Still, Marvel felt the drug reference violated the ethical code of the comic standards and gave its agents the right to refuse the issue. Next month, Spidey, along with every other comic on the rack, returned to its topical self-control.

For all the muscle-rippling comic book heroes, testosterone seems re-directed from the pelvic region to the legs. In one typical story arc, the fetching Scarlet Witch marries the android hero, The Vision (*The Scarlet Witch and The Vision*, Mini-Series, 1986; Englehart/Howell/Monney). This particular robotic unit does not come equipped with a mechanical phallus, but the couple somehow produce a child by sheer dint of their emotional exertions.

Instead of discussing the physiology of reproduction (the biology course designated Sex 101 on college campuses), Marvel used the romance of The Vision and the Scarlet Witch to discuss interracial relationships.[10] When Wanda (a.k.a. the Scarlet Witch) and her husband try to buy a house in an all-white neighborhood, the residents confront them with homemade weapons, threatening, "We don't want your kind around here." In what sounds very much like language from the civil rights movement, Wanda replies, "You can accept The Vision and myself for what we are — people

8. This was a ridiculous state of affairs, considering the comics that were popular among teens in the sexually liberated 1960s.

9. "Mary Jane" is also an old-fashioned way of referring to marijuana, but the irony may be unintentional. On a related point, Spider-Man was used in anti-drug ads in 1999. See "Spider-Man to fight youth drug abuse," August 31, 1999, CNN: http://www.cnn.com/US/9908/31/ spiderman.drugs/

10. One could say that sex between witch and a robot is more inter-species than interracial, but even so, the lack of sexual relations between an android and a witch directs attention to arrangements that are, given the society in which we live, unusual.

The Vision and Scarlet Witch, a mixed couple, find themselves confronting angry whites in suburbia. (By permission of Marvel Comics.)

like yourselves...! Sure, I have mutant powers, and he lives inside a synthetic shell, but we're all part of the same club — parents!! And we all want the same thing — a quiet and secure place to raise our families! That's what I wish for you, and that's what I want from you!" Convinced by her passion and cowed by her threatening power, the rednecks with baseball bats agree that it is unfair to hurt a pregnant lady. No like provision is made for her husband, whom they presumably still want to kill.

The Vision's sexuality is mysterious enough, but what ensues is a real head-scratcher. When the babies are born (Wanda has twins), Wanda's brother, himself a superhero named Quicksilver, objects that the twins, Tommy and Billy, are named "from his side of the family! But what can I expect?"

What nonsense! The Vision *has* no family! He's a product, something manufactured, like a clock radio. What family can The Vision have? His mother was a supercomputer, his father an oil can. We might suspend disbelief here in favor of magic realism and simply accept that Quicksilver feels slighted. Many parents want their children to marry within their faith, within their race, certainly within their species. But to marry inorganic matter? How can a computer create and transfer DNA code to organic matter? But we're being too literal again. We can dismiss the logic of The Vision's procreative abilities; we don't need to know how and why he creates a neosperm, just that he does so.

Things get even sillier in *The Vision and the Scarlet Witch* #1 (1982, Mantlo/Leonardi/Akin and Garvey). In this short-lived series, the happy couple moves into their new home. The Vision is hungry — though what he eats is unclear — and Wanda agrees to cook him up something, even if it means they must "postpone their lovemaking until tonight." While busy in the kitchen, she thinks back on her life: one of the original Brotherhood of Mutants, she then joined The Avengers, and learned to control her powers under the tutelage of the witch Agatha Harkness. Meanwhile, upstairs in an empty library, The Vision — now renamed as just "Vision"— reflects that he's not human but an extremely life-like android, built by the automaton Ultron 5.

We further learn that Ultron 5 used parts of the original Human Torch, an android built by the allies in the Second World War. (Never mind that he's a machine but called the *Human* Torch!) His full legacy is as follows: The first Human Torch was built by Professor Horton and fought the Nazis as part of a team called the All-Winner's Squad, a supergroup that included Captain America, a youthful Namor, the Whizzer, and Miss America. (The latter two were married and sired Quicksilver and the Scarlet Witch.) Rounding out the group were Cap and the Torch's respective sidekicks, Bucky and Toro.

After the war, the Torch and Toro scorched commie butt, until the Torch was doused with a fire retardant called "Solution X-R," specially concocted for the purpose by the USSR. Thereafter, he was buried in the desert and left for dead. But those commies didn't do their homework: They carelessly buried him on an atomic test site; the terrible power of a mushroom cloud reactivated our hero. But the Torch's now-atomic body was never intended to handle this awesome power and he eventually went nova. Eleven years later, the evil scientist known as the Mad Thinker reactivated and reprogrammed the Torch to attack The Fantastic Four. The team had no choice but to deactivate him again, but, since he was a war hero, they gave him a funeral of sorts. Since the Torch came from a lab, Reed Richards sealed him into one — a fitting funeral for a machine — lab to lab, dust to dust. Soon after, the mega-automaton Ultron 5 came across him and modified him yet again. He was no longer the Human Torch. He had become The Vision.[11]

So, The Vision or "Vision," isn't just a machine; he's recycled parts, now wandering around his new suburban home. Machine or not, when demons come a-calling on Halloween and Wanda is injured, not only does the android rush to his wife's side, he even sheds tears. Our narrator tells us that "even a synthozoid can cry." Eventually, Vision and Wanda drive the demons from their homestead, but, needless to say, after this ordeal, they are simply too tired to make love.

Super Reasons to Avoid Sex

If you're rolling your eyes, we share your frustration. After all, machines don't cry, and it's difficult to accept that there is any passion in this marriage. Besides, even if The (cold-hearted) Vision has sex with Wanda on some quieter night, he can't enjoy it. He lacks the requisite circuitry. But what about a hero like Captain America, whose testosterone level sustains his superhuman strength? Cap dates attractive women, but these relationships never develop very far. Or do they?

In *What If* #38 (1983; Margopoulos/Reed/Esposito), we are asked to imagine Captain America married with children and ready to retire. As we might expect, the Red Skull exploits Cap's love of his family to bring the hero to his knees. But in this alternate universe, the Red Skull has a family as well. His son carries on the family tradition by attacking the aging Cap. With his family at risk, our hero has no choice but to keep on fighting, not for the love of freedom, but for the preservation of his family. The

11. The full story, with footnotes concerning the stages of The Vision's development, is found in *Avengers* #134 (1974; Englehart/Buscema/Station).

message is clear: This "What If" Cap would have been better off had he remained celibate.

Nor is it only in the "What If" world that Cap faces temptation. In *Avengers West Coast* #56 (1990; Byrne/Ryan), we learn that Wanda has left The Vision; the marriage is "no longer viable," but we're not given any details as to what went wrong. But soon after, she hooks up with Captain America. Our hero may even have had sex with the Scarlet Witch. He's not sure: it seems Wanda has temporarily lost control of her psychic powers, and reality itself is now up for grabs. Thus, Cap remains unsure whether he has in fact done the deed, and even if he has, it's not his fault. Wanda was controlling his mind and presumably his body (*Captain America and the Falcon* #8, 2004; Priest/DiVito/Kolish).

His ex-partner, the Falcon, has sex regularly. For example, in *Captain America and the Falcon* #12 (2005; Priest/Bennett/Jadson), the Falcon takes time out from saving the world to have a quickie with a Navy Seal hottie. But as we've seen in our chapter on black superheroes, the rules are different when it comes to the Falcon and Luke Cage, who are always depicted as less stable, less trustworthy, and more sensual than their caped Caucasian counterparts.

Unless he's under mind control, however, Cap is celibate, though not always by choice. On one occasion, he almost makes love to his blonde supermodel girlfriend, secret agent Sharon Carter, but the intimate scene is interrupted by Scorpion, a supervillain, equipped with a huge, reptilian tail—the one phallic feature of the tale.[12] And, as we have seen, Spider-Man solemnly resolves to avoid intimacy with any woman, fearing that, should she discover his identity, his enemies could hurt her, or use her to manipulate him. Since either scenario is undesireable, sex is out of the question. Likewise, Banner is attracted to Betty, but as The (bulging) Hulk, there is no question of his doing much about it.[13]

The X-Men are perhaps most sexually frustrated of Marvel's heroes. Being prisoner to, or imprisoning, our sexual desires is also at the heart of the very popular *X-Men* comic, which envisions and justifies physical freedoms. Bryan Singer's big screen *X-Men* neatly melds our interests in strength, size, and sex. With the skin-tight costumes clinging to Halle Berry (Storm), Rebecca Romijn-Stamos (Mystique), and Famke Janssen (Dr. Jean Gray), no one can miss the meaning of the multiracial, even multi-species, dimen-

12. Captain America finally sleeps with someone! See his tryst with the voluptuous Diamondback in *Captain America* #30 (2004; Kirkman/Eaton/Geraci). Oops! Turns out she is a robot. See *Captain America* #31 (2004; Kirkman/Eaton/Geraci).

13. Since Banner takes the growth serum in order to impress Betty, his sexual diffidence is perhaps a veiled reference to steroid use in America, which turns male athletes, including bodybuilders, into huge specimens, even as it shrivels and deactivates the testicles.

sion of the film's supercharged sexuality. This is a real buzz-kill for Professor X, who is paralyzed from the waist down. He's the only *Homo superior* (i.e. mutant) who isn't either naked, like Mystique, or suggestively leathered and ready but oddly unwilling to contribute to the gene pool and evolution.

DC Comics seemed to move in a different direction, making sure that the 1990s Batman cavorted with Catwoman. Yet even here, where sexual interest was explicit, sexual contact was rarely on the menu. Then we have Superman, who, if we were to go by his name alone, should set the standard in performance. He has the model physique, and his stamina is quite literally out of this world. Plus, Clark Kent grew up on a farm and, presumably, knows all about animal husbandry. But, like most superheroes, he seems uninterested in sex. Why should this be? Why doesn't Superman exploit his good looks and physical prowess? To answer this question, we need to consider the historical context of Superman's origins.

Superman and his Rural Upbringing

Superman's origins are intricately connected to America's international and domestic security. The first Superman comic (*Action* #1) appeared in 1938, but the hero gained national fame circa 1945. America was winning a world war at the time, having developed an atomic weapon, and its industry was turning out war material at a superhuman rate. In short, Superman appeared at a time when America was flexing its own strength. And yet, this child of Krypton does not land in any industrial or urban center, but in a version of America's past, the farmland of Smallville. The people who find him, Jonathan and Martha Kent, are prototypical of a Jeffersonian America: farmers—independent, strong, healthy, moral. Quite a different world would have confronted Clark had he landed in New York, with its filth, factories, and suburban sprawl. In fact, in many ways, Superman, whose descriptive hype—"faster than a speeding bullet, more powerful than a locomotive, able to leap tall buildings at a single bound"[14]—is indelibly linked to urbanized landscapes, gives us a sense of America as a violent, industrial and intimidating place. The cover of *Action Comics* # 1 (1938; Siegel/Shuster), does not present the hero fighting for "Truth, Justice, and the American Way," but out to stop the technological and urban marvels which have ruined traditional gender roles. Superman is a luddite

---

14. The famous phrase was first used for the animated Max and Dave Fleischer series, released by Paramount Pictures in 1941. The phrase as found in the pilot (September 26, 1941) originally cast Superman as a force of nature: "Faster than a streak of lightning, more powerful than the pounding surf; mightier than a roaring hurricane," but was rewritten for the second installment, "The Mechanical Monsters," November 28, 1941.

avenger; his job is not to put America in the driver's seat, but to smash all cars and, in so doing, drive Americans back to the farm and its traditional values. This anti-industrialism is also present in the animated film features, produced by Paramount Pictures from 1941 to 1943. An early story, "The Mechanical Monsters," has Superman fighting a bank-robbing robot mob. Lois steals aboard one of the flying robots and is soon captured by the robot's designing industrialist, who attempts to dip Lois in molten lead. Arriving at the factory of the mastermind villain, Superman demolishes the robots and rescues Lois. He then picks her up and returns her to the purity of the countryside, symbolized by blue skies. And so it goes: in "Billion Dollar Limited" (January 9, 1942), Superman foils the robbery of a train on its way to the U.S. mint. Superman disables the train, whose mechanical processes have been harnessed by the thieves, and lugs it to the mint like a caped mule. In "The Bulleteers" (March 27, 1942), Superman defeats a gang of criminals whose secret weapon is a car that morphs into a plane and a rocket. In "The Magnetic Telescope" (April 24, 1942), a mad scientist uses a device to harness magnetic rays of a passing comet. The device, his foe warns, is tantamount to "tampering with nature." Superman destroys the machine and restores the natural order. The story is repeated in "The Electric Earthquake" (May 15, 1942), in which American Indians, anxious to reconquer New York, use modern science to destroy white civilization. Superman sympathizes, longing to see the "old island" looking "good," but he realizes that the Indians, who now use advanced technology, are not likely to return the island to its verdant youth.[15]

What also strikes us as important about *Action Comics # 1* is the terror Superman causes in men. What are these fleeing men afraid of? Superman never harms anyone except criminals. Does the cover suggest all men are criminals? If so, what is their crime? Another early cover depicts Superman grabbing a woman violently. Again, what is her crime? We suggest that, in Superman's eyes, Metropolis is in fact filled with criminals, or at least moral deviants.

Superman and Feminism

During the Second World War, America's women left the domesticity of the home for factory work. Posters showing muscular women, epitomized by Rosie the Riveter, suggested that women could do the work, even if it

15. There are exceptions to Superman's Agrarian tendencies. For example, in "The Underground World" (June 18, 1943), Superman discovers an underground world of birdmen. Rather than leave them be, he uses a grenade to destroy their world. The idea that Superman fights technology was revived in a 1982 issue of *Superman Family* (#217; Bridwell/Schaffenberger/ Chairmonte), in which the Man of Steel takes on Metalo, a man in an iron suit.

meant sacrificing femininity for the good of the country. Some women became quite skilled and thus were a threat to men, who saw these assertive women as taking their rightful places in society. When Clark comes to Metropolis, he gets a job as a reporter at the *Daily Planet*, but quickly becomes emasculated by Lois Lane, a new-age virago whose moxie wins her the top cover stories. Clark, meanwhile, is typically given some lesser task formerly reserved for women. To a man raised in a Jeffersonian Smallville, the big city is problematic because the roles of women and men have been turned upside down.

Women have become men, but these "butch" women don't need these "feminized" men. Superman's love interest, Lois, is a prime example. Her masculine behavior suggests autonomous completion. She doesn't need a man to feel complete. As a consequence, the emasculated man is unable to attract women like Lois. Clark's submissive responses to Lois are legendary: "Whatever you say, Lois"; "Gee whiz, Lois." Since women do not need men, all the Average Joe can do is bond with other emasculated men or boys. Thus, Clark forms a relationship with Jimmy Olsen. Together, they discuss why neither of them is capable of seducing Lois, whom they both seem to adore. In the animated feature "The Arctic Giant" (February 27, 1942), Clark asks Lois if she needs some company in reporting on a story concerning a monster. "Oh, no, Clark," she replies, "you'd probably faint if you saw the monster. You scare so easily." Lois leaves, and Clark takes heart in the fact that she may be right about his "mild-mannered" persona, but "Superman hasn't fainted one time yet."

It can't be fun being either of these guys. A typical *Daily Planet* day begins with Lois beating out Clark for a story. Lois then gets kidnapped — Lois is always being caught by bank robbers, master criminals or aliens— and Superman saves the day. Then Lois writes her story, which can usually be summarized: "Reporter Kidnapped; Superman Saves!" Meanwhile, Clark writes about some farm report. Before the printers roll, Clark and Jimmy sit around reading the copy, remarking on how great Superman is, while Lois goes for a drink and hunts for yet another lead.

What interests us is the two men reading Lois' reports about Superman, who typically shows up just in time to save her. This repeated scenario suggests a fantasy in which women still need big, strong men to save them. Clark and Jimmy are neither big nor strong; consequently, their reading of the daily news is yet another reminder of what's wrong with them. It's another form of self-flagellating humiliation.

Have you ever wondered wonder why Clark wants to be a reporter? He was raised on a farm and should be good with his hands. Yet the physical demands of reporting, at least as depicted here, require only a pencil and a piece of paper. Lois can beat men in the medium because she can compete within its skills range without having to compete physically. Reporting, like many newly-created city jobs, was and is non-gender-specific. That

Clark would take the job suggests that he's not comfortable in the ways of rural America, even if his whole personality has been shaped by Smallville's rugged Jeffersonian ideology.

Of course, Clark's disguise is understandable. He must seem weak so that no one suspects that he's really Superman. But this rationalization is interesting in itself. Does it suggest that male, urban readers saw Superman as a fantasy in which they too might rise above their emasculated realities, into a fantasy of violent males who assert physical dominance over women?

Things are better for Clark than they are for Jimmy. At least Clark is secretly Superman. Even better, Superman has a girlfriend — sort of. His one affirming relationship is not with Lois nor Lana, his Smallville friend of the comics — we'll get to the television series and films in due course — but with Wonder Woman, the Amazonian Warrior Princess and proto–New Age woman.

Her invisible plane suggests that she is on some level to be associated with the female factory workers who built America's B-17s and other weaponry in the war. Her association to the mythical Amazons, a tribe that tried to dominate men in Greece, suggests that men should fear her. Her lasso, though seemingly innocuous, is nonetheless magical, thus linking her to witchcraft and perhaps even hinting at S&M. For Clark, who has all the hallmarks of submission, what could be better? But do these two have sex or get married?[16] No. Rather, Wonder Woman is happy at home in the company of women, leaving Superman to mope around his apartment, waiting for Lois not to call, or in his Fortress of Solitude, an icy palace that suggests the sterility of his domestic circumstances.

The Superman Movies

Nothing, it seemed, was ever going to change. However much Clark lived in the city, he was still a small-town goof. Similarly, however much Superman saved America, he was never able to redeem his country's morals. Both Clark and Superman, at least as depicted from 1938 to 1980, are impotent failures. As of this writing, DC continues to wrestle with making Superman more attractive. On July 21, 2004, the *L.A. Times* ran an article entitled "Back to the Launch Pad for 'Superman,'" in which John Horn declared that "the character doesn't have the kind of edgy appeal of a Batman or the 'X-Men' crew. He's an old-fashioned do-gooder, sort of a nerdish superhero."

16. The cover of *Superman Family Giant* #181 (1982; Bates/Delbo and Colleta) depicts Lois, dressed as a bride, next to Superman. A priest pronounces them man and wife. But Lois is horrified to find that Superman has been turned into a gnome. The cover is misleading: within the comic itself, Superman and Lois do not marry, though Superman is turned, albeit temporarily, into a gnome.

Superman's inability to turn back the sexual clock is apparent in the Christopher Reeves vehicle, *Superman: The Movie* (1978), which sticks to the same formula as the comic book. In *Superman II* (1981), however, Lois (Margot Kidder) finds out about Clark's alter ego, and they fall in love. Superman gives up his superhuman abilities and becomes a regular human. Although they have coitus, Clark is oddly dissatisfied with being a normal man, and Lois too misses some of her independence. Thus *Superman II* is really a reaffirmation of the original Superman premise. When the world is in trouble, Superman must break off his relationship with Lois for good. The world needs saving more than Clark needs a wife.

Superman Gets a Wife

In the AIDS-sensitive environment of the 1990s, safe sex was the new message, and *Superman* again was revamped. In the TV series *Lois & Clark: The New Adventures of Superman*, starring Dean Cain, the writers handle the no sex/no love issue in a different way. In the fourth season episode, "Swear to God, This Time We're Not Kidding," Clark and Lois finally get married, but they don't have sex. In the next episode, "Soul Mates," Clark and Lois are on their honeymoon, but before coitus can occur, Superman has to go somewhere to save the day. In the season-finale episode, "The Family Hour," the two attempt to have children, but we never know if normal coitus is achieved, since the show was then taken off the air. Clearly, ratings dip when Superman has, or attempts to have, sex with a woman. Since Superman's demographics are predominantly male, this inversion suggests that Superman's emasculation is more central to the character than his sex appeal.

The newest series entitled *Smallville* also deals with the adventures of Superman's sexuality. Most of these adventures deal with how Clark learns about his powers and their limitations. So how does this series deal with the normal sex drive of a teenage male? In the episode entitled "Heat," Clark is sexually attracted to his very appealing chemistry teacher. Poor Clark! When he gets all worked up, his eyes shoot out flames. Fearful of setting his town on fire with his X-rated vision, Clark is forced to cool down his sexual passions. Later in the episode, the teacher comes on to Clark (every young boy's fantasy), but he has no problem resisting her "kryptonite-inspired pheromone powers."[17] The only other time he gets physically passionate is in the episode "Red," when he is poisoned by red kryptonite. Not to worry;

17. Kryptonite was "invented" not for the comic, but for the *Superman* radio series. Julius Schwartz relates that the rock was introduced so that the character's voice, Bud Collier, could go on vacation for two weeks. In his absence, radio listeners were told that Superman was locked in a room and was so weakened he could not escape. In Collier's temporary absence, a fill-in groaned heroically until Jimmy and the gang could save him. Schwartz, 132–3.

even if Clark wants sex, no one else in Smallville does. The only time any of the characters get "sexed-up" is when they too are under the influence of some weird mind control agent: Lex and Chloe in "Hug," Lana, Pete and Jonathan in "Nicodemus," Lex and Jonathan in "Heat."

Raising the Flagg

We have seen, then, that even in the sexually permissive '70s and '80s, tales of comic book superheroes, though replete with skin-tight costumes covering desirable bodies, were not tales of sexual beings. From a typically male adolescent perspective, this is pathetic. What's the point of being beautiful if you won't allow yourself to be sexually active? The comics allow for sexual magnetism, but either they come up with bizarre explanations, as in the case of The Vision, or with reasons within the storyline that love cannot not move from the Platonic to the physical.

Thank God for the sexually active Flagg, who seems to have taken it upon himself to make up for the rest of these altruistic eunuchs. He doesn't even need a cape or super strength. Wherever he goes, Flagg meets fans who want to help him and, if he can manage it, to sleep with him. In scene after scene, Chaykin sketches Flagg giving in to available, gorgeous women attired in scanty lingerie.

Where's the Meat?

There's a double standard at play here. For all the naked women in these tableaux, we see very little naked Flagg. As in films, here too female nudity seems acceptable, but male nudity less so. Presumably, women sleep with Flagg because they want to, which means, among other things, that they find no fault in his private parts. We are not talking about a hero, like Jake Barnes in Hemingway's *The Sun Also Rises*, who must be loved despite a war wound to his pelvic region that has left him impotent. As one critic explains, even in pornographic films, in which nothing is left to the imagination, male genitalia have special significance:

> Every scene ends with a so-called "money shot," in which intercourse ends and the male is masturbated to ejaculation on the woman's body or face. These shots are prominent, and occasionally given further emphasis by being repeated or depicted in slow-motion.[18]

18. Chris Nagel, "Pornographic Experience" (Web- journal, *Journal of Mundane Behavior*, 2000).

According to Chris Nagel, the logic of pornography requires that, regardless of their age or station in life, all women become whores as soon as they see an engorged penis. And the corollary of that proposition is also true: Size matters. From a traditionally pornographic perspective, the bigger the erection, the more the woman is aroused. Since Reuben Flagg made his living and became famous as a porn star, it seems odd to see him discreetly swaddled in a blanket while cavorting with his bare-breasted girlfriends. There are two possibilities here that the blanket hides: Reuben either is or is not "ready for his close-up."

Racy or prudish, the *Flagg* series ran to fifty issues. Although marked by early success, the series waned after Chaykin decided to write the story only and leave the artwork to others. Fans, unhappy with the less erotic artwork, were disaffected. Sales fell and Chaykin, with some grumbling, returned for the last five issues.

However, Chaykin chose not to "up" the panty count. Instead, with the series cancellation set, Chaykin turned to the question of Flagg's true motivations. At the outset of Volume 2 (1986), Chaykin places Flagg in the middle of a threesome with two stunning women. Reuben says, "Do I deserve this, or what?" One woman replies, "That's why we're so fond of you, Reuben — you're a selfish pig." Similarly, in #7 (1986) of the same volume, we find Reuben on the beach, making love with a woman. The scene could be from one of the adult films of Reuben's earlier days, as it relies on the same clichés: "Oh god, Reuben, it's like May Day fireworks, Pow! Pow! Pow!" Reuben grunts, "Uhhh — Your moves are great — but your metaphors leave something to be desired."

It seems unlikely that the ex-porn star is taking this moment to remark on his lover's trite pillow talk. The superhero seems to be talking about the difference between her efforts and his satisfaction. If she spoke better, would he be more satisfied? The reader may guess that Reuben, jaded by so many lovely women, needs that "something [else] to be desired." Of course, there is always the danger of reading too much into a text, but *American Flagg* is replete with gay themes, gay men, and gay sex. First, Flagg's best friend is Jules Folquet, a gay basketball star turned cop. Another friend, Media Blitz, also a cop, is a black lesbian. When she is taken prisoner in one story arc — in a scene that fits Wertham's thesis to perfection — Media Blitz is tied to a chair, while her kidnapper, a redheaded woman dressed in purple leather, says, "You want to sell out ... I couldn't care less— me — I want a piece of your sweet ass. You know what they say — once you've had black, you never go back."

Wertham and Gay Pride

Turning the inquiry from the comics to Wertham, we note that he argues that comic books have taught generations of young readers how to feel and how to act in sexual situations. By the same logic, when he provides specific examples, drawing attention to the very few sexually explicit panels in a thirty-page story arc to prove his point, isn't he also seducing his reader?

And would it be calumnious to suggest that Wertham concentrates on these salacious panels because pictures of men in tights, rather than, say, rural landscapes, interest him? Certainly, Wertham's interviews with young boys, who are repeatedly questioned concerning their sexual escapades and fantasies, including sexual deviancy, demonstrates Wertham's interest in such subject matter. After all, most adults do not seek out conversations with young boys (or girls) on these subjects.

Flagg as Fag?

We all have sexual predilections and interests, and, by his own logic, Wertham's interest in young men's interests is interesting — perhaps even, in the clinical sense, revealing. Ironically, Howie Chaykin's porn hero, Rueben Flagg, might suffer a similarly repressive blind spot. Consider the absurdly self-destructive ends to which Flagg goes to prove his masculinity. Is Reuben merely a Hemingwayesque repressed homosexual? Certainly Flagg's friends, and even his lovers, come to question the hero's sexual identity.

In #4 of volume 2 (1988), we find Reuben behind bars in Odessa, a territory run by the Turks. In a scene reminiscent of the 1978 film *Midnight Express*, a large Turkish guard enters Flagg's cell with a bat. "Don't try to fight this, Reuben," he says. "You were meant to be mine." He is thinking of possession in a sexual sense, of course: "We're talking fate — Karma — Kismet — Flagg, you is my woman now." Before the jailer can rape Flagg, a beautiful, half-naked woman appears, offering herself to the guard. The guard, drooling, accepts; Flagg assaults him and escapes with the woman, who turns out to be one of Flagg's former sex partners.

She saves him from this ordeal, but in the end, no one can save Flagg from himself. In an issue published only four months before the series ended (2.46; 1987), we encounter a very different Flagg. On the issue's cover, a dishy dominatrix stands, facing a weak-kneed Reuben. The dominatrix has only one word for him: "Wimp!" But, significantly, the word balloon is pointed to her crotch, not, as is the comic-book norm, to her mouth.

Since Reuben has been a notorious stud, what is the dominatrix complaining about? However lamely, the cover tells an obvious joke: Reuben is weak in more than his knees. Accordingly, as the story unfolds, we enter Ruben's mind. He's lying in bed, dreaming. It's a wet dream. Reuben is copulating with a beautiful woman and calls out her name in ecstasy. Just as he reaches orgasm, he awakens. To his astonishment, he finds himself at his desk, kissing a man, who, looking in Reuben's eyes, asks, "What are you, a fag?"

A Gay X-Man

Homosexuality is also discussed in Marvel's *Alpha Flight*, a series concerning Canadian X-Men. In #106 (1992; Lobdell/Pacella), Northstar saves a baby from the evil clutches of the supervillain, Mr. Hyde. Tests later confirm that the baby has AIDS. When Northstar's crime-fighting partners blame homosexuals for spreading the "gay plague," Northstar reveals that he has a secret.[19] He's gay!

Major Mapleleaf is horrified that one of his agents participates in such immoral activities. Northstar fights his former ally, but between punches, he resists him also with argument: "Do not presume to lecture me on the hardships a homosexual must bear! [*Punch!*] No one knows them better than I. [*Punch!*] For while I am not inclined to discuss my sexuality with people for whom it is none of their business, I am gay! [*Leaping toward Major Mapleleaf.*] Be that as it may, AIDS is not a disease restricted to homosexuals, as much as it seems at times the rest of the world wishes that were so! [*Punch!*]" He is, of course, stating a statistical fact. In Africa, for example, AIDS is predominantly a disease suffered by heterosexuals.

In subsequent panels, it becomes clear that this sexual plague crosses traditional masculine boundaries. We see the heterosexual Major Mapleleaf comforting Northstar in a suggestively sexual pose, legs spread, Northstar's phallic-less crotch in pictorial focus, his head buried submissively. Sympathy with the gay lifestyle, the image suggests, has the power to make straights gay.[20]

Killing Off Northstar

Marvel, however, has backed off breaking gender stereotypes. In *Alpha Flight*, Northstar was older, taller, buff, a heroic statue, someone who looked

19. The "gay plague" is also discussed metaphorically in *Daredevil* # 324 (1993; Chichester/McDaniel), in which we meet an old Marvel hero, Mobius, a vampire who can only feed on the blood of criminals. The implication is that AIDS attacks only the guilty, that it is, in effect, a God-like plague attacking the wicked. It took DC fourteen years to catch up but, as of this writing, Green Arrow is about to get an HIV-infected sidekick. See "Comic Book to Feature HIV-Positive Hero," Yahoo! News, Wed., Oct. 13, 2004. http://news.yahoo.com/news?tmpl=story&u=/ap/20041013/ap_en_ot/hiv_positive_superhero_5
20. The story ends with the two of them promising to fight together to defeat the "homophobic politicians who refuse to address the AIDS crisis." It turns out that scientists, presumably American, not only have the AIDS antidote, but they actually created the virus as a weapon.

Major Mapleleaf comforting his gay friend, or learning how to be gay? The idea that
arch-heterosexuals Reuben Flagg and Major Mapleleaf might become gay harks
directly back to Fredric Wertham's hypothesis that comic books teach deviant sexual behavior. (By permission of Marvel Comics.)

like Charles Atlas.[21] We remember those ads in the comics. Skinny guy gets sand kicked in his face, loses the girl, works out, drinks Charles Atlas shakes, beats up the bully, gets the dream girl. These ads suggest that having muscles means attracting girls, as well as gaining the grudging respect of rivals. It is true that bodybuilding also has a gay aesthetic, the idea that the male body can be admired, and envied. Nonetheless, we think of the most famous bodybuilders, Arnold Schwarzenegger, Lou Ferrigno, and Atlas himself, as "chick magnets." The link between bodybuilders and comics is clear. Not only do bodybuilding and exercise companies advertise their supplements and equipment in the comics, their champions are often cast as movie superheroes: Arnold played Conan, Stallone played Judge Dredd, Lou Ferrigno played The Incredible Hulk.

So heterosexuals are big and powerful, and the bigger they are the more powerful and the more heterosexual. With the original Northstar, Marvel shattered that image. Here was a guy as powerful as Wolverine, but he liked men. It didn't detract from his power to fight evil or lift a bridge. His sexual identity was divisible from both his physical presence and his moral character.

By 2005, however, Marvel soured on the idea. In *Wolverine* #25 (2005; Miller/Romita Jr./Janson), Northstar is brought back, this time as an "out-of-the-closet" teacher in Charles Xavier's mutant school. But the new Northstar looks nothing like the *Alpha Flight* version. The new Northsar is svelte, androgynously lacking in facial or body hair. With his tidy and pretty coif, Northstar may or may not look gay, but he certainly doesn't look tough. We learn a lot from his new French name, Jean-Paul Beaubier: "beau" means beautiful in French, "bier" means a stand on which a corpse or a coffin containing a corpse is placed before burial. The message is clear: Jean-Paul is already a walking cadaver, and he won't be around for very long. This is a cold and cynical way of looking at AIDS and HIV sufferers. We don't view people with cancer or typhoid like this. No, we find ways to keep them alive. Many, if not most, still don't feel that way about HIV or AIDS sufferers. And among that many, if not most, we can place Marvel itself, which, it seems, would rather kill a gay superhero with AIDS than deal with him.

The Plight of Speedy

If Marvel was washing its hands of its first gay hero, Northstar's death at the spiked hands of Wolverine still leaves an ideological mess. When

21. The DC hero Flex Mentallo was inspired by Charles Atlas. Jason Croft points out that "Atlas represents two ideas, seemingly conflicting, that are major themes in Flex: (a) that superhero comic books are essentially product, debris, inseparable from their presence as stuff; they are consumed and then left as a constant reminder of "junk culture"; (b) that superhero comic books are potentially transformative, that they engage in a multilayered system of representation and crossover that, in the end, implicates even the reader." "The Annotated Flex Mentallo." http://www.cwrl.utexas.edu/~craft/flex/background.html.

Wolverine stabs Northstar with his own phallic blades, we have to wonder why he picked Northstar. In the context of the story, he could have just as easily killed a whole array of mutants, both adult and teen. Is Wolverine homophobic? Even if this isn't the initial reason for the attack on this boyish girlie-man, when Wolverine's blades retract into his own body, they presumably are covered in blood infected with the HIV running through Northstar's body. Wolverine may have killed a gay man, but he's now a carrier of the virus. The series is ongoing, and we'll see where Marvel goes from here.

All things considered, at least as things stand now, DC has the more enlightened attitude on the AIDS issue. This situation isn't a result of DC's catching up so much as Marvel's falling back. In *Green Arrow* #44 (2005; Winick/Hester/Parks), Speedy is diagnosed with HIV. When Ollie, a.k.a. the Green Arrow, asks if she caught it from the "glass that cut you," she replies testily that it wasn't from a cut, or a mosquito bite, or a blood transfusion during a heart transplant. It was from hooking and drugs. "What drugs?" asks Ollie. "Meth", she replies, adding, "I was living on the streets, stupid. I shot speed, we all shot speed. Staying awake is a pretty high priority. Keeps the number of rapes down to a minimum." Ollie knew Speedy was a street kid when he adopted her. He just never figured out that her nickname was connected to her drug of choice. Ollie may be a hero from the '50s who lived through the wild sexual energy of the '60s and '70s, but he still has a hard time grasping the nature of AIDS and HIV. He's frustrated with himself and his inability to cope with this new enemy. Instead of studying up on the matter, he sublimates his anger in brutal physical routines. Speedy copes as best she can. She's tough, after all, and what with the prostitution and the meth, she knew that this day was coming. Nonetheless, she confides to her stepbrother that she feels "dirty", that she's "infected": "Who's gonna love me now?" Her stepbrother hugs her and kisses her tenderly. Speedy is pleasantly shocked. "Does this mean that you're my boyfriend now?" The reply is no. "So it was just one of those symbolic things to make me feel better?" "Yeah." "Well, that stinks."

We could dwell on the poignancy of the scene and its deft humor. But it's Speedy's notion that she's "dirty" that concerns us here. There is another fictional character with poisoned blood, who, like Speedy, calls herself "unclean." It is Mina Harker, one of Dracula's victims. After a series of visits by the famous Count, she finds herself being transformed into one of the living dead:

> Oh, what will tomorrow bring to us...? As for me, I am not worthy in His sight. Alas! I am unclean to His eyes, and shall be until He may deign to let me stand forth in His sight as one of those who have not incurred His wrath.[22]

22. Bram Stoker, *Dracula*, intro. by Leonard Wolf (New York: Signet/Penguin, 1992), 266–7.

Mina conflates her husband, Jonathan, with God, the capitalized "He," but the message is plain enough: Mina sees the tainting of her blood by Dracula as a sign of infidelity. The mingling of blood is an intimate experience, in her mind probably associated with the traditional breaking of the virginal hymen on the wedding night. Sharing her blood with Dracula's means that another man has known her body. Speedy's reaction, that no one will want to love her now, suggests the same. She's used goods, no longer fresh, innocent, virginal. She's tainted, corrupt, diseased.

The plight of HIV infection also turns up in another comic. In 1993, award-winning Image Comics launched the third series of *Shadowhawk*, the story of Paul, a district attorney who can't be bought by the mob. Gangsters kidnap and inject him with the AIDS virus. Paul seeks justice in the courts, but when that fails, he dons a costume and begins his counterattack. Most of the series, however, is concerned with his inner struggle against the AIDS virus. In the follow-up, entitled "Brothers Under the Skin" (1995; issue #12), Paul teams up with yet another HIV-infected hero, Chapel. Together, they seek a treatment for HIV and AIDS. Amazingly, they discover that the government has developed a cure, but our heroes can't get their hands on it. In Issue #13, Shadowhawk attempts to transfer his consciousness into a robot body, hence freeing himself from the virus. But the experiment is a failure. A cure comes in an encounter with the undead beauty, Vampirella. She turns him into a vampire and the undead blood kills the AIDS virus; but, in the following issue, #18, the process reverses itself and the virus ends up killing him.

In the case of Speedy, we doubt DC Comics will go the vampire route, but as of this writing, the story is ongoing. Early indications suggest, however, that DC has big plans for Speedy. In the same month that Marvel was killing off Northstar, DC had Speedy joining the Teen Titans. But Speedy is not impressed with her new companions. Even as she's meeting them, she can't help but feel how removed they are from the real threats to our society — poverty, drugs, prostitution, HIV, AIDS. Comparatively, the villains the Teen Titans face are pint-size playground stuff:

> I'm interested in becoming better — and getting back to Star City where I can do things that really matter. Help kids on the streets, stop corrupt fat cats and wash the dirt out of the alleys no one bothers to look down. Fighting super-villains with these guys? Not my thing. But for the weekends? I can handle it.

The point of being with the Teen Titans is more than just to indulge in yuppie-weekend-paintball-warrior stuff. The real worth of hanging with the Teen Titans is learning how other kids deal with the world. As Cyborg councils, "Being a young hero, trying to find your place in the world, it's hard." But, as he reminds Speedy, the young, even those with HIV or AIDS, soon become old. This is, or soon will be, their world, and what kind of world it is will depend very much upon what they do in it: "It's a new generation's team. A new Teen Titans. And you're welcome to be a part of it" (*Teen Titans* #21; 2005; Johns/McKone/Alquiza). That offer stands, whether Speedy has HIV or not.

THINKING, DEBATING, WRITING

1. Write an essay arguing for or against the proposition that comic books, or their film counterparts, can teach or otherwise induce young people to be gay.

2. Consult someone from the psychology department on your campus and inquire about the validity of Freudian theory. Then write a paper considering the hypothesis that you and your friends are trying to find someone like your mother or your father to marry.

3. Find out if your classmates or friends are interested in the sex lives of superheroes. Write a paper in which you compare the reactions of men and women.

4. Find out what scientific research says about the sources of sexual arousal: Which of the five senses counts most? Least? Do the findings vary by sex?

5. Wertham thinks that, left to their own devices, kids will read material that is bad for them. If you had your choice of reading materials, what would you read? Why?

6. Watch *The Hulk* movie and argue that its central concern is father-son, not, as we have argued, mother-child.

7. Study media images of gay culture. What do the images suggest in terms of power and masculinity?

8. Argue for or against the proposition that the president of the United States should be married with kids.

9. Where does AIDS come from? Contact the local hospital and find out about AIDS treatment. Is AIDS a "gay plague"?

10. Is it possible to have a popular and gay superhero? If not, why not?

5

Dr. Strange, or How I Learned to Love Democracy and Demonology

Heroes are not merely an expression of power. And yet, in the comics, might make right. Villains yield not to entreaties but to blows. What do the comics have to say about the nature of "good" in relation to "power"? Are they the same?

In the Warner Brothers' movie *Superman: Last Son of Krypton* (1996), Lois sees a flying man in a red and blue cape and remarks: "He's the Nietzschean ideal all wrapped up in a red cape; the superman." Lois knows her philosophy. The etymology of the word "superman" is commonly ascribed to the nineteenth-century German philosopher Friedrich Nietzsche, who contemplated the rise of a new man, the *Übermensch*. The translation is not exact: *Übermensch* literally means "over-man" or "above-man." But, it's logical to conclude that Nietzsche means a superior man or "superman." Indeed, it's not far-fetched to imagine Nietzsche writing for Marvel or DC Comics. We even have a sense of the characters he'd create. In *Twilight of the Idols*, Nietzsche tells us of a man who sounds like a superhero of sorts: "What does not destroy me makes me stronger." Let us call him Strongerman.

Often referred to as the father of postmodern philosophy, Friedrich Wilhelm Nietzsche (1844–1900) wrote voluminously, challenging many of the established norms of moral and religious thought. He accomplished what he called "the revaluation of all values," in part by a reversal of the customary way of looking at things. Whereas society traditionally asserts that we must help the weak, Nietzsche insists that we must strengthen the strong. Above all, Nietzsche believed that living things aim to exercise their strength and express their "will to power." A "superhero," in Nietzsche's universe, is no better or worse than a "supervillain," because terms such as hero and villain are meaningless for Nietzsche. All that counts is that the person be "super," whether for heroic or villainous ends is immaterial.

Nietzsche's superman — with his focus on exercising power, rather than restraining it — is far more prototypical villain than hero. Restraint, in Nietzsche's system, is a socially imposed barrier that demands the exceptional act ordinary, that a person's God-given or manmade potential remain just that — potential, and wasted potential at that. Thus, Strongerman is not concerned with saving the lives of ordinary people. Quite the opposite, our hero believes that ordinary people are merely maggots, "swarming in the foreground":

> He has indeed a certain right to feel thus, insofar as he feels himself elevated above the surfeit of ill-constituted, sickly, weary and exhausted people of which Europe is beginning to stink today....[1]

Strongerman's disgust with the weak sets him apart from his superhero brethren. Many superheroes are more sick men than supermen. Bruce Banner often loathes his normal self and longs to be The Hulk. Likewise, Bruce Wayne despises the effete playboy that he is in daily life, but obviously enjoys his resort to the Batcave, where he assumes the costume and prerogatives of Batman, scourge of Gotham's underworld. Even fairly well-adjusted heroes, such as Daredevil, have to deal with leading two lives.

This raises a complicated but essential problem. Is Strongerman a hero? We might begin by asking whether Strongerman has an alter ego. The hero, we have noted, has an alter ego, but the supervillain rarely, and often only initially, has a secret identity. He makes no attempt to fit into his world. His job is to express himself as a superior entity, not to hide in a suit and tie and assume an anonymous office job. The supervillain has no bills to pay, no checking account, no status in society. In contrast, we want to know how Peter Parker is doing in school, how Steve Rogers helps firemen after 9-11, if Matt Murdock's love life is picking up.

In the DC Universe, the perfect anti–Nietzschean is paradoxically the strongest hero: Superman. We think J.M. DeMatteis gets it right when he suggests that Superman, in Metropolis, "[w]ith his extraordinary powers, ... could have easily set himself up as a God. And I suspect we would have gladly let him ... Maybe that was just a psychological trick: His way of dealing with his true nature. To assume the modest persona of a Kansas farmboy. And a God. Maybe the only way to function as a God ... to carry out God's responsibilities and remain same ... was to deny that he was one" (2003; *JLA and The Spectre,* graphic novel, Dematteis/Banks/Nearly and Feeny).

Former *Batman* and *American Flagg* writer Howie Chaykin suggests that the villain is born from the stultifying of potential. In his Wildstorm/

---

1. Friedrich Nietzsche, *Genealogy of Morals, Basic Writings of Nietzsche* , ed. Walter Kaufman (New York: The Modern Library, 2000), 479.

DC Comic *Legend* #1 (2005; Chaykin/Heath), we meet Dr. Mudge, an odd-ball scientist who experiments with strength serums. As his work progresses, he needs a human test subject and decides upon surreptitiously injecting his pregnant wife. The result is that his son is born with superhuman strength. The mother attempts to teach the boy to hide his super powers. Even when bullies pick on him, he initially refuses to fight back. When he does, the results are predictable: A bully is sent sailing across the play-ground. A teacher then disciplines the boy by lashing him with a belt — the story is set in the 1950s, so let's not ask why the teacher isn't sued. No mat-ter how hard he is beaten, the boy refuses to tear up or even cry out. This stoicism has nothing to do with his super strength. His nervous system is like anyone else's. He still feels pain. He's just tough. Hard as nails. And the townsfolk are scared of him. As one parochially-minded schoolmarm puts it, "Something must be done to weaken him ... Something's got to be done to weaken the boy."

His father warns him, "You must never forget that you're not an ordi-nary man. When people find out, they'll ... fear you." Chaykin's lines echo Marlon Brando's portrayal of Superman's father, Jor-El, in *Superman: The Movie* (1978). Krypton is dying and Jor-El completes his rocket to fly the boy to earth. Jor-El explains that the yellow light of the sun will give the boy extraordinary powers:

WIFE: But why earth, Jor-El? They're primitive, thousands of years behind us.
JOR-EL: He will need that advantage to survive ...
WIFE: He will defy their gravity.
JOR-EL: He will look like one of them.
WIFE: He won't be one of them.... He will be odd, different.
JOR-EL: He will be fast, virtually invulnerable.

Later in the movie, a young Clark feels that he is wasting his talents. Every time he touches the football, he can score a touchdown. But he keeps his powers hidden and serves as the team water boy. Frustrated, he asks his father, "Is it so wrong to use your talents? Is it wrong for a bird to fly?"

Life is equally unsatisfying for Chaykin's nameless boy, who tests the limits of his powers by pushing down redwoods and jumping over farm-houses. But each time he displays his powers, he makes a new enemy: Men fear his strength, women think he's unnatural, even his parents exacerbate him with warnings. All the boy longs to do is be himself. Enough is enough. When two men cross his path, he warns that that he will "break both of your rotten necks.... I'll wreck your house ... I swear to God." The oath doesn't mean much, as earlier in the issue, he asks his father if he's stronger than God. His father replies that he doesn't know if God even exists. The boy, we assume, has digested this statement fully. The God he has heard about in Sunday school is a God of power. But if God is a fiction, and his power is fake, the boy's strength is real, as is the fear he instills in others. He has a choice: be like everyone else and hide his power, or be himself and accept that Godlike power has its uses. After all, God uses his powers, so why shouldn't someone who is stronger than God?

Given these examples, it's clear that in the world of the comic book, the hero's ability to defeat the villain is not based on his costumed identity but on his alter ego. In terms of ethics, the superhero is presumed to be better than the villain not because he is stronger, but because he is morally superior. In some sense, then, the philosophical must be acknowledged even in the comic-book worlds of deltoids and steroids, machines and cosmic cubes. Obviously, the hero's virtue cannot win the day alone; he must also be armed with a variety of superweapons or superpowers. Yet in the comics, even comparatively weak heroes defeat more powerful villains. Captain America should be no match for Dr. Doom; Magneto should be able to whip Daredevil. Why, then, doesn't the supervillain simply pick on a hero who is far weaker than himself? The answer, in short, is that it would make no difference. Were Doom to meet Captain America, he'd lose, as would Magneto in an encounter with Daredevil. Even the archer Hawkeye has been known to beat The Hulk, when the green-skinned behemoth temporarily turned bad or, more precisely, evil. Marvel and DC's *Übermenschen* or supermen, in short, get us to think about the power of morality and the role it plays in society.

Killing Off the Alter Ego

The vast majority of comic book titles concern heroes, but a few concern our favorite villains. Yet, why should this be the case? Aren't villains evil? The fact that supervillains, such as Doctor Doom, get their own comic books—which sells better than many traditional hero titles—indicates that on some level we enjoy and admire villains, even see hero and villain as similar. They are, at the very least, protagonists in their own world, demonstrating at all times their potential to destroy or to maintain social stability. The supervillain's excellence is measured in terms of excess; the more damage he causes, the better. The greater Doctor Doom's scheme to defeat The Fantastic Four, the more readers admire him, if only covertly. The supervillian flexes his muscle and tests himself against society; the hero, on the other hand, is measured by his restraint. No matter what the circumstances, he will not kill, rape, or pillage.[2] His heroism consists of pretending to be, so far as he can, ordinary. To measure physical strength, we

2. There are exceptions: see our Chapter 7, "Comics and the Prison System."

need look at a villain; to measure the hero, we just need to look at the alter ego.

It may not be enough to say that we identify with the hero's alter ego. Although the alter ego resembles us more than his indomitable, costumed self, even his Joe-Average disguise makes us look morally weak. After all, even though we might not consider ourselves the moral equal of Mother Theresa, we more than likely think of ourselves as decent citizens. Yet most of us have done something we're ashamed of: not returned excessive change when a clerk makes an error in our favor, slipped in the side door of the movie theater left open by our high-school friend, slept with people whom we knew we never wanted to see again, ignored the homeless person holding the sign asking for food, lied about a forgotten social engagement. The list of venial sins goes on, but we know that superheroes, whether in costume or going about their boring, daily lives, do none of these things, and never have. In this sense, then, it is not quite right to say that the superhero's alter ego is ordinary. Even though he may have a job and a definite place in society, the superhero is not simply a man like us. Rather, he or she is above the norm, above us, so that with or without the mask, the hero is always moral and, therefore, is not tempted to succumb to our petty thieveries and moral failings. We see this in the alter egos of many of the heroes: Spider-Man's alter ego is the irreproachable Peter Parker, always ready to assist Aunt May with her shopping. Thor's alter ego, Dr. Donald Blake, is always willing to help the sick, who can seldom pay him. Matt Murdock is the kind of lawyer who insists on representing the innocent and the poor. In his decades of flying around in Metropolis, Clark Kent has not even once betrayed Lois Lane, cheated on his taxes, or driven drunk.

And yet we note a surprising change lately in the concept of the superhero: Marvel has re-launched its heroes, many of them revealing or abandoning their alter egos. In the movie *Spider-Man II*, the hero reveals his face, if not his name, to a train car full of people. His best friend, his girlfriend, and his aunt all learn his secret as well. Captain America has recently revealed his identity; Tony Stark now admits that he's Iron Man; and Thor has given up switching identities with Donald Blake. While we suspect that Marvel developed this trend in order to add more action to the stories, we find the thinking fundamentally flawed. If superheroes have no secret identity, then there is no reason to suspect that there are heroes among us. Does Marvel understand that it is now measuring heroes only by their aggressive, often unsavory capacities? Perhaps Marvel simply wants its heroes to be larger than life all the time. No more boring pages of Peter helping his aunt.

Living up to your potential is a laudable goal. But what if that potential is harmful to those around you? From a Nietzschean perspective, the question has no meaning. This may be one of the reasons Marvel is unsure whether the Scarlet Witch is a villain or not. She, like all of Marvel's mutants, has no conventional alter ego, and, like her brother and sister mutants, in many stories she turns against the heroes with Nietzschean bravado. In *Avengers West Coast* #56 (1990; Byrne/Ryan), the Scarlet Witch enthuses, "So this is power! What a pleasing thing it is. How foolish to have so long denied myself its pleasures. How unfortunate for you, my former friends, that you did not see fit to encourage me in realizing my full potential." She then launches into an orgy of violence and cruelty. But those value-laden words have no meaning for the new Scarlet Witch.[3] What is important is that she exercises her full potential. The Scarlet Witch is out of control and we recognize that were she sane and healthy, she'd exert self-control along the lines of DC Comics' Flash, who worries that "[b]ehind the mask, you believe you can do anything. And truth be told, you can ... But that doesn't mean you should" (#219; Johns/Justiniano/Livesay/Wong).[4]

Society and the Hero

As we saw in our discussion of black superheroes, this kind of goodness is in part measured in terms of economic success and function. The hero, with the exception of black heroes like Luke Cage, operates above economic considerations. The alter ego excels within him. The superhero is like a knight who never had to shoe a horse. His alter ego serves as the trusty squire who saddles up the horse and cleans out the stable. It appears, then, that strength cannot be measured in muscle density alone. In the end, it is self-control — and its accompanying virtue of humility — that separates the hero from the antihero. The superhero's alter ego is manifestly of a higher type than the "strong man," because he chooses to deal with the world from a position of weakness. The strong man annihilates what he doesn't like; his alter ego negotiates the world, full as it is with what he doesn't like. Moreover, sometimes the hero's alter ego is handicapped, or turned into a weak or "sick" man: Matt Murdock is blind; Donald Blake is lame; Peter Parker and Clark Kent are inept putzes. Such quirks of fortune stress the need to cope in a world in which the hero must survive under

3. The idea of an out-of-control Scarlet Witch was too tasty for Marvel, who has returned to the concept. In the ongoing *Avengers Disassembled*, Wanda is responsible for the "deaths" (they'll all be back) of several Avengers. See "Tom Brevoort on House of M," Newsarama.com. http://www.newsarama.com/Marvel/HouseofM/Bre_HoM.htm.
4. In the same issue, we meet the Anti-Flash, Zoom, who is only interested in making others better. Meeting the villainess Cheetah, he promises in speech so fast it's almost a blur: "IWILLMAKE THE FLASH A BETTER HERO. BUT I CAN MAKEYOUU BETTER ... TOO." But Zoom is a villain, and we know that the Flash is the voice of reason.

dreadfully adverse circumstances. Given his infirmities, the hero's morality is all the more remarkable. Although superheroes are not morally flawed like us, they share with us a marked anonymity. And for their notable virtue, they receive no reward, no praise, no notice, except of the most fleeting kind. It is the supervillain who most often feels comfort and takes joy in the expression of power. There is no equivalent reward for the hero. As far as this world goes, anyone who makes an out-and-out "good guy" of himself does so at the peril of becoming a martyr. If not for his secret heroic otherness, the hero may appear insignificant and contemptible. We could go further and suggest that, were it not for his secret persona, the good man would sink from the merely insignificant to the contemptible, for he would be, like us, willing to tolerate the injustice of society. In the comic-book world, absent the costumed alter ego, nice guys finish last.

Elektra: Female Anti-Nietzschean

If you're wondering how women fare in the Nietzschean system, the answer is: not very well. The philosopher simply never envisioned a "superwoman," though, of course, the comics have. Supergirl first appeared in May 1959 in *Action Comics* #252. She's Clark's cousin and was hurled to earth from the exploding Krypton in a huge bubble of air. (Comet, the superhorse, and Krypto, the superdog, later join her.) Similarly, Marvel has the She-Hulk, Jennifer Walters, the meek and mousy lawyer cousin of Bruce Banner, who made her first appearance in *Savage She-Hulk* #1 (1980). And there is Wonder Woman, Queen of the Amazons, who first appeared in *All Star Comics* #8 (1941). Though virtually immortal, she isn't known for her all-encompassing knowledge or wisdom. Batgirl, who first appeared in the *Batman* TV series in 1967, is no more than another sidekick and, as the name implies, is emotionally immature. As of late, however, we can applaud the comics not simply for coming up with strong heroic female characters, but also in investing some of them with penetrating philosophical insights and transcendent mystical powers. This development is particularly evident in the movie, *Elektra* (2005), starring Jennifer Garner.

As *Elektra* opens, we are told: "For centuries a war has been waging in the shadows by two armies born of incredible powers. Yet it is said there lives a warrior who can tip the balance of power. But first she must choose." That choice is rather stark. She can kill "because" — and these are her words—"it's what I'm good at." Or she can seek enlightenment. As her Master Sensae explains, "You understand violence and rage, but that is not the way." So, while Elektra kicks, cuts and stabs a variety of assassins straight to hell, we are aware that all this violence, while exciting visually, is not the real test she faces. In essence, the real epic struggle is within Elektra, the drama of which is expressed through the metaphor of violence.

Elektra's inner struggle has nothing to do with excellence. She knows where her gifts lie. She's a killer. But is taking life, no matter how artful, any way to live? Such questions pulse throughout the comic and churn with brooding energy in the recent movie. But in both instances we may further ask why the comics, a visually-driven medium, even bother to ask such questions.

Action-oriented stories have, throughout history, been subject to similar queries. At heart is a sense that action, particularly violent action, is a poor vehicle for philosophical introspection. And yet without such introspection, we have nothing more than a spectacle of violence, which, while visually interesting, is hardly something most of would call meaningful art. The problem hovers like a black cloud not just over the comics but also over many so-called classic texts. In the Renaissance, scholars read Homer's *Iliad* and were troubled by the unrelenting action. His heroes were just killing machines. Thus, translators such as George Chapman added moments of reflection, pauses both in the battle and in the narrative wherein the reader could see that Achilles suffered when he had to choose whether he would live a long but undistinguished life or die young but be remembered forever.

Glory is not Elektra's nemesis. Her humanity is. After seeing her mother killed by assassins, Elektra retreats into herself. Eventually, she becomes an assassin, and her main target is Elektra. She has been slowing killing herself, cutting herself off from humanity, until she is more a creature of the spirit world than a living, loving human being. She can even become a disembodied spirit and see, albeit imperfectly, into the near future. When she is ordered to kill a man and his daughter, she finds herself wondering why they must die — not because she values their lives, but because she values her soul. What will be the cost to her in terms of what little is left of her humanity? Is she irredeemably steeped in sin? Can she rejoin humanity? She takes a chance and decides that saving life is far more noble than taking it. And the life she saves is her own.

Catwoman: A Villain Because She Is Free

Those of us who remember the old *Batman* TV show starring Adam West will recall a number of actresses who played Catwoman. There was Julie Newmar's sexy Catwoman in tight spandex, Eartha Kitt's purring but sharp-clawed Catwoman, and Lee Meriwether, who played her as a spoiled kitten. In *Batman Returns* (1992), Michelle Pfeiffer played Catwoman as a feline comfortable in her skin, prowling with feral aggression. All these actresses played

Catwoman as a creature defined by her body, not her mind. To be sure, there is some of that feline physicality in Halle Berry's Catwoman as well, in the 2004 film in which she plays the title role. There are early, comical scenes of Berry hungrily picking at can after can of tuna, hissing at passing dogs, etc. And certainly, the film is not shy to exploit her considerable physical beauty. A former Miss America runner-up, Berry is sexy in her leather outfit and knows it. But, for the first time, we also learn of the mystical nature of her powers.

As the film opens, we meet Berry's character, Patience Phillips, a talented but ditzy artist paying the bills by doing product ads for a cosmetics company. Arriving late one night to drop off the revised ads for the company's newest product, Beau-Line, she overhears the company's dark secret: Yes, Beau-Line will keep you beautiful as long as you take it, but as soon as you stop, it will scar your skin permanently. Nonetheless, the company plans to launch on schedule. After all, if a woman has to use Beau-line forever, that's a small price to pay for immortally young skin. Besides, what better way to guarantee customer loyalty? And if the customer can't afford to pay for Beau-Line, that's really not the company's problem. We've been here before, of course. It's Spider-Man's corporate responsibility problem transferred to the beauty industry.

Of course, now that Berry's Patience knows the company's secret, she must die. But soon after death, the guiding spirit of Bast, the ancient Egyptian goddess of cats, revives our heroine. As Ophelia Powers, the aging priestess of the cat cult, explains, Patience has received a gift that goes well beyond a love of tuna. Women live in a caged world; only by accepting the worship of Bast can she realize her true potential: "Catwomen are not contained by the rules of society. You will follow your own desires.... But you will experience a freedom few women will know.... You spent a lifetime caged. By accepting who you are, all of who you are, you can be free. And freedom is power." And that is why Catwoman is a villain: because she is free.

Democracy Versus the Philosophy of Freedom

All villains yearn for world domination; all heroes are more interested in controlling themselves. As such, all heroes are democratic, since a democracy, a society in which the people choose who will rule over them, can only function properly among individuals who first decide to rule themselves. Thus, the first rule of tyranny is to obey your ruler; the first and second rules of democracy are rule yourself and then choose who will rule over you. It's for this reason that democratic leaders try to appeal to voters by seeming like Average Joes. The winner of every election is the man or woman who most embodies the principles and self-control inculcated in the electorate. And yet it would be a mistake to say that this self-discipline is the automatic result of democracy. Indeed, as this pop project demonstrates, comics teach certain core values of society while often proactively seeking to change society on issues as diverse as international affairs, racism, and gay rights.

Ironically, it is through characters like Elektra and Catwoman that the reader is taught the basics of what our society considers to be normal behavior or "human nature." Comic books operate like the mad scientists and schemers who are often at the heart of their plots. They are social engineers, imposing order, teaching moral lessons, and then calling that order or those lessons natural or commonsensical. And yet there is little that is natural or commonsensical about these comic book heroes: nerds bitten by radioactive spiders, visitors from far-distant planets, psychopaths scarred by traumatic childhoods, snitches saved by ancient cat goddesses. If "human nature" existed, we wouldn't need heroes. If the love of a mother for her child were natural, there would be no abandoned babies left in dumpsters. But there are. If self-preservation were a "natural" instinct, people would never eat fatty foods, smoke cigarettes, or get hooked on deadly drugs. We equate "natural" with the right to do what we please, and the right to do what we please with "freedom." But these concepts are not interchangeable.

Indeed, as Thomas Hobbes suggested in *Leviathan* (1651), in his natural state, man's life is solitary, poor, nasty, and short. Or, as Gilbert and Sullivan wrote in their obscure operetta *Iolanthe* (1882):

> Man is coarse and Man is plain;
> Man is more or less insane;
> Man's a ribald and Man's a rake;
> Man is Nature's sole mistake.

Hence, the role of society is to impose rule on man, to make the natural order unnatural. Heroes are supermen or superwomen because they control themselves and work to suppress the "natural" part in themselves. The role of the superhero is to lead the way, to make everyone a superhero, because it is heroic self-control that makes the superhero not merely super, but unnatural. If the "natural order" is only imposed order, then the true natural order is disorder. Consequently, those who exert power (i.e. villains) are symbols of the natural disorder, which threatens in all societies to bring chaos back to the imposed order of man. The "natural order" is an historic triumph over the disorder of nature.

Oddly, it seems we have come full circle. If imposed order is civilized and unnatural, we would expect villains to want to wreck order and to return societies to chaos. However, this is not the case. Villains may want to smash the societal imposition of order, but they mean to do so by imposing a more restrictive sense of order. Their love of power is not an embrace of the natural, but the ultimate expression of their unnatural and, hence, civilized behavior. Thus, all heroes are protovillains, teaching the man in the street that the ultimate society is not one of heroes, but of villains, who are both unnatural and all-controlling. Superheroes, after all, are the ultimate cops, inspiring awe, respect, and fear. Yet, if we were all cops, we wouldn't need any. Likewise, superheroes depend upon everyone relying on them, even as they supposedly inspire heroism in others.

Accepting this as an accurate state of affairs, we can now understand why, in both the Marvel and DC Universes, the police and the media hate many of their heroes. Whether it is Spider-Man or Batman, these so-called vigilantes not only threaten to make autocratic organizations such as big business and the police state a thing of the past, but threaten to unmask these organizations, supposedly functioning for the public good as tyrannical forms of imposition. Once the man on the street learns that he has the power to control his own destiny, he is less likely to embrace democracy, a system whereby he voluntarily surrenders power. Whereas we have been told repeatedly that lessening democratic turnout is a sign of voter apathy, the supervillains would call it something else — a refusal to voluntarily give up power. To vote is to exercise your power, but that exercise lessens the very power it relies upon. Thus, democracy attempts to sustain itself by teaching core values such as human rights, but sustains itself ultimately by teaching voters that self-immolation, self-restraint, abdication are natural and desirable. If power is an expression of nature, then democracy, which allows voters to elect those who will have power over them, is a suicide pact, a self-abasement which keeps men and women artificially dependent upon others, a servile social chain which we ironically call "freedom."

Doctor Strange: The Moral Superhero

We can say that one hero bows where he may command, another delves into philosophical questions, yet another walks a mystical path. But is there one hero who does all these things? Yes, and his name is Doctor Strange, Sorcerer Supreme. He has no formal superhero name, no costume, albeit he occasionally wears a "cloak of levitation" which is, in all but name, a cape. Strange is of less than average build, and were it not for his Elvis-like sideburns and predisposition to wearing gloves, utterly unnoticeable.

We first meet Strange in *Strange Tales* #115 (1963; Lee/Ditko). He's a doctor and an egomaniac with all the makings of a supervillain. Strange is a surgeon, and we see him, after an operation, lighting up a cigarette as if it were a post-coital pleasure. His assistant beams, "The operation was a success, Doctor! Your patient wants to thank you!" But Strange replies, "I can't be bothered! Just be sure he pays the bills." The money, not the patient, is all that concerns Strange. After a freak car accident that ruins his hands, he is offered a job as a technical consultant, but refuses. "Stephen Strange assists nobody," he says.

Having exhausted the limits of medical science, Strange travels to Tibet in hopes of a cure. He has heard that there is a guru — the Ancient One — with surprising powers. At first, he finds the old man to be a joke. "All he does is study those meaningless scrolls and recite his empty dirges! What a waste of time." Witnessing acts that defy logic and the laws of the material universe, Strange concludes, "It's probably nothing more than simple hypnotism!" In Tibet, he saves the Ancient One and becomes his pupil. Thereafter, Strange is initiated into a world of magic and metaphysics.

Strange returns to New York, newly armed with incantations for virtually every evil. But the foes he fights do not rob banks or blow up buildings. In fact, they don't seem to do anything at all, since they exist either in another dimension or within his own mind. A typical Strange battle is hardly a traditional knock-down-drag out: In *Strange Tales* #114, an outsider witnesses Strange and Baron Mordo battling. Since she can't see the astral world, " ... it seems that Dr. Strange and Baron Mordo are simply standing still, just staring! But on another planet, in another mystic dimension, one of the most titanic battles of all times is taking place, silently ... desperately."

Doctor Strange's Greatest Foe: His Deepest Fears

Strange does battle against spiritual villains, but just as often, he engages destructive aspects of his own mind. In particular, Nightmare is his most formidable enemy. In *Strange Tales* #116 (1964; Lee/Ditko), Strange successfully travels to the realm of Nightmare to free captured human souls, which he then returns to their sleeping bodies. The narrative in *Strange Tales* # 122 (1964; Lee/Ditko) is more complicated. Forgetting to cast the proper protective spells before going to sleep, Strange is kidnapped by Nightmare. We learn only later why Nightmare is preoccupied with Strange. Nightmare is, in fact, Dr. Strange's own dark side, his negative energies manifesting themselves in mystical dreams. As he proclaims in issue #122, "It is as I suspected! I am entering the Nightmare world! I've been captured in my sleep."

Doctor Strange and the Capitalism Demon

If Strange battles most of his foes in dreams, he is also aware of an evil pervading the United States, a demon called the "American Dream." Among

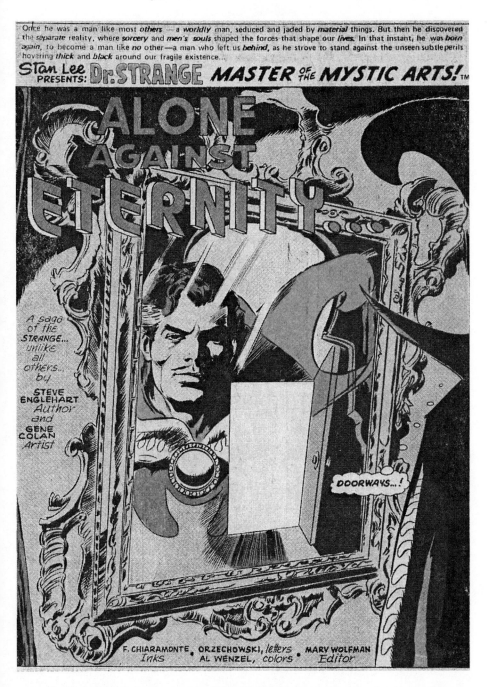

A typically introspective Dr. Strange fights his battles by staring into the mirror. (By permission of Marvel Comics.)

Strange's first adventures (*Strange Tales* #110, 1963; Lee/Ditko), we see a banker haunted by bad dreams because of the many lives he has ruined. His demons are nothing other than his conscience, which warns him that capitalism is tyrannical and ultimately self-destructive. Strengthening this motif, the ruin of Strange's rival Baron Mordo is described in capitalistic terms. In *Doctor Strange* #8 (1989;Thomas/Guice/Marzan), Satannish and Mephisto fight over Mordo, who has sold his soul to both. As Mordo explains in *Doctor Strange* #5, "In exchange for twenty-four hours of vastly augmented magical power ... I mortgaged my essence to that devil-may-care demon, Satannish the Supreme. Unfortunately, in my exuberance, I promptly yielded to the temptation of doing the very same thing with another old friend of yours—Mephisto." Mordo has lured himself into the capitalist trap of maxing out his credit cards and leveraging his debt.

The implicit association of Satan with banking is not new. Marlowe's Faustus makes a similar bargain with the devil. That being said, Doc Strange's writers extend the analysis to include virtually all aspects of the American lifestyle. In *Doctor Strange* #3 (Gillis/Case/Emberlin), we learn that Hell is created by each soul. For one with a truly profound intellect, Hell can be a never-ending metaphysical puzzle; but for many Americans, trained on consumerism, Hell is just bad food. One departed soul complains bitterly that, in Hell, "You can't get a decent burrito here for love or money."

Doctor's Strange's Return to American Values

In *Doctor Strange* #17–18 (1976; Englehart/Colan), an explorer declares that, in the founding of the American colonies, "We shall see this utopia rise from that virgin soil, and flourish...! A great civilization, which shall free itself from our old world, and grow to a vast continent with its sister to the north — before becoming a peace-maker to the world entire."

But Strange prefers Tibet to America. If this makes Dr. Strange some-what like the Beatles, giving up penthouse apartments to seek inner peace at the feet of the Maharishi, we may recall that the episode is a product of the age of "flower power." Strange's fascination with eastern mysticism allies him with that generation's interest in Zen, transcendental meditation, Bud-dhism, tai chi, Yoga, and the Age of Aquarius. Even his residence in the heart of Greenwich Village, then home to the East Coast's folk art and music movement, makes Strange a hippie superhero, more inclined to fight the demon within than injustices of the outside world. Like the Love Genera-tion that flocked to Woodstock, Strange's spiritual focus suggests a New Age criticism of consumerist American culture. Yet to abandon capitalist accumulation is not, in and of itself, to abandon all American values. In issue #16 (1976; Englehart/Colan/Palmer), we learn that Satan and Strange fight over which reality will master humankind: Strange's world of the spirit, or Satan's world of material pleasures and pains.

Aiding Strange in his battle against Satan is Benjamin Franklin. Together, they attempt to block Satan and thus liberate America from the tyranny of Satan's materialism. Strange picked Franklin because he thought this American would embody all the virtues of a philosophically robust society. But in this regard, Franklin is a disappointment. While Strange is off fighting Satan, Franklin seduces Strange's wife, Clea.

Many must be doing a double-take: Strange is married? Strange first meets his wife Clea in *Strange Tales* #126, when she helps Strange defeat Dormammu, a tyrant of a mystic dimension who plans to invade the earth. But Strange's main concerns are more metaphysical than physical. He barely eats; he never sleeps, unless meditation can be called sleep. He never kisses Clea good morning or looks romantically into her eyes. He never buys her flowers or takes her to bed. From Clea's point of view, Franklin's down-to-earth charm is an attractive alternative to Strange's otherworldly preoccupation. Strange, on the other hand, finds Franklin to be a shabby little man, more concerned with the pleasures of the flesh than with freedom.

The Defeat of the Spiritual

Satan can think of no greater punishment than to allow Strange, defeated, to return to his own home — not New York, but the astral realm. After all, if Strange lives in a kind of Oz, then he is the Wizard and Dorothy simultaneously, fighting a variety of wicked witches and saving a variety of cowardly lions. But at the conclusion of *The Wizard of Oz*, Dorothy learns that there is no place like home. There can be no similar return for Strange: he is caught on the opposite side of the fence. Having lived in the astral world, it is impossible for him to forget it or to prefer the material illusions of New York. Dorothy prefers Kansas, but a source of the movie's sustained popularity has been its ability to draw the audience into the magical world of Oz, a wonderful land that is at once more fantastical and more vibrant, more colorful, and more real than Kansas. Strange's world is not only more weird than ours, it is more interesting. Although Strange's Greenwich Village house is a mansion, the reader knows that its rooms, regal as they are, are merely portals to even more interesting and exotic worlds. Readers of *Doctor Strange* are encouraged to see the world as their master does, measuring reality not by earthly riches but by meditative rewards.

However, Marvel's portrayal of the metaphysical is not all positive. The rewards, while not inconsequential, are immaterial. Consider: Strange is married to a sorceress, Clea. On the surface, their marriage seems to be a happy one. They call each other by endearing names, such as "beloved," but all the while, their relationship is Platonic, that is, non-sexual. Indeed, Dr. Strange makes it no secret that he prefers astral projection to sexual intercourse. When the villain D'spyre wants to attack Strange (*Doctor Strange* #37; 1979; Stern/Macchio/Colon and Green), he knows of only one weakness—the nearly-extinguished spark of Strange's sexuality. It is not a mere coincidence that D'spyre sends a femme fatale, Victoria Bentley, to weaken the master mystic's resolve. Clea understands the threat immediately and worries that Victoria's sensual vibrations will somehow weaken her husband's powers. She's right. With Strange obviously sexually attracted and mentally distracted, his many astral foes lie in wait. D'spyre, watching all from the darkness of his own dimension, cackles: "The seeds I have planted have fast taken root. Strange doubts himself now, and his ability to cope. For a mystic, such festering thoughts are the first step towards death." Only when sexual temptation is removed does Strange have the wherewithal to defeat his foes.

This detail may suggest that Marvel is bending to the old comic-book code, a point we discussed in Chapter Four, but it isn't. In fact, both Strange and Clea are sexually frustrated, which makes them normal. Strange accepts the tradeoff, but Clea is dissatisfied and makes no secret of it. In *Doc Strange Special Edition* #1 (1983; Giodano/Costanza/Wein), Strange concedes that he has been a bad husband: "Clea, I've neglected you, both as a man and as mentor in the mystic arts. I've been preoccupied." In *Doctor Strange* # 64 (1984; Nocenti/ Salmons), we learn that Clea has finally left him. In the same issue we learn why. Adrienne, a beautiful blonde, attempts to seduce him:

> STRANGE: My dear, with all my years as master of the mystic arts, do you presume to think I can be taken in by the sorcery of female magic? Potent as it may be, I am certainly invulnerable to the mystique and magnetisms you are attempting to conjure.
> ADRIENNE: It isn't even working a tinsy bit...?
> STRANGE: No.

With little or no sex drive, Strange is unable to satisfy his wife or pursue new romances. His world is the mystic arts. We're not trying to overvalue sex in and of itself. That being said, going through life without a partner, without an intimate friend, doesn't seem entirely healthy.

Doctor Strange's Exile from Humanity

Dr. Strange is not even interested in punishing criminals. In *Strange Tales* # 119 (1964; Lee/Ditko), a couple of thieves break into Dr. Strange's home, his "Sanctum Sanctorum," and steal a gem that opens up a gateway to the Purple Dimension. Dr. Strange gives chase and confronts Aggamon, a fiend who has taken the thieves captive. Strange defeats Aggamon and returns to Earth with the thieves, but he never punishes their crime. In fact, he envies these criminals. They live in an uncomplicated world of objects. They have not had to deal with the stresses of the enlightened intellect as has Strange, who must fight the forces of evil in every waking and even sleeping moment. Strange may counter by arguing, as he does in *Dr. Strange* #13, that reality itself is only a dream, but this argument only makes him even less capable of interacting with other people. Rather than the truth setting Strange free, it has trapped him in his own awareness—a triumph of metaphysical philosophy that leads him to social failure.

If the spiritual world means nothing to the thieves he saved from Aggamon, the physical world means as little to Strange. In *Doctor Strange Annual* #4 (1994; Quinn/Hotz/Age), Strange finds himself looking at one aspect of himself as "driven as a computer drives a 'slave' machine ... it tortures me to see and feel from within ... my twisted, selfish, arrogant ancillary self." Similarly, in *Dr. Strange Vs. Dracula* #1 (1994; Wolfman/Colan/Palmer), Strange fights the Lord of the Undead, but he also recognizes that Dracula lives in (and on) the world of flesh and blood, whereas Strange knows that he lives "outside the human reality."

Strange's early temporary anhedonia — a clinical term referring to an inability to experience the world as anything other than remote, sinister, strange, and dull —calls into question the nature of a worthwhile or "good" life. Aware of the transience of things and goods, hemmed in by demons and fiends and devils from other dimensions, Strange is often depressed and anxious, not exactly the life of the party. Strange is so morose that it often seems that he needs a strict Freudian therapist, or perhaps pep pills, more than magical spells. Marvel recognized this problem. In an ill-fated Universal Pictures TV movie, *Dr. Strange* (1978), Peter Hooten starred as psychiatrist Stephen Strange, treating a woman who is afraid she will die in her sleep. Realizing that there is truth in her claim, Strange seeks out the aid of a sorcerer, Lender, who in turn senses that Strange has latent magical abilities. He asks, "What if I were to tell you that your ignorance has been a kind of protection for you, and that there's a price you have to pay if you are to understand your destiny? Would you still choose to pay it?" Strange replies, "Yes." And yet, at the end of the film, he still ends up with the good-looking blonde.

Some fans were disappointed in the portrayal of Strange as a psychiatrist, rather than as a mystic, but essentially the movie makes an incisive critical commentary on the comic's lack of vitality. Strange never seems to get out of his chair, hardly the hero for either comics or movies, both of which need action to propel their stories. Strange's mental battles suggest that in our world, with our imperfect view of the astral plane, we would see Strange not as a wizard of wisdom, but as a nut case in need of psychiatry. If Strange is a psychiatrist, the physician can heal himself.

The convergence of Strange's clinical need with his professional training presents us with new questions, which are at once social and philosophical. First, what constitutes mental health? Is there a necessary connection between happiness and mental health? Certainly, we can say that one reason Strange is strange is that he can experience no happiness in the physical world. He knows that fixing bones does not heal people, that only by mending souls does one genuinely cure. Strange's war is against the dark potentialities of the mind, the propensities that contribute to sorrow, suffering, corruption, and sin. Rejected by normally happy people, who find him obsessively morbid, Dr. Strange lives a monastic life, often not leaving his room for weeks on end.

Explaining Life, Death, the Universe: Doctor Strange Meets God

If *Doctor Strange* does not offer the comic reader conventional stories, it does offer surprisingly sophisticated solutions to some of life's most fundamental questions. The comic is, in this sense, a philosophical text, one in which even the nature of God is explored. Fans generally agree that the best *Dr. Strange* story is "A Separate Reality" (1973–74; Englehart/Brunner; *Marvel Premiere* #9 and 10 and 12–14).

If you have questions about what and who God is, here's the comic's answer: God is Dr. Strange's Tibetan master. When the Ancient One died, his negative, power-hungry essence began to absorb the magical power of every age. After sucking up all the spiritual power of the present age, he moved back in time, seeking more power to feed his desire. Thus, he grew stronger and younger as he moved back in time.

But what about the vexing problem of evil? Why does it exist? Why does an omnipotent, omni-benevolent God allow bad things to happen to good people? The answer: The Ancient One only allows bad things to happen in order to gauge people's reaction and learn whether he should intervene in other ages. This also explains why "God" may seem so hard to see and hear — so absent — from our age, but is seen and heard in other ages. It's not because "God" is any less real, but only more active, in one age than in another. This attempt to define god-like interventions as a learning phase in the education of the Ancient One allows a "God" that is fallible, a powerful but nonetheless imperfect being.

Why Strange's God Doesn't Count: Satan's Nietzschean End Game

Although Dr. Strange arms himself with his knowledge of who and what God is, Satan remains firmly unimpressed. Indeed, he heckles good-naturedly, "Your faith is becoming fanaticism, don't you think? You can talk all the brave talk you want, but you haven't really gotten anywhere in all this time." Satan braces Strange with the unvarnished truth that he is a nobody, with no experience of the world, no reputation, and no power. High-minded and immaterial concepts, such as "freedom" or the "soul," cannot stop Satan's domination. Strange might know the truth concerning "God," but so what? What practical use is such knowledge on earth? As far as Satan is concerned, Strange has wasted his time: "You haven't learned a thing."

THINKING, DEBATING, WRITING

1. We suggested that aggression, if left unchecked, creates a social monster. Look up the history of a famous tyrant (e.g. Hitler, Stalin, Pol Pot) and discuss what he was like growing up. Is it possible to spot a villain in the making, or to stop someone from becoming a villain?

2. Our society celebrates beauty and physical prowess. Write an essay in celebration of the intellectual over the physical.

3. Write an essay explaining what you would do to deal with evil in society.

4. Who was Mother Theresa of Calcutta? Why did people admire her? Write an essay arguing that Mother Theresa was or was not a super-hero.

5. Look up the term "flower power." Write a paper about the significance of the term, telling what happened to it, and to the values that surrounded it.

6. Do our remarks on Dr. Strange "read too much into" the comic-book action? Write an essay on how you would decide when an interpretation offers "too much" explanation.

7. Read Book III of *Paradise Lost* and discuss Satan's strength and his failings.

8. Nietzsche argues that we must strengthen the strong. What role does society play in protecting the weak?

9. Strange has no friends, no social life, no interest in day-to-day events, no interest in politics, films, sports, culture, or art. Write an

essay in which you argue that Strange's choice is wrong-headed or enlightened.

10. Discuss Strange's concept of God with a local clergyman. In what ways do Strange's views agree or disagree with your own religious background?

6

9-11 and the Man Without Fear

In a widely-publicized and controversial book entitled The Clash of Civilizations *(1998), Samuel Huntington predicted a new Cold War, one unlike the political conflict between East and West. This emerging conflict would more closely resemble the Crusades, when men like Richard the Lion-Hearted led armies to the Holy Land in an attempt to retake Jerusalem. Because this new conflict would emanate from religious differences, modern ideology would be rendered all but passé. Instead of Marxist determinism and Stalinist military divisions, Huntington argued, the West would soon face hordes of militant Muslims, who think of Western ways with revulsion and resentment.*

Until recently, comic books held it taboo to criticize or undermine culture, race, or religion. Even an expression such as "clash of civilizations," would have been unthinkable, much less printable. But 9-11 rendered that gentleman's agreement no longer viable. When the Twin Towers went down, they took the rules of engagement in comic books with them.

Marvel Predicts 9-11

Even before 9-11, Marvel Enterprises had — on more than one occasion — imagined New York City blown to bits. The opening panels of *Daredevil* #321 (1983; Chichester/McDaniel) represent a variety of attacks on New York. In the first, Namor the Sub-Mariner attacks the city. In the second, Galactus, an alien who consumes planets to obtain fuel, begins his absorption of the planet Earth at its economic and political epicenter, New York. In the third, paranormal Kulan Gath lands in New York and begins to take over the world through spiritual means. But all such uses of force — natural, alien, and paranormal — fail to take down the indomitable New

Yorkers. Daredevil comments: "The Big Apple's had its share of hard times. Neighborhoods attacked.... In a typical twisted fashion, New Yorkers have come to take pride in their larger-than-life-disasters."[1] How, then, we might ask, did the comics react to 9-11? The question is doubly pertinent, since both Marvel and DC Comics, the twin towers of the industry, are based in New York. The answer is more complex than one might expect.

The Return of Hal Jordan

In our chapter on comics and the Cold War, we promised that we'd return to Hal Jordan, America's favorite Green Lantern. Since Hal's crime was that he wiped out millions of aliens to save an American city, it was only a matter of time before DC connected him to 9-11. There have been other Lanterns since Hal's death: John Stewart, Guy Gardner, and even a female, teenage Green Lantern named Jade. But, in truth, all attempts to replace Hal have met with failure. The most noticeable failure, because it was the longest-running, was that of Kyle Raynor, an American teenager.

Initially excited by the power of being a Green Lantern, Kyle soon learns that wearing the ring does not make him ready to use it properly. He's raw, and the other heroes know it. In issue #67 (1995; Marz/Pelletier/Tanghal), Sonar, a master of sonic power, attacks New York, and the Flash, worried that Kyle can't handle him, intervenes. What follows is a story of trust. Initially, the Flash tells Kyle to stand back and "[l]et somebody who knows what he's doing take over." Later, he tells him that he'd "better learn that ring doesn't make you a hero. Just somebody with a powerful toy." It soon is apparent that Sonar is more powerful than the Flash or the Green Lantern. Only by working together can they defeat him. In terms of geopolitics, this is prescient of the second Gulf War coalition. America, widely accused of going it alone, can't defeat her enemies without trusting her friends to help out. The theme is repeated three issues later, when John Stewart, the former Green Lantern, explains that "the ring isn't what makes you a hero. Don't depend on it too much. Arrogance has tragic consequences. I learned that the hard way. The ring's just a tool, Kyle. A hero depends on what's in your heart, and in your mind." But more temptations await the hero. Kyle, as we learn in #70 (1996; Marz/Pelletier/Tanghal), is studying to be an artist — it's just like a comic book writer to imagine that heroes not otherwise saving the planet practice drawing comics! When his girlfriend objects to his drawing nude models, Kyle admits that he's not

---

1. Daredevil's list misses a few attacks. In *Doc Strange* #2 (Gillis/Case/Emberlin), the dread Dormammu, for example, mounted a New York–based assault against the world.

cut out to be the Green Lantern. After all, if he can't even handle the ups and downs of having a girlfriend, how is he supposed to be mature enough to save the planet? With his doubts growing, Kyle meets his long-estranged father, a former hippie rock star, Johnny Walden, in *Green Lantern* #77 (1996; Marz/Pelletier/Tanghal).

Walden plays on his son's longings for a traditional family. He needs the Green Lantern to aid him in his plan to overthrow the government. Similar to the Kingpin, Walden argues that the American Dream has been killed by "a liberal federal government, foreign interest, the media, the worldwide banking conspiracy ... but the Dream's not dead ... America can be great again, but it needs help from the common man. It needs everyone who believes in America to stand up and do their part. My country needs me ... and it needs you."[2] Kyle agrees to help. When his sometime partner the Green Arrow asks how he could join this radical militia, Kyle just shrugs, "Family's what's important. Green Arrow's just a guy." The larger point is that Kyle is also "just a guy"— not a hero. By *Green Lantern* #107 (1998; Marz/Johnson/Batista/Lowe/Wiacek), Kyle is literally begging former Lanterns Alan Scott and John Stewart to take his ring away. They refuse.

Kyle's tenure as the Green Lantern can be summed up as a remarkably long story arc of a man given extraordinary powers, but still ill-equipped to be a hero. After years of replacements, DC finally had to admit the truth: There is only one Green Lantern, and his name is Hal Jordan. DC finally pulled the plug on Kyle in November 2004, with *Green Lantern* # 181 (Marz/Ross/Ramos). The story was called "Endings," and for Kyle, the title fits. He's not even in the story.

But wasn't Hal killed saving the earth? After his death, Jordan was transformed into The Spectre, but after suffering for decades, he is transformed back into the Green Lantern. Interestingly, Jordan's musings respond to Kyle's aforementioned doubts. What a great reversal! Jordan's heroic assurance has been haunting Kyle for a decade; but now, upon his return, Hal's thoughts reply to Kyle's haunting doubts. And having literally returned from the dead, what has Hal learned? The very thing that has eluded Kyle and the other pretenders to his title: "Tragedy goes with the job. But I've been looking for someone to blame for the things that were taken away from me.... But when it really came down to it, I blamed the ring. I lost sight of what a gift it is."

But that gift is not just power. Kyle has been misusing the ring. The secret of the Lanterns is not power in any physical sense. As he explains, the green power of the ring is "willpower from every living being in the universe converted into energy. Amplified by our own a million times over.

2. See the Kingpin's remarks in our Chapter 3, "Spider-Man and Corporate Responsibility."

There's an emotional electromagnetic spectrum out there that can be harnessed and used. Green willpower is the most pure." Hal, then, is the Daredevil of the DC Universe, The Man Without Fear, the perfect weapon against the threat of the Cold War and present-day terrorism because he has willpower: the ability to confront difficult moral problems and then make hard choices decisively. No turning back.

The argument is expanded to reflect geopolitical concerns in *Green Lantern Rebirth* #1 (2004; Johns/Van Sciver). Kyle Raynor suggests that the reason why John Stewart will never be a great Green Lantern, like Hal Jordan, is that he's basically slavish. "You look to others to lead you around," Kyle says. The racism couldn't be more blatant. John, a black man, is a good soldier who takes his orders but won't—or worse, can't—think for himself. He is, at least compared with Hal Jordan, "less American," in that he is willing to put the Green Lanterns before American interests. He does the same in the Justice League, where he always does what he is told, never challenging the established power structures, represented by the white and moneyed power elitist, Batman. Kyle accuses, "And what's your role as Green Lantern with the Justice League, huh? You're just a good, little soldier, Stewart. And let that Dark Knight [Batman] tell you what to do. You never even challenge him." The WASPish Kyle, on the other hand, sounds more like George W. Bush rejecting the dictates of the U.N.: "Screw the [Green Lantern] Corps," he says, "I don't miss the guardians and their stupid rules."

But if Guy Gardner and the other Lanterns have failed to live up to their capabilities, at least they're not guilty of wholesale slaughter, as Hal is. Perhaps Hal is unaware that he has betrayed the values, not of the Corps, whose rules are, as Kyle points out, intellectually and ethically vapid. Perhaps Hal has betrayed the "emotional electromagnetic spectrum" of the Lantern—the willpower of the universe to overcome fear now "throughout God's universe."[3]

This theological line also links Hal Jordan to Dr. Strange, who, we recall, finds that the greatest enemy in the universe is Satan, also known as the "Great Fear." What is this fear that has infected Jordan and forced him to kill the other Green Lanterns? The mystery is explored in *Green Lantern Rebirth* #1, in which Hal Jordan, once the icon of American freedom and power, now metes out justice in Islamic fashion. He even makes a gruesome pun on the ancient rule of "an eye for an eye" by chopping a hand off a thief named William Hand. Horrified by Hal's actions, the Green Arrow still admires the "sadistic sense of humor" in the act. To others, he's a mes-

---

3. The Corps, desperate to stop Hal, releases his greatest enemy, Sinestro, perhaps in the vain hope that one renegade Corps member could stop another. The plan is a failure. Jordan snaps Sinestro's neck. See *Green Lantern Rebirth* #3 (2005; Johns/Van Sciver/Rollins).

sianic figure. At a ball game, he finds that everyone begins to confess his or her sins to him. One says he's been embezzling funds form his company, another that he cheated on his wife. Are these such great sins? And what should their punishments be? Castration for the fornicator, the chopping off of hands for thieves?

The story evolves in *Green Lantern Rebirth* #4 (2005; Johns/Van Sciver/ Rollins). According to Hal, the Corps itself became a stumbling block to peace. From Hal's perspective, he did the universe a favor by wiping out the Corps. Paradoxically, he accuses the Corps of manipulating him into becoming a murderer: "Lies. You forget nothing. You allowed this to happen. Without chaos, without evil in the universe — you have no reason to exist." So Hal is both avenger and victim. He avenges Coast City by murdering the entire Green Lantern Corps, who, according to Hal, want to be murdered to allow evil back into the universe. This claim is convenient, in that it allows Hal to operate with moral impunity. He's not to blame for the murder of millions; the Green Lanterns are. Hal might have pulled the trigger, but he's the real victim. At the same time, Hal believes that the Corps is evil and gets what it deserves.[4] All this has a 9-11 feel to it — Osama bin Laden preaching the Koran but practicing violence, gloating over the murder of thousands, while arguing that the Americans brought 9-11 on themselves.

In God We Trust?

Marvel has also looked at 9-11 both as a military strike and a religious act. In *Iron Man* #407 (2003; Grell/Ryan/Parsons), Iraqi sailors, using a refurbished North Korean submarine, plan a nuclear strike on New York. Intercepted by a Coast Guard cutter, the Iraqis open fire, sinking the boat. The captain and the first mate have the following exchange:

CAPTAIN: We must have struck the magazine. A lucky shot.
FIRST MATE: Allah is with us.
CAPTAIN: Don't delude yourself. A just God would strike us dead for what we are about to do.

This exchange could not have occurred in a comic book before 9-11. It is controversial to the core. Some readers might take the captain's remark, in the context of holy war, as conciliatory, and therefore reasonable: "We've

4. In *Action Comics* #596 (1987; Byrne/Williams/Costanza), we learn that the Guardians themselves were formed because a being of immense power named Krona unleashed a nameless evil upon the universe. In part to atone for that act, Krona thereafter formed the Green Lantern Corps. So Hal's attack on the Lanterns can be read as part of a cosmic comeuppance: Krona's cronies finally paying for his crime of unleashing evil into the cosmos.

been lucky so far, but let's not kid ourselves: God won't like or support this." The captain's reluctance to attribute victory to Allah places him in a dubious situation. From media reports on bin Laden, we hear that he draws recruits and attracts financial support from religious zealots. Many in the ranks of al Qaeda are adherents of a fundamentalist faction of the Muslim religion known as Wahhabi. From their point of view, the war—*jihad*—is not about land or oil, but about the far more important issues of right and wrong. The very presence of American and European troops, whom they regard as infidels, in places like Saudi Arabia (site of the holy city of Mecca) amounts to desecration. Yet this Iraqi captain rejects that ideology.

Then again, the captain isn't really opening a serious discussion. As he well knows, there is not much use debating with a holy warrior on a suicide mission. In any event, this brief exchange in the heat of battle is a private one between trusted coworkers.

If the captain privately doubts his actions, publicly he sings a different tune. Using an American network bandwidth, he broadcasts a message to all Americans:

> People of New York! Once again we bring terror to the heart of America, retribution for the destruction of our homes, death for the daughter of our brothers. When the sun rises over the destruction we have wrought, you will know that there is no safe place, no haven in which to hide. You will question how God could allow such a thing ... but the hand that strikes you is not the Angel of Death ... it is the hand of retribution.

Here we find more than the usual anti-American rant, "America is no longer safe from terror." The terrorist also emphasizes that his war is a just cause, settled the old-fashioned way: an eye for an eye. At the same time, the captain implies that the destruction that he brings (a nuclear attack) will shake the faith of Americans: "[Americans] will question how God could allow such a thing." In effect, by destroying an American city live on TV, he hopes to strike at one of the country's core beliefs: "In God We Trust."

Whom Gods Destroy

If the captain's private religious doubts don't dovetail with his public declarations, we can nevertheless recognize an American influence here. The captain has gone Hollywood. When the cameras roll, he's always ready with a clip that will make the network execs happy. A picture is worth a thousand words, the more so if it's on video.

But it is an *audio* clip that helps defeat the terrorists. New York is saved, not by an act of God, but by a man made of iron, who expresses another American core value: rock'n'roll. Smashing through the sub, Tony Stark, playboy-billionaire, a.k.a. Iron Man, declares, "In the immortal words of Mick Jagger, 'You can't always get what you want.'" It would appear that Iron Man counters the captain's argument by invoking a god of his own: Mick Jagger, a Dionysian symbol of capitalist drive. The song's lyrics go on to remind us that if we *try*, we might get what we *need*. These lyrics may not hold true for the Iraqi captain and his men, who want retribution. Clearly, the Gods of Rock'n'Roll side with the American record-buying public.

The same partiality is evident in the subplot, in which Iron Man/Tony Stark befriends an apparent orphan named "Angel." Stark takes her to a homeless shelter his firm manages, then buys all the homeless people in the shelter Christmas gifts. While Iron Man is off fighting the Iraqis, a news service reports that a statue of an angel has been stolen from a church. After Iron Man defeats the Iraqis, Angel disappears, and the statue reappears. As the reader may have fathomed, Angel is indeed an "Angel," but one that is virtually powerless in New York City. Destitute, hungry, and cold, she has to seek shelter with Stark. In the Big Apple, theology gives way to practical concerns: food, shelter, money. When Stark gives the homeless gifts for the holidays, he doesn't give anything of spiritual significance: no Bibles or rosary beads or crucifixes. He gives "feel-good" gifts: radios, televisions, Disney sweaters. Spirituality is a non-issue; it's not what you want, but what you need that matters. New Yorkers may think they want an angel, but what they need is Iron Man and rock'n'roll. The angel's inability to stop the Iraqis makes it clear that this is not a theological fight, not a matter of good and evil. Invoking the former junkie, the oft-demonized Mick Jagger, America can hardly argue that it is a religious society.

Comics and the Terrorist War

The subject of the aforementioned *Iron Man* story concerns terrorism on American soil. But comic book heroes are taking the fight to Europe and to the Middle East as well. After 9-11, the comic series *Captain America* was relaunched to reflect on the new dangers facing America. As the first issue (2002; Rieber/Cassaday) opens, Steve Rogers, a.k.a. Captain America, is at Ground Zero, helping firefighters dig out the dead. Nick Fury soon calls on him to hunt down the terrorist leader responsible, Fayal al-Tariq.

But before he can even begin the task, al-Tariq's men strike again, this time in a picturesque midwestern town, where his followers have taken a church full of worshippers hostage. They've wired the sanctuary with explosives. It's clear that there is to be no negotiation. The terrorists only wait for the media to arrive before they blow the building sky-high. The media arrive, and so does Captain America, who kills all the terrorists. As one goes for a gun, our hero, just before killing him, imparts a last piece of advice: "It [the gun] may be loaded. But it won't make you a soldier."

The Ethics of Terrorism

Captain America distances himself from these other combatants by claiming a kind of civility. He is a soldier, not a terrorist. He believes that American soldiers would never fight a war as terrorists do, not simply because they are Americans, but because they are warriors, who fight according to civilized rules.

From the terrorists' perspective, this is just stupid. They believe in killing their enemies by any means necessary. And as for civilians, well, no one is really innocent. Surprisingly, the rest of the issue demonstrates the legitimacy of that assumption. As it turns out, the town's main source of employment is a munitions factory, which makes the bombs that Israelis drop on Palestinians. Could it be that America is not so innocent after all?

This theme develops in issue #5 (2002; Rieber and Cassaday), in which Captain America follows the terrorist trail to Europe. As his plane descends into Dresden, he cannot forget the firebombing of that city in World War II, which some historians have called terrorism: "Dresden ... You would have said that we were doing what we had to do—To defeat Hitler and the Nazis. Crush the Axis. End their evil. But now—What do you see? February the thirteenth and fourteenth. 1945. These people weren't soldiers." Recalling how he helped the firemen after 9-11, Captain America reflects bitterly that, as Dresden burned, many German firefighters died trying to save women and children. "History," he concludes, "repeats itself like a machine gun."

But the new war on terror is not the same as World War II, and our hero's inability to see that is glaringly obvious in a conversation he has with a German woman. She does not understand why America feels it needs to bully everyone around the world. While they talk, the two play a game of chess, which Captain America wins, but the geopolitical discussion hardly ends in a checkmate.[5] Reiterating that the rules of war

5. The argument is more ironic when one considers that the background to that month's issue was the highly controversial book by Robert Kegan, *Of Paradise and Power*, which was featured in book reviews in the *New York Times* and *Los Angeles Times*. Kegan argues that America's desire to protect itself with first-strike capability has led many world leaders and much of the world's populace to view America as a terrorist nation, intent not upon simply defending itself, but aggressively expanding its control of the world's economics and natural resources, an economic empire enforced by the largest, most powerful military on the planet.

have changed, in *Captain America* #6, the protagonist comes face to face with yet another terrorist, who reminds him of other American atrocities in Guatemala and Kurdistan: "You know your history, Captain America.... The sun never set on your political *chessboard*—your empire of blood" [emphasis added]. Captain America replies: "My people never knew."

Nick Fury and S.H.I.E.L.D.

Nonsense! After all, Cap is a government agent, and as such, he has worked on covert operations before. So he is well aware of the secret ops army created to fight terrorism: S.H.I.E.L.D., led by World War II veteran Nick Fury. S.H.I.E.L.D. began as a Cold War operation but quickly adapted itself in the late 1960s to fight autonomous terrorist organizations such as HYDRA, a group that has no allegiance to any single government, land mass, or even ideology. If HYDRA anticipates al Qaeda, S.H.I.E.L.D. closely resembles some of the campaigns undertaken by the C.I.A. in the 1980s, particularly the operation which we now refer to as "Iran-Contra."

For those who have forgotten the scandal, while Central American nations yearned to overthrow their communist oppressors, the U.S. Congress was none too happy to find that its money was being used to fund terror campaigns in which villages were burned, women and children slaughtered, all in the name of U.S. geopolitical interests. When funding was stopped, Oliver ("Ollie") North, possibly on President Reagan's orders (accounts vary), set up an elaborate scheme of secretly selling arms to Iran, then using the profits to buy arms for liberation forces in Nicaragua. In hearing after hearing, North claimed that he was doing it for the good of America, and eventually Congress agreed. The matter was closed, and today North is a national radio talk show host and a regular guest on the nationally televised Fox News show, Hannity and Colmes.

It did not take Marvel Enterprises long to catch the similarities between North's covert operations and Nick Fury's S.H.I.E.L.D. Originally, Fury was a good guy. After Iran-Contra, Fury became a more shadowy, more complex figure. In *Daredevil* #326 (1994; Chichester/McDaniel/Oakley), Fury's covert forces have been tracking a terrorist organization intent on controlling the Internet. They find that Daredevil is on the trail of one of their agents, John Garrett, who has taken matters into his own hands. S.H.I.E.L.D. is not concerned when Daredevil beats one of their operatives to a pulp. Garrett can take care of himself. The greater concern is that S.H.I.E.L.D.'s cover has been blown.

American Torture

Garrett is collected by his S.H.I.E.L.D. operatives, who take him to the huge S.H.I.E.L.D helicarrier, a flying fortress, equipped with the latest gadgetry, where he is brutally tortured. Garrett remains unrepentant:

GARRETT: I played fast and loose with the rules? How's that make me different than an Ollie North? He's wearin' medals on TV and gettin' movie deals! I'm in the mud wearin' a cheap suit, about to be buried under the salt flats.

That Garrett expects to be executed tells quite us a bit about S.H.I.E.L.D. and Nick Fury, who started his career fighting Nazis and now uses their tactics of torture and execution. Of course, Garrett knows that all transgressions are forgivable. After all, Nick has crossed the line often, and, more importantly, he has the power to open any file and destroy any document:

GARRETT: You're a covert, manipulative S.O.B., Fury ... you can pull the strings to make like I never existed! Or look me in the eye and give me some due for what I did accomplish for this country, no matter how I got it done.

Not surprisingly, Nick relents. After all, Garrett is right. Fury does have the power. S.H.I.E.L.D., we learn, controls all governmental records and has new plans to expand its reach by installing a secret surveillance chip in every cell phone, every fax machine, every computer, every TV: total surveillance in the name of freedom.

If questioned on the need, Fury points to HYDRA's plans to take over the Internet. If S.H.I.E.L.D. doesn't protect the Internet, it will be destroyed. There's just one problem. Unknown to S.H.I.E.L.D., HYDRA is the manufacturer of the chips needed for this surveillance operation.[6] The two organizations need each other: S.H.I.E.L.D. uses its intelligence to ask for yet more money to build yet more weapons to find yet more HYDRA terrorists; HYDRA uses the money to build yet more weapons, and to recruit yet more terrorists to expand its own V-chip market.

Total Security Has Its Price

That S.H.I.E.L.D. is, in effect, subsidizing terrorism does not bother Fury. If HYDRA is only aiming at S.H.I.E.L.D., then America is safe, even if S.H.I.E.L.D. is not. But to Fury's horror, he learns that this logic, heroic as it may seem, is a joke. Walking through his old neighborhood, he now

6. S.H.I.E.L.D. also buys weapons from AIM a terrorist organization. See *Captain America* #30 (2004; Kirkman/Eaton/Geraci).

finds street gangs better armed than the C.I.A. (*Fury: Agent of S.H.I.E.L.D.*
#4, 1995; Chaykin/Lehmuhl/Kenner). He recognizes the ordnance: stan-
dard HYDRA weapons, now funded in part by S.H.I.E.L.D.[7]

After 9-11, S.H.I.E.L.D has other weapons to worry about. One is a new
kind of dog tag which, once placed around a soldier's neck, becomes a permanent collar. The tag can be used to track a soldier's movements, allowing for faster coordination and extraction. But, in event of enemy capture,
the dog tag can also be set to kill. This clever device assures that a soldier
can never be taken prisoner, and never, under threat of torture, reveal military secrets. But who makes the tags and who sets the codes? The reader,
perhaps, has already guessed: the terrorist al-Tariq, who can now kill any,
maybe even all, U.S. military personnel with a single press of his Palm Pilot.

When Captain America learns of this terrible secret, he confronts Col-
onel Fury, who is unrepentant: "We have to have it because the enemy has
it."[8] Captain America no longer recognizes his old friend. "The man I knew
would never allow his soldiers to come in harm's way," he says. However,
Captain America admits, when it comes to fighting terrorists, the war "is
not that straightforward." The enemy is weapons-rich but target-poor. He
offers no capital cities to bomb, no airfields to level, no land to seize. He
pits the strength of the West against itself.

As we soon learn, the high-tech terrorist has yet other plans. With a
click of a keyboard, violent prisoners are freed from maximum-security
prisons. By the same method, ships are allowed into port without being
searched for drugs or weapons, money is reallocated from John Q. Six-
Pack to offshore accounts, and false electronic evidence is planted, which
in turn is used to frame powerful politicians and industrialists. Perhaps
even more insidiously, the terrorists have invested in porn sites that destroy
the morality of their enemies and entice their women to debase themselves
for cash. The profits go straight to the terror networks. This war is pernicious, because many of the actions of the enemy stem from the desires of
Americans.

S.H.I.E.L.D. is aware of what is going on, but can't effectively intervene without trouncing the Constitution. Thus, what S.H.I.E.L.D. longs for
is not unlike what HYDRA wants: a suspension of civil liberties, a fall into

---

7. It could be argued that Fury's logic is like that of some police departments, which some
accuse of allowing drugs and guns to flood the inner cities: "Let them kill each other," the logic
goes, "we'll come in and mop up the rest." The cynical calculus of acceptable causalities over-
rules saving anyone who gets caught in the crossfire.

8. Concurrent with *Captain America* #10, Fury also appeared in *Iron Man* #410 (Grell/Laws/
Ryan/Perrotta). In that issue, the same or similar device is also found on North Korean assassins
who have attacked capitalist military industrialist Tony Stark (a.k.a. Iron Man). Fury suspects
that the assassination attempt has been made in a effort to cover up Stark's illegal sale of
weapons of mass destruction to the North Koreans.

anarchy, the rise of a new totalitarian order. No wonder Captain America looks back on the Second World War with some nostalgia:

> World War II — the War that made the soldier — was different. Men faced men on the battlefield. Black and white. Good and evil. Now battles have begun to be fought with disembodied screens and lethal keyboards. The world just isn't as simple as it used to be. And it's not safe to assume the enemies are either.[9]

Captain America as a Terrorist

On many occasions, Cap has even fought side by side with Fury. In *Captain America* #440 (1995; Gruenwald/Hoover/Severin), S.H.I.E.L.D. recruits him to take on the terrorist group AIM, an offshoot of HYDRA. Like its parent organization, AIM has no nation, no president, no representative to the U.N. Rather, it is an army of hardcore terrorists, well-financed, well-disciplined, well-organized, and supremely dangerous. When S.H.I.E.L.D. gets word that AIM is going to attack, Fury sends in Captain America as his preemptive strike weapon.[10] He tells a friend, "I'm mounting an expedition to AIM Island. Something big is going on there that needs investigating and probably putting an end to."

Why turn to Captain America? He answers to no one, not even to Congress or to the President. He's a one-man army, more deadly than a dozen Rambos. He's the comic-book "Ollie" North, attired in the vestments of flag and country and acting decisively outside the law.

Yet who can challenge Captain America's interventionist policies? Since he is above the law, the answer must be no one. Like a good soldier, a man of action rather than words, Captain America doesn't ask too many questions. This makes Captain America, as Fury describes him, "a perfect soldier ... who loves a country run by a government that can't always be trusted" (*Captain America* #10, 2003; Austin/Lee/Villarrubia). Fury, however, would prefer a soldier who asks *no* questions at all. What he really wants is his own al Qaeda, a group of fanatical devotees, willing to give their life for the flag. As Fury explains, "The world is a different place now, Captain America. America needs killers who will murder for the right cause. The just cause" (*Captain America* #16; Austin/Lee/Villarrubia).

Cap is appalled, but he shouldn't be. After all, what did American soldiers do in World War II or Vietnam or Afghanistan? Hand out parking tickets? America's soldiers are trained to follow orders and to kill the enemy. Every army's soldiers are trained to do the same. The fact that Captain Amer-

---

9. Fury agrees. Faced with street thugs better armed than the CIA, Fury nostalgically longs for the calm clarity of World War II (*Fury: Agent of S.H.I.E.L.D.* #4; 1994; Chaykin/Lehmuhl/Kenner).
10. In 2003, America invaded Iraq for similar reasons. The Cap story was written in 1995.

ica believes that only other armies kill is ludicrous and self-deluded. Captain America is, therefore, in a strange position: To defend America, he must pretend that America is innocent and al-Tariq is merely an aberration. In terms of America's post–9-11 actions, Marvel's irony couldn't be more venomously pointed. While Colin Powell was failing to cobble together a coalition against Iraq, al-Tariq was arguing that there is already a coalition of the willing, made up of oppressed people united against terrorism, against imperialism — and their target is America.

Drug War/Terror War

Marvel Enterprises used other elements of this same Captain America story line to connect the War on Terror to the older War on Drugs. One of al-Tariq's soldiers boasts, "All power lies within the walls of Alamut." Although the unnamed terrorist then blows himself up, it is clear that his ideology survives and, indeed, cannot be extinguished. Like the city of Alamut, it is centuries old.

During the Crusades, Alamut was known as a training ground for terrorism. Recruits willingly came, not out of a sense of religious duty, but for sensual pleasures. Recruits were drugged with hashish. When they were nearly unconscious, they were then pleasured with sex slaves. When a recruit awoke from his orgy of sex and drugs, he was told that he had been to heaven, and that if he wished to return, he had to offer his life to the cult. As a foretaste of the heaven to come, each recruit was given a piece of hashish, which he could smoke, thereby reviving at least half of his carnal delights. Such recruits, who were willing to do anything to return to the paradise they had experienced, were named for the drug they carried with them: *hashshashin*, the etymological ancestor of the term, assassin. When al-Tariq's terror organization invokes Alamut, it is symbolically allying itself with the drug trade.

Marvel tied the War on Terror with the War on Drugs in other stories as well. In *Daredevil: The Target* #1 (2002; Smith/Glenn Fabry), terrorists join with drug dealers to take out a hit on Daredevil. It's a win-win situation. For criminal organizations, dealing with al Qaeda means access to a sophisticated international network that can be used to smuggle high-grade Afghan hashish and opium into the States. For the terrorists, the drugs further weaken America's fighting resolve and provide more funds for weapons. It should be admitted, however, that this coalition is not easy to hold together. As one underworld figure makes clear, the mob hates Muslim fundamentalists:

> First off, I'd like you to know that I'm an American — through and through. I love my country, and more than that, I love this city. I despise you people for what you did [on 9-11]. I hate everything you represent. But I'm a profes-

sional. I didn't get into this business to express my political views. So I don't like you. Big deal. We're not here to make friends.

In the end, business trumps flag and country. So with a grin, the hit man Bullseye replies, "I'll send him [Daredevil] straight to Allah."

Bullseye's adjustment to the lingo of Muslim terrorists suggests that, on some level, fundamentalist terrorists and professional criminals see the world in mutually compatible ways. They both gain by the symbiotic relationship of drugs and guns. For Bullseye, this is a business opportunity, simple work for profit. Just so for the terrorists, who are an all–Prophet organization. As media wonks were quick to point out, 9-11 was more than an attack on American government. It was first and foremost an attack on American business interests. The Twin Towers and the space between them symbolized the divide between rich and poor, east and west.

Why Do the Terrorists Want to Kill Daredevil?

The attack on the Twin Towers is intelligible, if reprehensible. It's a target with religious significance as a Temple of Mammon. But why the attack on Daredevil? The question never occurs to Bullseye. Money is all he discusses or cares about. If the terrorists want Daredevil dead and are willing to pay, why should the myopic Bullseye wonder why?

But we are not invested in the transaction and are therefore free to wonder: Why would terrorists want to kill Daredevil? He's not the same kind of superhero as Captain America, whose very name and costume signify a national importance. Nor does he have the same global reach as Iron Man or Thor. In fact, Daredevil is a local champion. As with the black heroes, such as Luke Cage or the Falcon, Daredevil's "turf" is a ghetto, Hell's Kitchen.

It might have something to do with the hero's full title: Daredevil, The Man Without Fear. The terrorist attack of 9-11 was not meant simply to destroy or to kill; its larger goal was to place fear into the minds of Americans, to make them feel unsafe in their daily lives. Killing Daredevil could also have that effect, although the name of his territory, Hell's Kitchen, should in and of itself make the pedestrian weary. No need terrorists there.

Daredevil as Catholic Hero

We suspect that the terrorists target The Man Without Fear for religious reasons.[11] No character in the Marvel pantheon is as closely allied as

---

11. In addition to *Daredevil*'s box-office success, that year's Oscar nominations all had strongly religious themes: *The Lord of the Rings: The Two Towers, Road to Perdition,* and *Gangs of New York.*

Daredevil with religious faith. After the death of his father, a club boxer who is beaten to death by gangsters for his refusal to throw a fight, Matt Murdock is raised by a church-funded orphanage, which instills in him a strict adherence to the Catholic faith. He regularly attends confession and uses the church as his private sanctuary. Daredevil's mother is not revealed until the 1987 graphic novel, *Born Again* (Miller/Mazzucchelli); predictably, she is a nun. Thus, the church is, quite literally, Daredevil's home.

The *Daredevil* movie goes further than the book, placing Gothic statuary and iconography in Murdock's apartment, and giving him a customized sarcophagus, complete with an inlaid crucifix, as a sleeping chamber. Further, although most of Daredevil's story arcs are secular, many of the story titles have distinctly religious overtones. For instance, in the first 100 hundred issues, we found such titles as: "The Stiltman Cometh" (#8), "That He May See ..." (#9), "And Men Shall Call Him ... Ox" (#15), "None are so Blind ..." (#17), "And There Shall Come a Gladiator" (#18), "Thou Shalt Not Covet thy Neighbor's Planet" (#28), "If There Should Be a God of Thunder" (#30), "The Exterminator and the Super-Powered Unholy Three" (#39), "Brother, Take My Hand" (#47), "As It Was in the Beginning" (#53), "Behold the Brotherhood" (#73), "In the Country of the Blind" (#74), and "He Who Saves" (#97).

These titles are not accidental. Daredevil's power of supersensitive hearing may result from a radioactive spill, but this power is only one manifestation — a symbol, so to speak — of the hero's spiritually-derived power. In *Daredevil* #338 (1995; Smithee/Jubran/Parks and Hudson), we learn that Daredevil's real power emanates from his capacity to hear and obey a *higher calling*. Here we see Daredevil, hovering over New York City. The narrative reads, "Manhattan. 34 stories up, with *nothing but prayer* between here and the cold, hard streets below. There's a reason they call this costumed avenger Daredevil" [emphasis added]. In *Daredevil* #364 (1997; Kese/Nord/Ryan), the hero sets a room ablaze and lets two assailants burn to a crisp. Smiling down upon them, Daredevil thinks to himself, "I'll put the fear of the devil in them soon enough. They had better pray." In *Daredevil* #76 (1971; Conway/Colan), Matt Murdock's alter ego is referred to as a "horned demon" who takes vengeance on the wicked. In *Daredevil* #335 (1994; Smithee/Jubran/Hudson/Severin), Bushwacker notes that Daredevil is unlike other heroes in that he has no super strength or technological gizmos. His greatest asset is his faith. "The real Daredevil didn't need protection. The real devil never took a single bullet."

Muslims as Villains

It need not be said that, since 9-11, many Americans have come to see Muslim culture as dangerous, and the recent wars in Afghanistan and Iraq

as fundamentally religious in nature. George W. Bush is a devout Christian, his enemies devoutly Muslim.[12] Even the secular rhetoric of these wars
revolves around such tropes as "evil" and "infidel." We point to a recent
spate of articles concerning terrorism and religious intolerance.

Prefacing our discussion of the articles themselves, we note that bel-
licose individuals can be found in any society, and that religious intolerance in America, as well as a lack of understanding concerning Islam, is not
new. Nonetheless, in comic books and pop culture, the fundamental question at stake is the rationale for terrorism. Are terrorists simply an evolution of war philosophy, or is terrorism an expression of religious
intolerance? If the former, the religious question becomes irrelevant. If the
latter, dividing the philosophy of war from religion becomes impossible.
The latter camp is what concerns us here: Popular religious broadcaster Pat
Robertson was reported as saying that "Adolf Hitler was bad, but what the
Muslims want to do to the Jews is worse." In an interview with the *Washington Times*, an unapologetic Robertson complained that Bush "is not
elected as chief theologian," and objected again to Bush's description of
Islam as a "religion of peace." Another religious conservative, the Rev. Jerry
Falwell, referred to the prophet Mohammed as a "terrorist"; Falwell later
apologized. The Rev. Franklin Graham, son of evangelist Billy Graham (the
latter a close personal friend of George W. Bush), has called Islam "evil."

A number of conservative — including some policy makers with close
ties to the Bush Administration — agree. Calling Islam a peaceful religion,
as President Bush has in his public addresses, "is an increasingly hard argument to make," said Kenneth Adelman, a former Reagan official who serves
on the Bush Pentagon's Defense Policy Board. "The more you examine the
religion, the more militaristic it seems. After all, its founder, Mohammed,
was a warrior, not a peace advocate like Jesus." Paul Weyrich, an activist
who is influential in the White House, wrote, "I have had much good to
say about President Bush in recent months. But one thing that concerned
me before September 11th and concerns me even more now is his administration's constant promotion of Islam as a religion of peace and tolerance
just like Judaism or Christianity. It is neither."[13] On Saturday, November
30, 2002, in an article entitled "Conservatives Dispute Bush Portrayal of
Islam as Peaceful," published in *The Washington Post*, reported that a large

12. To be more accurate, most of bin Laden's members come from the fundamentalist Wahhabi sect. The stronghold of Wahhabism is Saudi Arabia.

13. It would appear that President Bush is reluctant to call a spade a spade. And here, we can
think of a number of ungenerous characterizations of his supposed lack of candor. In comparison, Osama bin Laden seems eminently clear about the religious aims of his terror campaign. In
1998, he told his followers, "The call to wage war against America was made because America
has spearheaded the crusade against the Islamic nation, sending tens of thousands of its troops
to the land of the two holy mosques over and above its meddling in its affairs."

In reaction to 9-11, Iron Man takes on an Iraqi submarine commander as he begins his nuclear strike against New York City. (By permission of Marvel Comics.)

number of the President's foreign policy hawks disagreed with Bush's characterization of Islam as a "peaceful movement." Insiders reported that the
President didn't believe it either.

Daredevil's Long-Standing Fight With Arab Muslims

If present American policy all but equates Arab terrorism with Islam,
then Daredevil, we can easily infer, is in agreement. After all, he has had a
long history of dealing with Islamic extremism. In 1972, as the Israelis and
Arabs engaged in what became known as the Six Day War, Marvel weighed
in with a two-issue series, *Daredevil* #97 and 98 (Conway/Gerber), in which
the Satan-clad hero (Daredevil) encounters a group of religious enthusiasts,
led by "The Dark Messiah." Espousing a fanatical fundamentalism, The Dark
Messiah has recruited three disciples: "Josiah the Deceiver," "Macabee the
Tall," and "Uriah the Unfaithful." The Muslim theology here cannot be
ignored. Islam holds that Moses and Jesus were blessed forerunners of the
prophet Mohammad. We must, therefore, take account of the fact that The
Dark Messiah sees his followers, not only as disciples, but also as prefigura-
tions of the True Prophet. Just as in Milton's *Paradise Lost*, narratives of heroic
figures in Hebrew Scripture foreshadow the Gospel, moving the human race
"From shadowy Types to Truth," so too The Dark Messiah is a Mohammedan
figure. He rejects Daredevil as an infidel: "Fool! There is but one true living
hero–and he is our master. You are but an agent of Hell — A Servitor of Satan!"

In 2003, with three wars raging in or near the Middle East, American
audiences flocked to the movie *Daredevil*, starring Ben Affleck.[14] Like the
Spider-Man movie of a year earlier, *Daredevil* was a number one summer
movie in America, though not for the same reasons. In 2002, when *Spider-
Man* premiered, corporate corruption and 401(k)s were the main fare of
talk shows. In 2003, the subject was 9-11 and *jihad*. *Daredevil* also features
corporate corruption in the form of the Kingpin, but audiences, we suggest, were attracted to *Daredevil's* religious iconography. The "Guardian
Devil," as he is called in the movie, does not protect corporate America,
but offers Christians a kind of *jihad*, a Christian holy war against the faith-
less. He tells a rapist in court, "I hope for your sake that justice is found
here today, before justice finds you." Like the *jihadists* of the Islamic world,
Daredevil enforces the ancient cause of retributive justice: an eye for an eye.
"Justice," Murdock states, "is blind."

---

14. As of this writing, Israel is at war with the Palestinians, and America is at war with
Afghanistan and Iraq. Afghanistan is technically not in the Middle East, but the country became
a safe haven for Osama bin Laden and like-minded Saudis, as well as of their European and
American sympathizers.

The film opens with a shot of Daredevil clinging to a church steeple. At other points in the movie, he merges seamlessly with the church's gargoyles. The religious imagery is invoked throughout. Even the earliest trailers focus on this theme. One trailer shown at the L.A. Comic Convention in 2002 begins with the following voice-over: "For Daredevil, justice is blind ... and for the guilty, there's hell to pay."[15]

The idea couldn't be more Catholic. Mainstream Catholic thought requires that there be "payment" for sin. Christ had paid for man's sins, but man could set up a pre-payment option for his own misdemeanors.[16] In medieval times, in order to acquire funds for the refurbishment of St. Peter's Basilica, the Vatican established a system of *quid pro quo* for most sins, in the form of "indulgences." These could be awarded in exchange for donations above and beyond the usual tithes and gifts to the Church. Implicit in this association of redemption and personal payoff is an idea that, some would say, the Church shares with organized crime. The crime boss is a secular parallel to the Pope of pre–Reformation times, in the sense that he exercises earthly authority, collects revenues, and offers "protection" from real or imagined dangers. From an iconographical point of view, informed by cultural history, hitman-for-hire Bullseye is Daredevil's sinister double, serving that other "Pope" of America, the all-powerful Kingpin, and, through his intermediaries in the drug trade, al Qaeda.

Bullseye as Religious Warrior?

Okay, so if Daredevil is targeted because he's a Christian, why, out of the many thousands of supervillains available, is Bullseye hired to bump him off? In the recent *Daredevil* movie, we first meet Bullseye (Colin Farrell) in a London pub, drinking and throwing darts with the locals. Things turn ugly when the bar owner says he doesn't want "his [Bullseye's] kind" in the pub. Bullseye, who has a strong Irish accent, is presumably Catholic and, thus, despised by the presumably Protestant barkeep. A crosshair symbol — a cross within a circle — is embossed on Bullseye's forehead. It is as if his singular ability to throw darts and disks and knives with extraordinary force and accuracy were embossed, like the stigmata, in his flesh. After his arrival in New York, Bulleseye tells the Kingpin of Crime (Michael Clarke

15. Said Daredevil director Mark Steven Johnson, "I wanted to show that clip [of the church scene]. It's at the core of the film." The convention and the *Daredevil* sneak peek are ably covered at: http://www.comics2film.com/StoryFrame.php?f_id=2481

16. Mel Gibson's *The Passion of the Christ* (2004), one of the most successful films in history, makes this point devastatingly clear. The film was a major hit with Roman Catholics and fundamentalist Protestants. The idea here is that the atonement for man's sins was paid by the Passion of Christ.

Duncan) that he looks forward to killing Daredevil, and that he will do so
free of charge: "The Devil is mine." But if Daredevil is the devil, on some
level Bullseye sees himself as holy. This mirror opposition continues to the
climax of the film, wherein Bullseye uses the very materials of the church,
most specifically the stained glass, to attack Daredevil. In the battle, Bullseye is injured when bullets pierce his hands, on which the camera focuses.
The bullet holes, neatly centered in each hand, suggest the Savior's nail
prints. Ironically, Bullseye, an impaled anti-Christ, triumphs over the dark
Daredevil, and, if only temporarily, over God.

Daredevil as Satanic Figure?

Although Daredevil calls himself a "Guardian Devil," he is more like
the ancient Greek Furies, who chased the guilty. The Furies have also been
associated with early Christianity, particularly with the image of the gargoyle, which, as we have seen, the *Daredevil* movie uses to good effect.
Scholars suggest that gargoyles represent lost souls, condemned for their
sins by eternal banishment from the Church. Transformed into stone monsters, they could serve as symbols of temptation as well as the consequences
of surrender to temptation.[17] But if Matt Murdock is a devil, then...

Daredevil and Temptation

Who among us is just? In many stories, even Daredevil is tempted by the
same human failings we all have. In *Daredevil* #109 (1974; Steve Gerber/
Brown), we meet Nekra, Priestess of Darkness, who uses her power of hate to
transform New York into an earthly Hell. "Several thousands of New Yorkers
are made helpless captives of their own greed. Like animals, they shove and
tear at one another, clutching in frenzied ecstasy falling slips of green paper."
In *Daredevil* #265 (1989; Nocenti/Romita Jr./Rosen). New York becomes the
new Sodom. All the fetishes of capitalism, from cars to computers, are demons;
every person is a gargoyle of some sort or other. Only Daredevil, who remains
deaf, dumb, and blind throughout the issue, is unaffected. Yet, as a demonic
police officer tells him, "It don't matter. This city'll get you, if I don't. It ham-
mers you, day in, day out! All the little hassles, all the tension, the sheer chaos
... it beats you numb, in the end. Brutalizes you, day in, day out, Till you're

---

17. Other accounts suggest that gargoyles served as warnings to people, telling them to mend
their ways or else! Gargoyles may also have even been symbols honoring the pagan gods that
people worshiped before Christianity spread throughout Europe. Peter Winkler, "Monsters in
Stone," *National Geographic World*, October 1998, 8.

so hard, you're inhuman. A man made numb, a New Yorker." Daredevil himself is both the city's poster child and its one and only hope. But, as the day wears on, everyone notices that he's "zombified." Toward the close of the story, we find Daredevil in a bar, drowning himself in booze. Like his fellow city-dwellers, he lives in isolation, blocking out the cacophony of New York sirens, radio and TV reports of rape, race riots, and murders.

In the follow-up, "Beer with the Devil," we see Daredevil as a kind of medieval knight tempted by women, alcohol, and other intoxicating stimuli. It's Christmas Eve, and as Daredevil drinks his beer, a ravishing redhead strikes up a conversation:

> REDHEAD: I'll tell you why I'm here. I betrayed my husband. He left me. So I find myself alone, on Christmas. Have you ever betrayed anyone?
> DAREDEVIL: Yes, and I'm paying for it now.
> REDHEAD: Wasn't it fun, though?
> DAREDEVIL: Fun, lady? Well ... A horrible kind of fun. The kind of fun that makes you hate yourself. If you call that fun.
> REDHEAD: I'll miss my husband. We've been together for an eternity. We traveled all over the world ... I remember him on the beaches, in Cuba, in '60, '61. Guatemala in the fifties. We had a ranch outside Dallas in '63 ... all good times. [...] Sometimes, you draw lines for yourself that you won't cross.
> DAREDEVIL: Yes.
> REDHEAD: Then it seems as if you only drew them to step over them. Do you think that stealing a dollar is as bad as stealing a million?
> DAREDEVIL: Yes, maybe worse.

In the background, the television blares a live interview with a homicidal maniac: "Yeah, I'm waiting for the chair. It ain't so bad here. I'm not sorry for what I done. I didn't hurt anyone. I hadda kill him. I liked it. It was fun. I like killing ..."

> REDHEAD: (*Seductively slipping her hand over the hero's bicep*): What was the harm? I didn't think liking a man, having fun with him, would hurt anybody.... Do you think it matters? If you betray or don't, if you cross a line or don't? Can one person's acts really make a difference? You're a hero. Think you make a difference? Think with your finger on the scales, you could ever shift the weight of evil over to the other side, even a fraction?
> DAREDEVIL: I don't know anymore. I don't know if I make a difference. That's why I'm here, in this bar.
> REDHEAD: Me — I think it's too late for the world. The apple's rotten. There's no going back. Someone took a bite. And it's been rotten ever since. Forget the world, Daredevil. Let someone else be the hero. Take a bite, be selfish — kiss me.

For a while, Daredevil kisses her, then a fight breaks outs, and someone is stabbed. Uncharacteristically, Daredevil does nothing except continue to enjoy himself. We've seen aspects of this argument before in our chapters on Spider-Man and Dr. Strange: Sex must be sublimated because it distracts the hero from serving the needs of others. So, resisting her enchanting lips, Daredevil awakens as if from a nightmare: "Why do you try to seduce me? Get away from me!" Violently, he pushes her away.

The vignette is infused with the sensual overtones of Spenser's *Fairie Queene* (1590–6), in particular "The Legend of Sir Guyon in the Bower of Bliss." Here, the true Knight of Temperance, Sir Guyon, is tempted by an array of sinful pleasures. He meets a finely dressed lady who holds in her left hand a golden cup; with her right hand, she gathers ripe grapes and squeezes their juice into the cup. It is her custom to give a draught of this wine to every stranger who passes, but when she offers it to Guyon, he flings the cup to the ground and walks on. Temptations increase. He enters into the Bower of Bliss, a garden of resplendent beauty. He knows that if he strays from this path, he will be destroyed by pleasures. Guyon is further tempted when he meets two naked goddesses playfully swimming in a pond. One stands bold and topless; the other lures him by both inviting him and blushing at her own invitation.

Again, Guyon moves on, only to be enchanted by a music unlike any he has ever heard. It seems to be a harmony of the joyous singing of birds and angelic voices, of instruments and murmuring waters and whispering winds. Through it all comes the siren call of yet another temptress, Acrasia. At last, Sir Guyon arrives at her bed chamber. He sees her lying half asleep on a bed of roses, clad in a veil of silk and silver. Languidly, Acrasia offers herself to Sir Guyon, who understands the price of her embrace: if he sleeps with her, his innocence will be corrupted. Abruptly, Sir Guyon breaks away from Acrasia to destroy the Bower of Bliss, leaving nothing to tempt him further.

Similarly, with perhaps too much violence, Daredevil pushes the lovely redhead away. In turn, "she" morphs into "her" true form, that of the demon, Mephisto: "You thought you could punch away — Mephisto?! A true merry Christian would have turned the other cheek!"

Mephisto knows just where to direct his jest. It's not Daredevil's violence, but Matt Murdock's law practice, with its loopholes and justifications — its moral ambiguity — that Mephisto knows his adversary considers sinful:

> I've been watching you.... Your hypocritical whining over the violence in your life.... The lawyer in you always finding a loophole for your selfish self — Your self-indulgent cries.... One day, I'll tip the scales, and you'll welcome me into your arms, you'll embrace me, redman, willingly, like you just did at the bar.

The Devil grows gigantic, clutching Daredevil like a rag doll:

After conquering temptations of the flesh, Daredevil comes face to face with the Devil.
(By permission of Marvel Comics.)

> Do you see, Daredevil, how immense evil is? You used to believe that one
> man, no matter how small, could fight evil. Could defy it, stand up to it, and
> that you grow to an enormous size by that very defiance. But you're forgetting
> that, Daredevil. You're almost mine, Diablo.

Matt Murdock makes no reply. What reply can he give? He knows that he's
guilty; after all, who is free from sin? Certainly not Matt Murdock.

The Sins of Matt Murdock

We know that, in the physical sense, Daredevil cannot see. His superhero feats are made possible by a sonar system, which emerged in compensation for his lost sight. But in the moral sense, Matt Murdock is also
willfully purblind, in that he refuses to accept the demands of the legal system of which he is a part. There is a lack of moral clarity here, or, as Lady
MacBeth says, "Hell is murky." When Matt Murdock loses the case that justice says he ought to win, he can impose the values of the boxing ring,
taught by his father: "Never give up." But, of course, this means that the
legal system only works when Matt Murdock agrees with its outcome. His
indignation is, so to speak, beyond the law. Or like that of Judge Dredd, it
is the law.

The *Daredevil* movie suggests that Matt's vigilantism both redeems
and compounds his culpability. In one poignant scene, a child, hiding in a
corner, witnesses Daredevil attack a local loan shark. Aware of the child's
justified terror, Daredevil says, "I'm not the bad guy, kid." It is important
that this scene roughly corresponds to Matt's childhood discovery that his
father, a washed-up prizefighter, worked as a loan collector. In fact, Matt
was running from the scene of that revelation when, hit by the truck, he
lost his sight. So loan collectors are bad guys; but then Daredevil is behav-
ing in the same way that his father, the mob enforcer, did: with savage brutality, and outside the law. We remember Kingpin's acerbic remark: "I've
been in this business a long time, and I've learned that no one is innocent."
So how does this apparent moral relativism mesh with Daredevil's moral
indignation? Matt Murdock steadies himself with what the Kingpin might
think of as a pious platitude: "All you need is faith."

From Matt Murdock's perspective, it's certainly not faith in the courts
or faith in scripture. The Bible may say, "Vengeance is mine, saith the Lord,"
but it also says, "All have sinned and come short of the glory of God." As
the Kingpin says, "No one in this business is innocent," for "this business"
is nothing less than life itself. Moreover, Murdock spurns the spiritual coun-
sel of his priest, confessing only after it is too late — "You were right, Father;
you were right."

But admitting his mistake is not the same as confessing his guilt. Matt Murdock knows that from the perspective of a child, he might seem like a "bad guy," but that is not the same as admitting that that perception is correct. Were the legal system just, there would be no need for a hero like Daredevil, dedicated to the higher calling of an absolute, retributive justice. Hence, Murdock only pretends to have faith in the legal system. His very appearance in a court as an attorney masks his true belief, namely, that justice depends on an extra-legal exercise of relentless force. So he dons a second disguise, one more recognizably apart from the corrupt world of the court system; and it is in this performance as Daredevil that he finds hope and a reason to live.

And if this is so, then who, if anyone, is—or can be —"good"? The faith of Murdock's traditional upbringing provides him with an answer, but it can no longer be considered "the" answer. Murdock knows that there are devils, as well as angels, in the world. He has been taught that, under the stipulated protocols of contrition, penance, and repentance, sins can be forgiven. His beliefs also insist that these rituals must be rigorously followed. Unfortunately for Murdock, knowledge of his sinful nature has complicated his adherence to them. Indeed, Murdock assumes the outward signs of Satan — a red suit with horns on his head — even as he sets about doing God's work in a troubled world. A conscientious lawyer by day, Murdock fights for justice in court, warning perpetrators that, for their sake, he hopes that "justice prevails."

If Matt Murdock is fallen, that gives him one thing in common with everyone else, including the Kingpin. But he is also like his father, the fallen pugilist, down on the canvas— down, but not out. In a similar sense, even if Matt Murdock or his hooded persona, Daredevil, can't put Mephisto down for the count, he can, like his father, continue to pull himself to his feet. He can survive another round and even — who knows?— throw a lucky punch.

Daredevil, Hellspawn, New York and Terrorism

The idea that lawyers are irredeemably steeped in sin is not new, but it has a special resonance because of the 9-11 attacks, in which 3000 lawyers, investment officers, bankers, and their assistants were massacred. In the 1996 animated movie, *Spider-Man vs. Daredevil*, Daredevil notes that wherever he goes in New York, someone attacks him. He quips, "A lot of people react that way to lawyers." If Matt Murdock fears for his life from disgruntled clients, the Daredevil of issue #321 (Chichester/McDaniel/Oakley) connects that fear to terrorism. Written in 1994, the story arc, "Fall from Grace," concerns a terrorist attack on New York involving chemical pathogens. Infected by the virus, Daredevil's persona splits. The good Daredevil continues the campaign against crime; the other, Hellspawn, is strengthened by every blow that Daredevil strikes. When at last Daredevil confronts his beastly *doppelganger*, Hellspawn has much to say. He's been following Daredevil from years now, and has tracked his fall from grace: "in dee heavy beat of his heart, dee red-man makes excuses for his sins." Hellspawn sees right through Daredevil's actions to his motives. The costume is an excuse for Matt Murdock to do as he wishes, to doff his catechism along with his courtroom apparel. His crimes belong to someone else, that is, to Daredevil. When confronting Daredevil, Hellspawn explains that he is "what you see in dee mirror ... if you could see. We share dee same darkness. But to you, it be a trap. For me, dee place from where I strike!"

Matt Murdock/Daredevil couldn't agree more. While Daredevil fights terrorists, he also employs the strategy for which they are named; he strikes terror into their hearts. After Daredevil finds a cure for the pathogen, he returns to the church for spiritual solace and renewal. As he leaps from a skyscraper, the narrative reads, "Daredevil reaches out. New York touches him back. And the hero and the city belong to each other." We can, of course, read this statement in a number of ways. There is a sense, perhaps, that Daredevil and New York City deserve each other, in that they are equally fallen from grace. Then, too, Daredevil needs the city's corruption and violence in order to forget — or to justify — his shaky relationship with Christian doctrine, sternly propounded as it is in the confessional booth. Even in the most upbeat of scenarios, Mephisto's laughter resonates within his hypersensitive earshot. For if physical violence can seem, in the crucible of the city's flawed legal system, recompense for sin, then it follows that terrorism, motivated by religious zeal, cannot be, regardless of Daredevil's morally ambiguous campaign, defeated.

Batman Begins

We all know that successful films breed imitations. Like the *Daredevil* movie of 2003, the recent film *Batman Begins* (2005) is also enveloped with quasi-religious fanaticism. The ideology of the movie almost exactly mirrored that of the real-life *jihadists* who struck London's Underground on July 7, less than a month after *Batman Begins* opened in hundreds of theatres in the U.S. and U.K. As the film begins, Bruce Wayne's loving parents are shot down by a street thug. A scene in the opera the family is attending reminds young Bruce of his recent traumatic experience with thousands of bats flying around him. It is at his insistence that the family leaves the theatre; once outside, they encounter an armed robber. Although the Waynes offer no resistance, the happenstance mugging turns into a double murder. Bruce blames himself, since his fear is what prompted the family to step outside. Ironically, the assailant is exactly the kind of individual that the Waynes have used their wealth to try to help. So when he is old enough to act on his own, Bruce Wayne sets out on a quest to understand the criminal mind, which leads him to a prison in the Far East. As Gotham sinks into violence and corruption, Bruce Wayne seeks the remedy to evil.

And yet *Batman Begins* is only superficially about crime, in the trivial, legal sense of the term. This Christian Nolan film is a parable of the post–9-11 world, in which we are asked the question: Is terrorism justified? Raz Alcor (Liam Neeson), arch-villain of the piece, is the moral leader of the League of Shadows, a society dedicated to annihilating the corruption that threatens civilization. This secret order of warriors believes that evil cannot be vanquished by half measures, which are the means by which corrupt politicians and the police conspire with the rulers of the underworld to preserve the decadent *status quo*. When he attempts to recruit Bruce Wayne (Christian Bale) into the League of Shadows, Alcor insists that Wayne do more than master the martial arts. He must recognize that to win this holy war the warrior must triumph over fear, and, above all, over society's ingrained moral squeamishness. Bruce Wayne fails the latter test when he refuses to behead a criminal held in the League's private prison on the pinnacle of a Himalayan mountain, where he is instructed on how to go "beyond good and evil" (to use a Nietzschean term) and become what ordinary people would regard as a criminal.

With the extract of a blue flower grown on the slopes of the Himalayas—a nod to the aforementioned "*hash*"assins?—the League of Shadows produces a hallucinogen to destroy Gotham City, the very citadel of civilization. But to put that plan into operation, the League of Shadows needs the help of Carmine Falcone (Tom Wilkinson), crime boss of the corrupt world that the League hates. Playing on American greed, Raz Alcor besieges Gotham with a chemical "weapon of mass destruction" (WMD), a comic book version of the very toxins we fear bin Laden will create and deploy. And fear is the byword for this film. Batman may save the day, but his victory is only a reprieve. The blue flower of the Himalayas grows there still, the League of Shadows may be weakened but is not eradicated, and its ability to smuggle weapons into Gotham remains intact. Wayne may have picked a costume to strike fear into the criminal mind, but the idea that terrorists will acquire the mechanisms of postmodern warfare, pollute our water supply and turn our cities into madhouses and death chambers, gives us all reason to be afraid of much more than a man in a bat costume.

THINKING, DEBATING, WRITING

1. Draft a letter to the U.N. outlining why you believe the United States has the right to respond militarily if it feels itself to be in danger. If you do not agree with this position, respond to a paper written by one of your classmates who does take that view.

2. Our essay argues that religion is at the heart of the 2003 movie *Daredevil*. Rent the movie and then write an essay in which you disagree; if you wish, use evidence from outside sources to back your arguments.

3. Write an essay on the history of America's Middle Eastern policy. When did it start, and what changes has it undergone?

4. Did it surprise you that America sells its advanced weaponry to other nations? Look up the history of Lockheed Martin, Boeing, and other military contractors. Do American companies do America a disservice by selling weapons to other nations?

5. This chapter argues that New York is a "scary" place. Look up the crime statistics for the city of New York, and then ask your local police if New York deserves that descriptive.

6. Is Islam a misunderstood religion? Read a section of the Koran and come to your own conclusions. Contact a cleric at a local mosque and get his view as well. Present your findings to the class or to your friends.

7. All the examples in this chapter focus on military solutions to terrorism. Research and describe what political initiatives have been offered to end terrorism.

8. Write an essay either supporting or opposing the actions and policies of Oliver North during and after the Iran-Contra affair.

9. We write: "In terms of geopolitics, this is prescient of the second Gulf War coalition." Look up the definition of "analogy" and discuss when or if an analogy can go too far.

10. Captain America and Nick Fury look back nostalgically to the "good old days" of the Nazis. Look up the history of World War II and discuss whether the current situation is more or less dangerous.

7

Comics and the Prison System

At the end of the movie X-Men *(2000), we see Magneto (Ian McKellen), who has the power to control anything magnetic, locked away in a prison made of plastic and glass. He warns his nemesis, Professor Charles Xavier (Patrick Stewart), that the prison will not be able to hold him; he will soon find a way out. Xavier, who goes by the name of "Professor X," concedes that Magneto will not be in prison forever. Either the villain will break out, or he will serve his term and be released. Either way, Magneto is determined to impose his will on society, and all Xavier can do is "be waiting for him."*

Such cat-and-mouse scenarios demonstrate the raison d'être of comic book heroism. After all, without a villain, who needs a hero? At the same time, Magneto's imprisonment raises interesting philosophical questions about the nature and value of punishment. Given the fact that the movie came out during a renewed debate over California's "three strikes" law, it's hard to read Magneto's warning of future mayhem apart from one of the burning issues of our time: criminal recidivism and the death penalty.

X-Men asks us to judge whether prison is an ethically sound institution. The opening shot depicts a group of people walking in the rain like automatons. They are Jews, Poles, and Slavs who have been rounded up by the Nazis. We know that they are beginning an internment process that will probably end in their deaths. The movie goes on to ask us to equate the oppression of the mutants with the Nazi treatment of the Jews, Slavs and Poles—a "final solution" to a societal problem that presupposes that the "crime" of being Jewish or Polish or Slavic or mutant is beyond "cure." Hence, the "others" must be rounded up and quarantined, as if they suffered from a communicable disease. That disease — or sin — is difference. If difference is a sin, then ethnic minorities are born in sin, and so they must die.

Born Criminal?

The Christian doctrine of "original sin" presupposes that every human-being is "fallen" and, thus, in need of the rod of correction. Medieval practices of self-discipline, flagellation, and penance were designed to mortify the flesh and, thereby, to curb sin. The goal was to discipline the mind to exclude things that were sinful, to beat the flesh into compliance.

Putting aside religious beliefs for the moment, we can readily admit that self-control, of course, is vital in any society. From an early age, we are all disciplined to control our bodies, beginning with the regulation of food and sleep, which are meted out at regular intervals, and then to gain control over our bladders and bowels. We learn how to listen, how to talk in turn, how to respect our elders, etc., until we are properly trained cogs in the human machine, able to work long hours without stopping for food or bowel movements, able to take orders, able to discipline others. For those who cannot function in these socially appropriate ways, we have a variety of institutions. For those who can't regulate bowels or food intake, we have hospitals, where they are cared for by doctors and nurses. For the mentally undisciplined, we have mental hospitals, in which, again, the inmates are closely monitored, medicated and supervised. For social deviants, we have prisons, in which they are regulated, supervised and punished.[1]

Professor X as Guardian and Prison Guard

The connection to the X-Men is clear. The religiously-named Xavier (he shares his name with the founder of the Jesuits) has the ability to read people's minds, which enables him to gaze, godlike, into men's consciences. This power allows him to thwart crime before it happens, a form of prevention that is practiced, not just in his dealings with Magneto, but even within his own school.

Xavier runs a school for gifted youngsters, all of whom are products of serious genetic mutation.[2] Under his watchful eye, mutants from all over the country learn how to control their powers. But they also learn submission: Xavier enters their minds to teach them discipline, a pursuit shared by the adult X-Men, who systematically operate as the functional equivalents of guards in the school.

1. According to Michel Foucault's *Discipline and Punishment: The Birth of the Prison* (1975), prison and the punishment within were not designed to mete out pain for past offenses; they were designed to curb or to control future actions by modifying the deepest spaces of the unconscious.
2. As Xavier explains to the new recruit, Logan, a.k.a. Wolverine (Hugh Jackman), the school is just a cover. Deep below the building lies a hidden network of tunnels, high-tech weaponry, and surveillance technology.

Professor X, the Panopticon and Big Brother

Professor X's ability to read minds mirrors the ideals of Jeremy Bentham's creation, the Panopticon. The principal innovation of this "perfect prison" was a fully-glazed observation tower, with a 360-degree view of the environment. It functioned, in effect, like a house of mirrors, in which guards could watch, or appear to watch, prisoners twenty-four hours a day. In theory, we can see the logic: Someone must either watch the criminal, or the criminal must be convinced that someone is watching. Eventually, this method of disciplining through surveillance will become second nature, and the criminal will behave as if someone really is watching at all times.

The idea is akin to George Orwell's characterization, in *Nineteen Eighty-Four*, of the ubiquity of Big Brother's observation techniques. In this famous novel, Orwell imagines a society in which the state watches everyone, even members of the enforcers of that society, with the aim of curbing and controlling criminal behavior before it takes place. The Philip K. Dick-inspired film *Minority Report* (2003) starring Tom Cruise, explores the same idea, with its Department of Pre–Crime.

The *X-Men* film may owe more to the 1995 DC Comic turned live-action movie, *Judge Dredd*, starring Sylvester Stallone. Set in the near future, Dredd is a one-man justice system: police, jury, judge. As it happens, Dredd was genetically grown for the job, but he has an evil twin brother, as twisted as Dredd is straight-shooting: Ricco, whose philosophy is that judgment is a mere technicality. Sooner or later, everyone is guilty: "Crime and innocence are only a matter of timing." The assumption is that, left unguarded or unobserved, people naturally revert to criminal, sinful beings. The "cure" to this natural devolution is to deprive citizens of privacy, or of the sense of privacy, in order to ward off misconduct.

The above-cited movies suggest that surveillance is a human norm, not a mutant characteristic. Indeed, even within the *X-Men* world, the government, led by Senator Kelly, wants to create its own way of keeping tabs on mutants. The senator proposes a registration system that will catalogue the abilities of the mutants, abilities that the senator believes will only encourage and enable antisocial behavior on their part: "What," he asks, "is to stop a mutant from robbing a bank?" Since our sympathies lie with Professor Xavier, the senator's suspicions tells us more about him than they do about the mutants, whose unique talents can just as easily be marshaled in service of the human race. The senator focuses not on the promise of human mutation, but on the crime that an individual mutant may commit. Apparently he believes, with Jeremy Bentham, that without surveillance, humans naturally gravitate toward criminal activity. Nor is Xavier of a radically different opinion. He is, after all, a school administrator; and his mutant school, like any other school, requires discipline. Accordingly, we see Xavier scolding students who don't pay attention, students who let their normal natural adolescent exuberance control their behavior. The kids play practical jokes on one another, pass notes, make inappropriate gestures, jeer comically, and stare at students they find attractive. Naturally, Xavier frowns on such behavior, for it is his job to teach children to become adults. This area of training has nothing to do with math or grammar, but with discipline, a focus of attention, a control over one's own body that allows children to watch over themselves, to control and to discipline themselves, even when no one else is watching.

Isolation and the Prison

Other than locking people up, what is the function of prison? We would probably say that hospitals function to aid recovery from illness of the body or mind. The aim of treatment is a "healthy" or "normal" citizen, no longer a "committed" patient. In a mental hospital, the individual internalizes the demands of society, learning to take medicine in accord with orders and routine. Other aspects of behavior (dressing appropriately, eating properly, spearking in turn, not shouting) are subject to the same rigors of internalization.

In the *X-Men* movie, the point of locking up Magneto is to punish him. The nature of that punishment is isolation. Arguably, this confinement can be harder to bear than the tortures of the Nazi internment camps. As awful as they were, in those camps, although husbands and wives and children were usually separated, prisoners were not deprived of human contact. Magneto, however, spends his days alone, watched only by guards, with whom he cannot interact.

This is not just a fantasy of the comics. In our maximum-security prisons, isolation is the supreme form of American punishment. In California's notorious Pelican Bay, prisoners do not even see the guards, who push prisoners' meals on trays through narrow slots into their concrete-block cells. Lawsuits have been filed on behalf of Pelican Bay prisoners, arguing that isolation is Constitutionally-prohibited "cruel and unusual punishment."

The practice, however, is time-honored. In 1821, New York's Auburn prison instituted isolation for all its prisoners. According to Alexis de Tocqueville, the results of this policy "proved fatal for a majority of prisoners." The great nineteenth-century French historian of American democracy concluded that isolation did not reform prisoners, but made them either insane or suicidal:

> Their lives appeared to be in danger ... five [of the original eighty] of them had already died in one year. Their spiritual condition was no less disturbing:

one of them went out of his mind; another took advantage of a moment when a guard had brought him something to hurl himself out of his cell. Running the almost certain risk of a fatal fall [off a balcony].

If de Tocqueville saw the flaws in the system as early as 1821, why is isolation still a standard practice in American prisons? In its earlier practices, isolation was meant to provide a reflective environment. If the prisoner had nothing else to do and no means with which to torture others, he would punish himself. Through self-reflection, the prisoner would be given time to see what he had done, to mourn his own behavior and to reflect upon his aberrant actions. Once surveillance had been turned inward, the prisoner had no way of turning it off. He became his own worst enemy and his own worst guard, a prisoner who went on punishing himself in endless self-reflection. This isolation was not radically different in concept from monastic chanting vows of silence. The point was not merely punishment, but a turning inwards for the betterment of the soul. The reality, however, was that the isolated prisoner often did not become spiritually better. Suicide, after all, is traditionally considered a sin, and psychosis, while not a sin, hardly seemed like a helpful outcome for a term of self-reflection. In no way does either outcome allow for the "cure" of the criminal.

X-Men II and Rehabilitation

Magneto's only variation from the tedium of isolation is the regular visits of Professor Xavier, who spends the occasional hour or two playing chess with him. Chess is, of course, a board game requiring discipline. Every piece on the board possesses a certain capacity for power and movement, and the power of any piece changes with each move. The skill in chess lies in looking ahead, in coordinating one's pieces and in anticipating the adversary's moves.

For Magneto, however, the game with Xavier is an exercise in futility. Since the professor is a psychic, able to read his mind, there is no way for Magneto to disguise the aim of his strategy. He is, and always will be, one step behind. So, in effect, the two men are not playing chess in the ordinary way. The point of their game is not to pass the time, but to get Magneto to see the world from the perspective of an eternal checkmate. Perhaps, Xavier hopes, if Magneto sees that every move he makes has been anticipated, he'll stop trying to play a game of social change that he cannot possibly win. The experiment is a resounding failure. Once Magneto breaks out of prison, he, like all comic-book villains, slips into tights and starts blowing things up.

Things are no different in the DC Universe. Batman, for instance, spends much of his career in seemingly endless battle against villains, who have, if anything, the physical advantage of surprise attack. What happens to these villains when Batman captures them? However dissimilar their crimes may be — killing or robbing, destroying buildings, ruining rare and precious treasure, masterminding criminal organizations, or using gadgets that threaten world domination — their punishments all fall back on the old standard. They are all locked up in one big madhouse, Arkham Asylum, where they are kept in isolation. Like the supervillains in the Marvel Universe, these DC villains invariably escape, until Batman tracks them down and brings them back to the asylum.

What If....

Because he lacks actual superpowers, anyone, hypothetically, can become Batman. After all, none of us can become Superman. We're not born on Krypton. And we can't become Spider-Man or Captain America or Daredevil without a potent drug or a near-lethal, one-in-a-million chance exposure to radiation. Fat chance that someone will offer us Green Lantern's ring or Thor's magic hammer. We're not born with mutant powers, and we can't enroll in a correspondence course with the Ancient One. But anyone can become rich, either through inheritance, hard work, or just dumb luck. And given the right motivation, we could use our money to hire personal trainers, buy a souped-up car, train our bodies, and discipline our minds. In short, it seems there is something "do-able" about Batman: few people may achieve his heroic statue, but anyone can, to a lesser extent, be a hero.

For purposes of crime prevention, the question is whether, under a change of circumstances, law-abiding citizens might become villains. This is explored in Marvel's great but long-defunct series, *What If?* In #40 (1983; Gillis/Guice/Grainger), Marvel's creative team asked, "What if Dr. Strange Had Not Become Master of the Mystic Arts?"

At the story begins, Dr. Strange has his accident and seeks the Ancient One, but he does not become his pupil for very long. After learning that it is his heart and not his hands that holds him back, Strange returns to New York with a new sense of purpose. If he can't be the world's greatest surgeon, he can at least teach medicine to the next generation of doctors. All goes well until he is haunted by the demon Nightmare. Meanwhile, without Strange as a pupil, the Ancient One continues to teach Baron Mordo the mystic arts. In our dimension, we may recall, Mordo is Strange's enemy, but that was in part because of the Ancient One's sudden interest in Dr. Strange. Perhaps if the Ancient One, clearly a father figure, had been more attentive to Mordo, he would have been a model citizen. And will Strange be a good person in all circumstances? Amazingly, even with the focused attention of the Ancient One, Mordo still gives in to his lust for power; likewise, Strange's potent and positive mystic powers are activated without his seeming knowledge or acceptance. The message is clear: You are what you are from birth. Destiny rules. The fault, it seems, is in the stars, not in ourselves.

A similar story is told in *What If* #2 (1971; Thomas/Trimpe), which asks the question, "What If The Hulk Had the Brain of Bruce Banner?" As the story begins, Banner is zapped with gamma radiation and turns into The Hulk; but instead of becoming a mindless cretin, he retains Banner's brain. He continues to date Betty, though her father is horrified. Banner confronts him: "First, when I was a normal man, you berated me as a weakling — a jellyfish. And now that I've acquired inhuman strength, you revile me as a monster. What does it take to satisfy you, man? What??" The general sees the error of his ways and agrees that Banner, though green and eight feet tall, can marry his daughter. In the meantime, Banner defeats all the foes he would have defeated in our universe.

Banner, however, is still first and foremost a scientist. Joining his skills with those of Reed Richards, he cures Ben Grimm/The Thing of the hideous rocky skin that cover his body. Grimm is all smiles. But after a freakish lab accident, Grimm is again turned into The Thing, though this new incarnation is as imbecilic as the original Hulk. General Ross sends in the troops, with predictable consequences: The Thing is hunted as if he were The Hulk. Our narrator explains that "There is a Cosmic Scale … an inescapable balance which decrees for every gain, there must be a loss." If a criminal becomes a hero, a hero must become a criminal. Hence, even if we cure one criminal, the amount and type of crime will remain constant. Both these stories suggest that there really isn't much we can do to eradicate crime, a message which may well undermine the purpose of the hero. After all, if crime is a constant, then it makes no difference whether he fights it or not.

The Thunderbolts: Heroes or Villains?

In 1997, Marvel tried a bold experiment with one of its villainous gangs, The Masters of Evil. The group is led by the old Nazi villain Baron Zemo, the same character responsible for the death of Cap's original sidekick Bucky Barnes.[3] We're not talking about just another criminal

---

3. To get around the problem of Zemo's age, the original character is succeeded by his no-less-evil son, Helmut, who agrees with all of his father's teachings. To ensure that reader continue to think of Zemo as identical with the original, Helmut is given a pronounced Prussian accent and an authoritarian manner.

here. We are talking Hitler's right-hand man. Zemo's underlings include:

• Fixer: Also known as Techo, who wears a mechanical suit that allows him to assume any shape.
• Beetle: a former mechanic, tired of low-paying jobs, he builds himself an Iron Man-esque suit.
• Screaming Mimi: a former pro wrestler whose voice has been artificially enhanced, now able to create solid-sound constructs, including the wings she uses to fly.
• Goliath: a former soldier of fortune and smuggler, then a professional criminal, now an adventurer, able to change sizes at will.
• Moonstone: a.k.a. Karla Sofen, a former pupil of the evil psychiatrist Dr. Faustus, who used her training to steal the powers of the former hero Moonstone. Physically svelte, she is nonetheless the strongest of the group, and obviously the most manipulative.[4]

We have already seen that heroes, under the right circumstances, can be thought of as villains — e.g. Namor, the fugitive Spider-Man, the Punisher, and Luke Cage. But these are misunderstood characters. The Sub-mariner attacks New York to defend his underwater city, Atlantis. He doesn't attack for petty, personal gain, or even to extend his global power. All he wants is that Atlantis be left alone. Spider-Man, like the Punisher and most Marvel heroes, operates outside the law. Some want to bring him to justice, but most see that he's working for the public's greater good, and, certainly, he doesn't profit or attempt to profit from his powers. Luke may charge for his services, but he refuses to be employed for criminal exploits, even though he is wanted for breaking out of prison. But then again, he's also misunderstood. He was innocent of the crime that put him in jail in the first place.[5]

Even the Green Lantern, guilty of murder on an intergalactic level, kills to save life on Earth, and he atones for his sins after becoming The Spectre. In *Day of Judgment* #5 (1999; Johns/Smith/Jones), for example, Hal is called a "sinner," a "murderer," a "damned soul." He counters: "I regret what I became. If I could erase it I would. But I can't." As The Spectre, Hal now serves "the sprit of Redemption" (*JSA All Stars* #3; Johns/Goyer/Kitson/Cooke). Others remain unconvinced: "Do you think you've suddenly paid for your sins? That you've become a hero again? It's just a matter of time before you're slaughtering these mortals. You can deny The

4. For this biographical information, I am indebted to the Marvel Directory. http://www.marveldirectory.com
5. Innocent, unless you're following the more recent miniseries, discussed at the end of our chapter on comics and black heroes.

Spectre's true nature.... But not your own" (*Day of Judgment* #5; Johns/Smith/Jones).

As we might expect, Batman believes that Hal is irredeemable:

> BATMAN: You plan on infusing this maniac [Hal Jordan] with the power of The Spectre?
> HAL: This is my chance. Hal Jordan's second chance.
> BATMAN: The men and women you slaughtered didn't get a second chance, Jordan. (*Day of Judgment: Purgatory* #3; Johns/Smith/Jones)

Even if we see the logic of Batman's position, we can at least admit that Hal has worked on behalf of us all, and that his crimes, serious as they are, were not personal, vindictive, or avaricious. The Spectre is a new person, not just a new label.

The case of The Thunderbolts, however, is more akin to Batman's foe, Two-Face: change your name, and you thereby change your identity. The ultimate failure of Two-Face suggests that The Thunderbolts will return to crime in due course. In fact, that's the plan. With The Avengers and The Fantastic Four presumed dead, the plan is that The Masters of Evil, now calling themselves The Thunderbolts, will fill a hero vacuum and win the trust of New Yorkers and eventually the world. Once they have access to the world's military defense systems, they will reveal themselves as the villains they are and rule the world. Brilliant! There's just one fly in the ointment. As time goes on, the former villains begin to warm to the applause and approbation heralded upon them. They begin to like being heroes. Play-acting becomes real.[6] Moonstone, a trained psychotherapist, warns Zemo that his plans for world domination are being ruined by this conversion to heroism:

> Remember, most of them have been outcasts or rejects their entire lives, and the psychological power of role-playing ... combined with the massive societal approval....

Moonstone never gets to finish her report. Zemo cuts her off dismissively. Power, he suggests, will win out over virtue.

But he's wrong. Abe Jenkins, formerly the Beetle, is beginning to have feelings for Songbird, who is grieving the loss of her former boyfriend. As a villain, he should exploit her pain for his own gain, instead, the narrator tells us that: "He doesn't know what's going on — just that someone he's coming to care about is in pain, and that if he's any kind of man at all — He'll find a way to help her." Later, when Spider-Man is in the Beetle's power, he lets him go because he knows the webslinger is a hero. Jenkins

---

6. This is a process writer Kurt Busiek called "the seduction of good." See "Doing the Right Thing The Wrong Way — Avengers V. Thunderbolts," *Newsarama*.com., http://www.newsarama.com/forums/showthread.php?s=&threadid=7194

surprises himself: "This hero thing — I'm starting to think — well, I'm starting to think it's contagious." Likewise, Moonstone admits, "It's a heady
feeling to play hero— and to be accepted.... It feels good, that rush. Maybe
too good." Even Zemo gets in the act by defeating Armin Zola, the Bio-
Fanatic — described as "Hitler's geneticist." So Zemo, in effect, is fighting
his father's former Nazi colleague.

On the one hand, these adrenaline rushes and hormone releases imply
that these former villains aren't really converting to heroism, they are simply getting hooked on emotional highs. Good and evil aren't the issue, feed-
ing the ego and enjoying the rush is. The Thunderbolts make no personal
sacrifices but think they're heroes all the same. They're not. The Thunderbolts are more like the warriors described by Ulysses in Shakespeare's *Troilus
and Cressida*— men who let the ends justify the means, immoral monsters
who eventually betray each other and themselves:

> Force ... or rather right and wrong...
> Should loose their names, and so should justice too!
> Then every thing include itself in power,
> Power into will, will into appetite,
> And appetite, an universal wolf...
> Must make perforce an universal prey,
> And [at] last eat up himself [I.iii.111–24].[7]

We note their petty and sensual natures. Goliath uses his size to check
out topless sunbathers on building tops; even the Beetle, who magnani-
mously let Spider-Man go, steals $7,000 from a burglar (*The Thunderbolts*
#1–4; Busiek/Bagley/Deodato/Buscema). And when occasion serves, these
seeming heroes still consider murder a valid option. When they trap The
Hulk, they squabble over who should kill him, not how they can help him.
In the process of his capture, they also rupture a dam, which nearly kills
everyone is a nearby town. It'll take thirty million dollars to clean up, but
The Thunderbolts' only concern is whether the group got enough media
attention in the attack.

If The Thunderbolts get high by doing good, then we can say that their
rehabilitation is akin to a twelve-step program, albeit in reverse. The point
is not to get off addiction, but to get off *on* addiction. Their occasional petty
crimes are relapses, normal and natural enough in any sobriety program.
But will The Thunderbolts get hooked on the addiction of doing good deeds
or fall back into crime? In *The Thunderbolts* #50, the reformed members
receive an official presidential pardon for their previous criminal actions.

---

7. Indeed, as *The Thunderbolts* illustrator Fabian Nicieza explained: "unlike the Avengers, the
Thunderbolts are very willing to let the ends justify the means. They'll play a game of currying
favors between countries, blackmailing political or corporate leaders, etc." (*ibid.*).

But there is a hitch, and we've seen it before. As we recall from the chapter dealing with black heroes, Sam Wilson, despite all the good deeds he had done as the Falcon, had to answer for his crimes in a court of law. In the end, he was spared jail time, but only on the condition that he stop fighting crime. The same thing happens to The Thunderbolts. Their punishment is inaction and non-involvement. This goes against the very nature of both hero and villain, since both believe that an individual, for better or worse, can make a difference in the world.

In *The Thunderbolts*, everyone except Zemo and Techno ultimately turns hero. In the case of Techno, we feel some regret; after all, the world needs another Tony Stark. But Zemo? A neo–Nazi, whose father was aide-de-camp to Hitler and responsible for the death of Captain America's sidekick Bucky, can never be accepted by the public. This raises an interesting question. Are we willing to forgive criminals?

In the case of Zemo, we'll never know. In the end, Marvel has The Thunderbolts shipped off to counter-earth (don't ask!), where their criminal backgrounds are unknown. Only Songbird, who was never more than a petty thief, is spared this fate. So what are we to make of this exile? It seems to us that Marvel is suggesting that villains can reform, and that the odds are quite good — three out of five of The Thunderbolts reform. Getting the public to accept a rehabilitated crook is more difficult. At best, the public allows that criminals can stop being criminals, but would prefer they still not live among us.[8]

The Hulk as a Metaphor for Domestic Violence and Childhood Trauma

Recalling the beginning of the *X-Men* film, Ang Lee's 2003 movie version of *The Hulk* also asks us to consider the nature and origin of crime, and like *X-Men*, Ang Lee's film argues that crime is genetic in nature, and thus incurable. As the movie opens, we see a variety of microorganisms, simple and then more complex life forms. We're in the lab of brilliant but unethical scientist David Banner, who is working on genetic sequencing. His goal is to modify human DNA so that it is impervious to chemical weapons. Experiment after experiment fails until the doctor begins to work with lizards and other reptiles. To his astonishment, David Banner learns that reptile DNA, mixed with mammalian strands, allows his test animals

---

8. An exception would be Hawkeye, who began as a villain but only for one issue. For the past thirty years or so, he's been a hero. However, his criminal past was recently explored in *The Thunderbolts: Reassembled* #1 (2005; Nicieza/Grummett/Erskine). Thereafter, the character was killed off. Hawkeye is a fan favorite, so the safe money is on his return.

to regenerate damaged tissue. When he reaches the human test-trial phase, the government shuts down his research. Nonetheless, he uses himself as a guinea pig. The result is that he becomes reptilian, specifically, the upper encephalon, responsible for higher functions such as emotions, seem dramatically curtailed. Worse yet, he passes on his modified DNA to his son, Bruce. When the government learns of his continued tests, they threaten to arrest him. This finally pops the lid off the emotionally-bottled Banner. He goes home and strangles his wife, the crime partially witnessed by his four-year-old son, Bruce, who in turn bottles or represses the memory.

Bruce Banner (played by Eric Bana) grows up to be a seemingly model citizen, clean-cut, a non-smoker, abstemious, a respected scientist. But his ex-girlfriend, Betty (played by Jennifer Connelly), complains that he's repressed, emotionless. Without knowing it, Banner has become like his father. He's even a scientist, experimenting, like his father did, on modifying DNA. Betty's father General Ross (played by Sam Elliot) sees the uncanny resemblance:

> ROSS: He's his father's son, every goddamn molecule of him and he's....
> BETTY: What...? Predestined to follow in his father's footsteps... ?

That is, of course, Ross's fear — that Banner will kill the woman he loves — in this case, Ross's own daughter, Betty. For her part, Betty remains convinced that Bruce would never hurt her. As she says, "You're forgetting that he saved my life." Her father retorts, "Yeah, from a mutant poodle."

In the theater, Ross's line, at least at the showing we attended, got a laugh. But he is making a serious point. David Banner's serum is so toxic that it can turn a poodle, considered among the most domestic and harmless of pets, into a snarling, rabid, blood-hungry monster. Considering Banner's own pent-up rage, what is he capable of becoming? Even Banner is afraid. After killing the monstrous poodle, he finds himself squeezing Betty's neck. Before he goes too far, Bruce regains control and apologizes. Hours later, calm and sipping coffee at the breakfast table, Banner confesses to Betty: "When it [his transformation into The Hulk] comes over me and I totally lose control ... I like it." Never were the words of a domestic abuser put so succinctly.

Fearing for her own life, Betty phones her dad, who calls in the Army. But what can they do with him? General Ross threatens Banner: "I'll put you away for the rest of your natural life." It sounds extreme, but Ross has a point. After all, what if Banner has a temper tantrum in a city center like San Francisco? Of course, that's exactly what happens.

The larger question, of course, is not what we have to do with The Hulk. He's not real. But what do we do with our all-too-real Bruce Banners of the world? What do we do with parents who beat or molest their own children, and what do we do with those children, many of who grow up to become just like their parents? Should we punish an adult for his crimes, or treat that same person as a victim?

It really depends whether we think that people who commit evil acts are absolutely evil. The nineteenth-century English novelist Charles Dickens suggested that even the worst of killers were merely good people who lost their tempers. In Chapter 47 of *Oliver Twist*, he describes quite possibly the most violent murder in English literature, the death of Nancy by her brutal boyfriend Bill Sikes. In the following chapter, Dickens shows us a far different side of this seemingly inhuman killer:

> The sun — the bright sun, that brings back, not light alone, but new life, and hope, and freshness to man — burst upon the crowded city in clear and radiant glory. Through costly-coloured glass and paper-mended window, through cathedral dome and rotten crevice, it shed its equal ray. It lighted up the room where the murdered woman lay. It did. He tried to shut it out, but it would stream in. If the sight had been a ghastly one in the dull morning, what was it, now, in all that brilliant light!
>
> He had not moved; he had been afraid to stir. There had been a moan and motion of the hand; and, with terror added to rage, he had struck and struck again. Once he threw a rug over *it*; but it was worse to fancy the eyes, and imagine them moving towards him, than to see them glaring upward, as if watching the reflection of the pool of gore that quivered and danced in the sunlight on the ceiling. He had plucked it off again. And there was the body — mere flesh and blood, no more — but such flesh, and so much blood!

As harrowing as this narrative is — when Dickens read the passage aloud, acting out the parts, it was common for people in the audience to faint — his overall message is clear. In the calm, clear light of morning, even Sikes knows that what he did was wrong. He needs to be punished, absolutely, but is he a monster? No, for if he were, he would not feel any remorse for his actions.

Dickens' call to take pity on criminals, even violent criminals, seems the logical and humane course of action. It seems like a good idea to give these people therapy, but, as of this writing, no treatment seems to be successful — we regularly hear of pedophiles who are incarcerated, then treated, then released back into society unchanged and seemingly unwilling to change. And what of domestic abusers? Again, we often hear of women fearful of their very lives, or sometimes of men who fear the women they live with. It's easy to conclude that these abusers, raised on violence, not only express themselves violently, but feel like they are doing the right thing when they do so. It's as if they have a genetic marker that not only makes them commit these acts but also rewards them with an endorphin blast for doing it. As the saying goes: "If it feels good, do it." Or, as Banner says, "When it comes over me and I totally lose control ... I like it."

The Punisher Approach

If rehabilitation doesn't work, perhaps we should just kill convicts. The option is explored in Marvel Enterprise's 2004 movie *The Punisher*. As the film opens, we meet Frank Castle (Tom Jane), an FBI agent, strong, but otherwise normal, married, with a son who adores him. When a sting operation in which Castle is involved goes awry, Howard Saint (John Travolta), complying with the demands of his wife, Livia (Laura Harring), massacres Castle's entire family.

Unlike so many comic book heroes, Castle has no super power. He is no Wolverine, with the capacity to heal within seconds of his wounds, nor does he possess an extraordinary, Bruce-Waynesque intellect or financial resources. His power comes from his monastic sense of medieval sin. What the world needs is a good dose of punishment. Amid all the blood and bombs that make up the climax of the film, the Punisher makes a point of precisely mirroring a previous offense. You killed my family, now I kill yours. Tit for tat. Punishment for offense. No lawyers. No trials. No bullshit.

But what if the Punisher makes a mistake? In the Punisher's premiere (1974, in *Spider-Man* #129; Conway/Andru), our killer is after Spider-Man because he thinks the webslinger has killed his friend. He's wrong, as it turns out — a significant argument against the death penalty. The Punisher even comes to see that self-evident truth — that he would have killed Spider-Man for nothing, that he would, in fact, have been a murderer.[9] Having the Punisher avoid that epiphany has more to do with the work put into creating a new character than with the Punisher facing up to his flaws. After all, if the Punisher begins to doubt himself, then he has no reason to continue to be the Punisher. Instead, the Punisher merely turns his fury onto another target, in this case, the Jackal, the villain who gave the Punisher the wrong information. The Punisher never tells Spider-Man he's sorry for trying to kill him; he assumes it's enough that he tells Spider-Man that the Jackal "will pay" for his misdeeds. Well, we know what that means.

What matters, however, is not just the logic of killing, but how the Punisher kills. For the (original) Punisher, execution was quick and painless. And certainly the executioner took no pleasure in the process. Before the planned execution of Spider-Man, he says, "It's not something I like doing.... It's simply something that has to be done." Spidey escapes, but someone else is killed in the melee — a criminal, but according to the Punisher, a criminal who did not merit death: "I did not intend to become a common murderer — by allowing a man to fall to his death.... If I'm ever to live with myself, I have to know I'm doing the right thing."

---

9. Technically, he's still committing a crime: attempted murder is a felony.

So, the Punisher, at least in his 1974 premiere, had a conscience. How the character has changed with the times! In the video-game version of *The Punisher* (released in 2005), our hero not only takes pleasure in killing, but according to one game reviewer, "the special interrogations launch the game into a different plane of dark fun, brutally violent satisfaction, and grisly surprise. You'll wish there were more chances to pull these interrogations off *once you get a taste of them* [emphasis added]."[10] The game is filled with "dark delights" such as an interrogation that takes place on a drug boat. Frank is hot on the trail of a nuclear weapon and has tracked it to this boat. After killing all but one of the Russians aboard, Frank ties up his victim and rips his arms out of their sockets. In another scenario, the Punisher interrogates by kicking the back of the prone Russian's head. No answer, more kicks. He also crushes the same unfortunate Russian under a forklift. The point is to not to kill but to torture. The change in the Punisher can be attributed to a variety of factors: a more lenient Federal Communications Commission, which allows greater and greater violence on American airwaves; a fascination with gangsters, white, black, and Asian; the brutalizing conditions of war and the reportage that brings it home; the 2004 allegations of "torture" at Iraq's Abu Ghraib Prison, investigations of similar claims at the U.S. Marine base and prison at Guantanamo Bay, Cuba; and, finally, the video game industry itself, which rates games by the "kill" count. Whatever the factors, the Punisher for 2005 and beyond doesn't believe that death is a punishment. Death is merely the point where punishment stops.

Batman Embraces the Death Penalty

Enjoying this kind of violence is something we associate more with villains than heroes. The equivalent to the Punisher in the DC Universe is Batman, who takes no pleasure in killing, but also concludes that some people just need to die. In the first installment of the fan favorite *The Dark Knight Returns* (1986; Miller), we meet Harvey Dent, a former city prosecutor, who goes insane when half his face is disfigured by acid. Harvey used to believe in the criminal justice system, but, after this accident, he comes to see justice in terms not unlike those of the Punisher. There are only two options, to be decided by a flip of a coin. Heads, you live; tails, you die. After years of intense therapy that go nowhere, Bruce Wayne steps in with what seems a simple enough cure. If Harvey was good when he was handsome, let's give him plastic surgery to heal his physical and emotional scars.

10. Douglass C. Perry, "Want to see what The Punisher is all about? We've got five brutal interrogations that prove this game is for real." ign.com, http://ps2.ign.com/articles/577/577834p1.html? fromint=1.

Two-Face and the Superficial Cure

If Two-Face's problem is simply a few facial scars, that's curable enough. Indeed, after the operation, psychologists are in agreement: Two-Face has been "cured." This solution sounds facile, but aren't we told that most crimes are committed out of immediate want? If Harvey needs beauty the way an addict needs drugs, then giving Harvey a new face or the addict a bag of smack should, in theory, mean that neither is likely to kill the convenience store clerk.

Does this procedure end the menace of Two-Face? No. Despite enjoying poster-boy beauty, Two-Face returns to his murderous ways.

In the next installment, the Joker escapes from Arkham Asylum and sets out on a rampage of dismemberment, death, and bad jokes. In an amusement park funhouse — where else? — Batman faces the Joker for the *n*th time. To many readers' shock, this time Batman stabs the Joker in the chest, killing him. As if this were not sufficiently out of character, Batman actually wonders if he is doing the right thing: "I could save him, but I won't." Then, in the next issue, Batman kills yet again. This time, Batman buries the head of a muscular gang member in the mud. As the juvenile offender suffocates, Batman admits that "a voice inside my head told me to stop; I didn't listen." After all, who is better qualified than Batman to recognize the symptoms of the incurably insane criminal? Batman has been fighting these villains all his life.

What more could he do to establish his credentials as one who knows the criminal mind? Then again, some would say that Batman, a vigilante and now a murderer, is a criminal himself. In the last issue of *The Dark Knight Returns*, Batman even plots to kill Superman.

It belabors the obvious to point out that Frank Miller's Batman teaches us that when Batman commits murder he becomes a bad guy. The idea is hardly new. Two thousand years ago, the Roman satirist Juvenal asked, "*Sed quis custodiet ipsos custodes?*" ("Who will guard the guards?") Yet, more often than not, the comics don't even ask this basic question. No reader of *Batman* truly believes the nerdy psychologists who appear in Miller's comic, filled with psychobabble about how Batman is a menace. Nor does the reader actually side with the small-minded new chief of police who wants to take Batman down as a vigilante. These people may not be evil, but they are misguided by too much "liberal" gray matter. Batman is a man of few words. He knows the answers, even if, most of the time, he doesn't act on them.

Gotham's villains and psychologists both argue that Batman should be stopped, though not, of course, for the same reasons. The psychologists may actually believe that Batman is ill; they may feel sorry for him and want to treat him. To this, we respond by admitting that Batman's reluctance to kill might be rooted in childhood trauma. His own parents, as we all know, were murdered in front of him. Does this mean that he's an emotional mess? Sure! What's your point?

When looking at Batman, who is masked as are the villains he pursues, it's sometimes easy to see anyone in a mask as engaging in the same duplicity, but when measuring the actions of Batman and the Joker, there is a world of difference. Indeed, we were somewhat exasperated by Batman's tolerance. Our reaction to Batman's murder of the Joker was, "What took so long?" Of course, with the Joker dead, *Batman* fans lose one of their best villains. Not to worry, boys and girls. The Joker can always be brought back in a number of ways. The Joker can be genetically cloned or miraculously reanimated. A time warp might save him, or Batman might have killed a decoy. One way or another, he'll be back, a smiley-face of incurable fury and bad punch-lines.

Prison as Social System

Overall, it seems that Marvel Comics were far more liberal than DC Comics in the 1960s, '70s, '80s and '90s. As we argued, in terms of sexual politics, there has been some retrenchment on Marvel's part and some effort on DC's part to close the ideological gender gap. As of this writing, most of DC's major characters are firmly in favor of the death penalty, although with moments of hand-wringing. As we have seen, Batman (at least in the *Dark Knight* series) is pro-death penalty. Even the peace-loving Flash, among the less violent and levelheaded of the Justice League, agrees that some criminals just can't be helped: "The death penalty is unpopular among the [Justice] League [led by Superman], but ... some people need to die." Wonder Woman agrees: "There [villains] are monsters.... And if they cannot be contained, they must be destroyed" (*The Flash* #219; Johns/Justiniano/Livesay/Wong).

On the other hand, as Robin points out in *Teen Titans* #21 (2005; Johns/McKone/Alquiza), supervillains have their own equivalent of a clubhouse: "Just not in Big Buildings shaped like a 'T.'" Robin means, of course, the Teen Titan Headquarters, similar to The Avengers' mansion, or The Fantastic Four's high-rise Baxter Building. Robin's point is, villains need friends as well, if only to discuss the ways in which they could solely or jointly take over the world. And, after all, they are competitive egomaniacs. Without someone to dominate, what's the point of all that power? This is a theme we explored to some extent when we looked at the friendship/rivalry of Clark Kent and Lex Luthor. For now, it's enough to point out that villains need friends and that this characteristic may in and of itself suggest that villains are not all bad.

Anther sympathetic portrayal of the standard villain is found in *JSA All Stars* #4 (Johns/Goyer/McKone/Faucher/Robinson/Harris), in which we meet Courtney Whitmore, All-American Girl, the stepdaughter of the Star Spangled Kid, who is now too old for that name. Courtney's real father is a petty criminal in a supervillain club calling itself the Royal Flush. Not only is he a criminal, he's not even an important one. Courtney confronts her loser dad. Everyone in the gang is ranked according to a deck of cards, with Kings the highest; Courtney's dad is a two. She complains, "Do you know how embarrassing this is? My dad's a thug for the Royal Flush Gang. Not even a Jack, or at least a five." We've seen this kind of thinking before in our look at Nietzschean villains. But what follows is more complex than simply saying that Courtney's dad is a loser. He replies:

> We both try to belong. Don't we? We join a gang. Wear the colors. We're just pretending to be important. Like father like daughter.

Reading just the dialogue, Courney's father may seem cold-hearted, even malicious. But if you look at the art, you get a different impression. Courtney's dad's eyes are soft, tender, tear-swelled. He really believes that wanting to be a hero or a villain is really about belonging, having friends, hanging out, even if it is in prison.

The Profitable Prison

At least as seen through the eyes of the Punisher and Batman, sometimes there is nothing else to do with a dangerous felon but kill him. In the comics, however, we can see that this logic can't be put into large-scale practice. Killing all the supervillains would mean that the heroes would have no one to fight. Since comics are a business, the justice of the comic-book world cannot be absolute. This situation should not surprise us. What may surprise us is that money is an equally important — sometimes the determining — factor in prison operations.

The warden of many of America's prisons is a CEO, who disciplines his prisoners to be model workers and model consumers. Put it this way: In the case of the comics, the Joker he is not just a repeat offender; he's a loyal customer. In some ways, this might remind the reader of the 1994 Stephen King movie, *The Shawshank Redemption*, wherein the warden used prisoners to build roads, wash laundry — all for his personal profit. David Werner, author of numerous books on the history of American prisons, explains that in the latter half of the nineteenth century, penal experts were preoccupied with the financial demands and opportunities of the prison system: "The profitable prison was the well-disciplined prison."[11]

Nor has much changed. Today, more and more prisons are run for profit. Private investors now build prisons, pay guards, educate inmates, and provide food, medical treatment, clothing, even recreation. Today, the prison industry employs hundreds of thousands of workers, either directly or indirectly: financiers, contractors, managers, catering companies, uniform companies, security and surveillance companies, manufacturers and purveyors of body orifice scanners, makers of razor wire, and the list goes on. To increase revenues, and under the guise of "job training," some prisons subcontract their prisoners as laborers. Prisons now assemble a variety of products, ranging from toys to high-tech gear.

In return, the state pays investors a set fee for each prisoner. Since this fee adds up to less than the state would have to pay to build and run the prisons, it would seem that private prisons provide taxpayers with a win-win situation. The public demonstrates little interest in the issue: As long as these offenders are off the streets, who cares who owns the bars they're kept behind? But this is a big business, and one that is not necessarily interested in keeping citizens safe. The number of people incarcerated in America is staggering, and growing larger every year. In 1998, according to a Justice Department report, 1.8 million Americans were behind bars, more than double the total in 1985. America has the world's largest inmate count, higher than the 1.4 million in China, whose population is nearly five times that of the United States. The states are spending nearly $30 billion a year to keep people imprisoned — about twice the amount spent a decade ago.[12]

But is any of this making us any safer? Critics observe that this prison model encourages criminals to be more violent. Criminal charges, for example, were lodged against guards at Corcoran Prison in California, where prisoners were forced into "ultimate fighting," which is, even outside of prison, allowed as a spectator sport in only five states. At Corcoran, the fights provided both amusement and the opportunity to bet on the outcomes (illegal in California). Worse, since prisons are run for profit, it's not in their interest to "cure" the inmates. What they want is repeat business. Statistics demonstrate that once a man enters prison, he will in all likelihood (in seven out of eight cases), be back sometime in his life. We're not paying to cure crime, we're paying to make life-long consumers who need the services of the institution.

Of course, society claims that prison is for the prisoner's—and our— own good. Returning to the supervillains of the comics, however, we see

11. Conversation conducted on University of La Verne main campus, December 11, 2003.
12. See "The Real Price of Prisons," *Mother Jones*, http://www.motherjones.com/news/special_reports/prisons.

another principle at work. The most successful villains (the "super" villains) aren't model workers; they are model and disciplined consumers. Ironically, the ideal citizen is not Batman, but his enemies: the Joker, with his predictably wide smile of customer satisfaction; Two-Face, the ultimate capitalist, who decides his life by flipping a silver dollar; Catwoman, who needs money, not love, to feel good; the Penguin, who dresses like a monocled millionaire and is always ready to make a killing; the Riddler, the bowler-hatted proto-lawyer, whose paperwork is always mired in brain-teasing enigmas. No wonder the Joker has that idiotic grin. Batman's foes are perhaps insane, but (look at them smile!) happy. They are on top of things, perhaps not beautiful, but very much in charge, at least for the moment. And, having internalized the discipline of a competitive world, they are ready to demonstrate many of the qualities admired in polite society.

The Prison as Social Laboratory

Magneto, locked in his plastic prison, also recognizes the economic nature of the prison. He remembers the forced labor camps of the Nazis. Prisoners in Auschwitz, we recall, were also forced to dig ditches and work in factories for companies such as Volkswagen, which today refuses to pay any damages to survivors of the labor camps. There is some small upside to Magneto's prison. At least he isn't forced to assemble trucks for GM. However, the comics do discuss the ethics of exploiting prisoners, not necessarily as slave labor, but as test subjects for human experimentation. For that part of the story, we need to return to Ang Lee movie, *The Hulk*.

As we recall, the government spends fortunes on capturing the green behemoth, but to what end? The Hulk seems happy enough bounding around the desert. He's really not very interested in humans or cities. Why even go after him? The answer is profit. The government, or at least the companies with which it subcontracted the work, has a lot invested in the serum running through The Hulk's system, and it wants a return on its investment.

When The Hulk is captured, he is incarcerated in a specially-designed underground prison. He is then prodded and poked by a biotech corporation that wishes to patent The Hulk's power and sell it back to the government, which will then make an army of Hulks. Everyone wins in this scenario, except The Hulk himself, who will probably be killed if all goes right. Of course, nothing goes right, and The Hulk wrecks the base and escapes.

Film director Ang Lee has been criticized for turning *The Hulk* into a father-son relationship story, but elements of the script, particularly the recurrent need to exploit the military potential of The Hulk, harkens to the original book. In the comic, the government builds a number of huge bases in New Mexico, known as Gamma Bases, manned by both United States Army and Air Force personnel. In story after story, The Hulk is captured, brought to a Gamma Base and prodded; he then escapes and destroys the base. Typical is *The Hulk* #104 (1968; Friedrick/Severin/Giacoia), in which the Army captures The Hulk; in the next issue he escapes. In issue #130 (1970; Thomas/Trimpe), a physicist bombards Banner with his new Gammatron that separates Banner from The Hulk. The military tries to protect Banner, but The Hulk smashes everything, and Banner is forced to reverse the process.

Experiments on The Hulk yield the occasional success. One scientist injects himself with a modified strain of The Hulk serum and becomes the government-employed superhero Dr. Samson, normal enough except for a streak of green in his hair (#141, 1971; Roy Thomas/Herb Trimpe). In 1980, Banner met his cousin, Jennifer Walters, who needed an immediate blood transfusion. Banner rolled up his sleeve and saved her life, but she was then transformed permanently into the She-Hulk, green, massively powerful, but — unlike the male version — brainy.

When not attempting to capture The Hulk, the United States makes sure its valuable experiment doesn't fall into enemy hands. In *The Hulk* #106 (1968; Goodwin/Thomas/Severi/Trimpe), The Hulk is captured by the Russians, who are interested in what the U.S. has been spending its bioweapons money on. Nick Fury and the boys from S.H.I.E.L.D. then rescue The Hulk, but again fail to capture him.

Color-Coding The Hulk

Attempts have also been made to reform and rehabilitate The Hulk by teaching him to be nicer. This is obviously a metaphor for prison rehabilitation programs, many of which deal with anger management. In one long story arc (#325–380), Banner is cured through drugs and psychotherapy, but another Hulk emerges, a character fans call The Grey Hulk. The color change is significant, as it fits a widely recognized cultural stereotype: a black man as criminal. Was Marvel dealing the race card here? Perhaps. But The Grey Hulk *is* a much more productive citizen, at least in the sense that he listens, learns, takes orders, and enjoys society. Great, we might say; at last, hope that prisons can help people. A few problems, however, quickly become manifest. The Hulk is smarter and can control his temper, but what does he do with his new capabilities? He goes to Vegas and becomes an enforcer for the mob. Yes, prison can job-train criminals, but only, it seems, to be better criminals. Recently, a TV news segment aired on a similar plan to rehabilitate drug dealers by putting them through Marine boot camp. The suggestion was that women and children in the ghettos may someday be safe on their porches and in their cribs, because drug dealers can now be taught to run *and* shoot straight!

Marvel's decision to turn The Hulk back to green and to make him again a walking moron raises several cultural and racial questions about the ways in which our society frames violence. When Banner is The Grey (or black) Hulk, it's clear who the criminal is: It's The Grey Hulk. Can we say the same when Banner turns from the grey into The (green) Hulk? This situation suggests that we punish similar crimes on the basis of color, not guilt. The Grey Hulk may have more brains than The (green) Hulk, but we spend less time thinking about how to deal with him. When Banner, a white man, goes berserk, he's ill, a victim, a sufferer of phallic anxiety in need of medication; when he's The Grey (or black) Hulk, he's a criminal.

The World as Prison

It may be too easy to say that these villains return again and again because they have made a place for themselves in our fantasy lives, that they are too clever or vile for us to give them up. After all, we don't want them rehabilitated. No one argues that the Joker is innocent, only that he is interesting. But, in an even more telling drawback of the penal system, we learn — at least as presented in the comics — that these culturally isolated figures (labeled by society as "villains") don't want to be cured either. In the *X-Men* movie, someone asks the mutant Mystique (Rebecca Romijn-Stamos), who can assume any form, why she doesn't simply disguise herself as a non-mutant. She offers a bland but compelling response: "We shouldn't have to." The reply is laconic but clear enough: Mystique argues for difference over discipline. She feels she doesn't have to be like everyone else. Her freedom and identity are more important than fitting into a world of rigidity and repetitive discipline. Thus, her support of the chess-playing Magneto, whose goal is social integration — but not in the sense of fitting into a "normal" society.

Instead, Magneto wants everyone to be a mutant like him. Using a high-tech gadget of his own creation, he hopes to remake the world's leaders into mutants. His logic is simple. They hate what they don't understand. If they were mutants, then these leaders would understand persecution firsthand, and stop hunting mutants. Magneto is not, then, an advocate of leniency for criminals, but rather an avatar of reverse discrimination.

The Hulk reacts violently to attempts to cure him. In such cases, is the death penalty appropriate? (By permission of Marvel Comics.)

Although branded an arch-criminal and imprisoned at great expense to the government, Magneto argues that, if the mutants were running the world, it would be impossible — and unnecessary — to lock anyone up.

In essence, Magneto comes to the same solution undertaken by the inmates in Edgar Allan Poe's short story, "Professor Tarr and Dr. Fether." In Poe's story, the narrator is given a tour of a sanatorium, where he finds that every treatment strikes him as crazy. It turns out that the inmates, after taking control of the mental prison, have placed the doctors and staff in the cells that the inmates had formerly occupied. From the patients' point of view, "cure" is only a nice word for "punishment." If the doctors got a taste of their own punishment, they might think twice about the efficacy of this form of treatment. From a multicultural perspective of tolerance, it's difficult not to side with Magneto, Mystique, and The Grey Hulk. If mutation — change — is the norm, there will no longer be a need to isolate and to punish difference, for in their ascendancy, mutants would control the keys to the biggest prison of all, the world itself.

THINKING, DEBATING, WRITING

1. Does your state have the death penalty? Do you agree with your state's policy? How long has that policy been in effect? Does the state have a moral mandate to rehabilitate murderers?

2. We suggest that whites are treated better in the justice system than minorities. Write an essay in which you agree or disagree; use evidence from outside sources to back your arguments.

3. Discuss the rituals of capital punishment, such as legal appeals, candlelight vigils, the last meal, last rites, etc.

4. Did it surprise you that many prisons are run for profit? Contact any prison in your state and interview the CEO or CFO of that company, if not by phone, then by e-mail or mail. When did the company get into the prison industry, how much profit does the prison make, and how many people does the company employ? Do you think prisons are a "growth business"?

5. Why is there a need to isolate and to punish difference? Contrast Martin Luther King's "I have a dream" speech with the dream of Magneto's plan for a one-world, all-mutant society.

6. Frank Miller's *Batman* dismisses psychology and other therapeutic fields in favor of punishing criminals. Contact a psychologist in your area and ask for his/her side in this ongoing debate. Present your findings to the class.

7. All the examples in this chapter focus on men in prison. What

about women in prison? Are lighter or harsher terms meted out to woman killers? Are there proportionally more or fewer women on death row?

8. Read Edgar Allan Poe's "Professor Tarr and Doctor Fether." Argue whether a fictional piece can be used as evidence in the ongoing discussion of prison reform.

9. Read Frank Miller's *Dark Knight*, then play psychologist. Even if Bruce Wayne helps people, he may also need our help. Should we "cure" him or allow him to be "sick" simply because his "sickness" is a benefit to society?

10. We compared America's prison systems with that of the Nazi interment camps. Is the essay unfairly stretching the truth to make a point? Write an essay opposing or defending the American prison system.

Coda: Our Heroes, Ourselves

February 5, 2005: We are standing in front of a monument to our times, a building that expresses who we are, how we see ourselves, and how we want others to remember us. It is a monument to our genius and a gift to the ages, the West Coast equivalent of the Lincoln Memorial in Washington, D.C. It is the Disney animation studios in Burbank, California, home of Mickey Mouse, and birthplace of Pixar, makers of *Toy Story, Finding Nemo,* and the superhero spoof, *The Incredibles.* Some would say Disney has played no part in the recent evolution of superheroes, and perhaps they are right. Our discussion, which has focused on Marvel and DC heroes, does not touch on Disney characters. Architecturally, however, the Marvel building in New York makes no statement comparable to the Disney complex in Burbank, and DC's headquarters is similarly undistinguished. It seems to us that Disney's studio asserts the cultural power and importance of comic books. The building is a multi-columned structure, not unlike the tomb of the Roman Emperor Hadrian. Instead of the heroes or Roman gods, its statuary celebrates the Seven Dwarfs, with Dopey standing in pride of place.

We can probably concede that the Seven Dwarfs are lovable and heroic. Very few readers will admit to wishing them or Snow White harm. But why idolize them? Presumably, when we do so, we are not valuing their intelligence. Rather, when gazing on the Dwarfs, we are admiring their loyalty and their dependability, their honesty and their willingness to help. If so, we can say that these statues stand as metaphors for our cultural values, which hold that we should be sensitive to the plight of the weak, and which applaud the inclusion of everyone. But even if we affirm this analysis, we may still wonder if Dopey is the best choice as the Dwarfs' symbolic leader.

How dumb are we for reading comic books? As we have seen, comic books often focus on the "hot-button" issues of society, as addressed — and even "solved" — in comic books. In this book, we aimed to promote those literate and intelligent conversations going on in the comics and among their readers. We have a dream of turning comic book readers into readers of Shakespeare and Milton. Our aim is to save the world from illiteracy.

What we didn't say was why we need you to do this. You see, it's our fault. And we need your help to redeem us from our crimes.

In a recent article published in the *Harvard Education Letter*, Tom Newkirk, a professor of English at the University of New Hampshire in Durham, argued that students come to the classroom with their own ideas of what constitutes classic literature. When faced with what we honorifically call the "Canon" (Shakespeare, Milton, Austen, Dickens, Joyce, to name only a few), they turn their backs because these cultural impositions fail to meet either their social needs or aesthetic criteria.[1]

Part of the problem is that this clash of cultures is not fought between equals. Teachers are adults; students are kids. Teachers in grade school are not only bigger than their clients, but they are also armed with the power to assign grades. Students, on the other hand, are evaluated not only on their ability to understand and appreciate what they are told to read, but on the enthusiasm they register in response to the Canon's cultural uplift. Humiliation accompanies defeat, as teachers grade students on their ability to switch their allegiance from books they like to "literature" they are supposed to love. Of course, some students learn to play the game better than others, and some even excel according to the competitive standards imposed by its rules. But the poorly-kept dirty little secret is that many of our best students only pretend to be interested in these assigned "classics," and some good students register outright resentment.[2] "A lot of times we are snobs," Tom Newkirk admits. "We see ourselves as special, protecting our own forms of literacy and protecting literature.... Kids sense the disapproval. You want them to acknowledge your world, but you also have to acknowledge theirs." Bonny Norton's recent study of *Archie* comic-book readers includes the following critical assessment from a twelve-year-old: "*Archie* is more of a comic type thing, not a book type thing." When asked if comic books were not books, he responded, "It depends if it's supposed to be fun or not."[3]

Has reading always been so dull? We argue that the present problem is how we are training our teachers.

1. Sara-Ellen Amster, "Shakespeare vs. Teletubbies: Is There a Role for Pop Culture in the Classroom?" *Harvard Education Letter, Online Research,* http://www.adams5th.com/journalism.htm.

2. Ivey and Broaddus suggest that many students only pretend to read during assigned reading periods, and that the classroom was one of the least likely places students might find reading materials of interest. G. Ivey and K. Broaddus, " 'Just plain reading': A survey of what makes students want to read in middle school classrooms," *Reading Research Quarterly* 36 (2001), 350–77; 368.

3. See "The motivating power of comic books: Insights from Archie comic readers," *International Reading Association* (2003),140–7;141.

It was not always this way. It was in the Golden and Silver Age of comics (the 1950s and 1960s) that English departments first spread across America. While the initial spread of these institutions was not tied to the comic-book industry — whose works academics systematically disparaged as pulp filth — English departments nonetheless benefited from readers who began their passionate affair with the printed word as found in the monthly installments of *Superman*, *Batman*, *Wonder Woman*, *The Green Lantern*, and *Captain America*. While these generations of students might not have been offered a class in *Batman* or *The Flash*, these same readers could at least bring their narrative sensibilities and passions to the standard set of canonical texts. The teaching method of the day was "New Criticism," a species of formal analysis focused on texts as structures of human significance, as Aristotelian embodiments of human experience. Using a criticism that distinguished aspects of a work as timeless, the comic reader might still cherish his or her favorite comics as profound, if personal, reading experiences.

Today, English departments are more likely to teach quasi-political science, New Historicism, Deconstruction, Cultural Materialism — schools of analysis that distain any meaningful articulation of aesthetics, except in relation to economics or history. Freshman composition is usually taught by graduate students who merely replicate the learning models they have experienced. These trendy critiques avoid discussion of the literary merits of the work itself, which they likely hold to be a "social construction" (that is, a pious fiction foisted on hapless, helpless victims).

So if we're not teaching about literature — about right and wrong, good and evil — what are we teaching to the future teachers of the world? This brief conclusion is not the place to discuss the merits or demerits of literary theory, but we think it fair to point out that much of present academic praxis is designed, it often seems, to frustrate any understanding or enjoyment of the text. The well-respected Paul de Man has uttered such gems as, "Interpretation is nothing but the possibility of error," and "The allegory of reading narrates the impossibility of reading."[4] J. Hillis Miller states that "[t]he poem, like the text, is unreadable" — a view that makes preparing for class not only wholly unnecessary, but impossible.[5] If respected English professors say that it's impossible to write about or even read literature, why plow through *Great Expectations* when other classes' assignments are due tomorrow morning? Not to worry, since Foucault tells us that texts write themselves. (If only all homework were so simple!)

Another critic, Althusser, rejects the logic of looking for character,

---

4. Paul de Man, *Allegories of Reading* (Hew Haven: Yale University Press, 1979), 76–7 and 205.
5. J. Hillis Miller, "The Critic As Host," *Deconstruction and Criticism*, ed. Harold Bloom (New York : Seabury Press, 1979), 217–53; 226

plot, or setting. To him, the "fun" of literature consists in looking at its passivity:

> [the] social relations, *spoken* by pre-given linguistic structures, *thought* by ideologies, *dreamed* by myths, *gendered* by patriarchical sexual norms, *bonded* by affective obligations, *cultured* by *mentalités*, and *acted* by history's script.[6]

It's hard to imagine comic books being put together by themselves in this way, or that out of such passivity such violent tales could come. We have no doubt that if one of these critics told Dr. Doom that he was "gendered by patriarchical sexual norms," he'd pay an immediate and painful "affective obligation" for such insolence.

We need not imagine Dr. Doom kicking Paul de Man — as pleasurable as many of us might find such a fantasy — to defend the importance of the comics. All we need do is ask a twelve-year-old. When we ask even adult comic book readers and collectors what they like about comics, they say things which we do not presently teach or even informally discuss, such as "that scene where the Silver Surfer turns on Galactus and saves the earth made my heart leap"; "When Mary Jane tells Spider-Man that he deserves to be saved too, I began to cry"; "When Superman discovers Lois dead, and he freaks out, screaming, and then uses his powers to turn back time, I felt, you know, good."

"Heart"? "Deserves"? "Good"? These terms imply emotional and moral judgments. What these readers are reacting to is the aesthetics of comic books, that is, the way in which the climax of the story "fits." But fits *what*? In perhaps the most famous discussion of this phenomenon of the propriety of endings, Aristotle talks about the turnabout, or reversal, of an ongoing scheme of things, in which the fortunes of decent individuals change dramatically, leaving an audience with profound feelings of pity and terror. Oddly, these feelings, in combination, are pleasurable, as if one has been purged, or "saved" from a like fate. Aristotle called this sense *catharsis*.

Today, neither we nor literary critics in general deal with such matters very effectively, perhaps because they depend on a shared sense of truth and beauty, good and evil. Without shared perceptions, without a shared vocabulary, reading as a socially meaningful pastime may not be possible. In an increasingly fragmented culture, which promotes diversity and relativism as absolutes, discussions of a climax along Aristotelian lines will go nowhere because Aristotle insists that audience reactions of "pity and terror" must arise from moral judgments about the characters in conflict. So,

6. E.P. Thompson, *The Poverty of Theory* (London: Merlin Press, 1978), 153.

in their place, we are inclined to ask readers, who may intuitively "get" or experience the Aristotelian value of the work, to reassess it, to, in effect, "un-get" it. They are taught to de- and re-construct their experiences, to see the literary work not from the insider but from the vantage of the outsider looking in, to see and discuss the work's exclusionary mechanisms— how it denigrates women, or how it promotes a conservative perspective aimed at preserving social injustice, etc.

Yet even after expressing how empowered students feel when reading and discussing comic books, scholars traditionally conclude with an apology like this: While comic books certainly help "develop critical media literacy, including the ability to appraise the content of media messages ... we join [prior studies] in cautioning teachers not to require their students to overanalyze the very culture from which they derive so much pleasure and meaning."[7] It has come to this: the best literary critics can do is deny pleasure in reading *and* affirm no meaning in the search for it.

And so, in front of this Disney monument, we're making our (superheroic) stand. The war has begun and we need to organize a counteroffensive. A "Center for Cartoon Studies" already exists in Vermont, run by James Sturm, a comic book writer. But for the most part, comic book readers have learned to keep their interests to themselves, as if being a comic book reader was a secret identity. Jason Tondro and a few daring teachers at the University of California at Riverside use comics in their freshman courses, but, as Tondro explains, that is only because his "our superiors *haven't caught us yet*"[8] [emphasis added]. Would that he were joking! The way things stand at the moment, reading comics is a literary crime. We, the authors of this study, want to register our outrage: that present critical practice should systematically beat the life out of literature, and make students ignore any pleasure in reading in favor of searching out yet more examples of race, class, or gender oppression, is neither professionally nor ethically harmless. On the contrary, it is a literary offense, an attack on literacy.

We wrote this book for voluntary readers. As voluntary readers, you are already voluntary heroes in the cause. Yes, the war to save literacy has started, and we're hoping you'll continue to fight the good fight. In fact, we're counting on it. Make no mistake: we, as teachers and custodians of canonical literature, need comic book readers more than you need us. Comic book readers— one of the few remaining, voluntarily literate communities— are too extraordinary in numbers to shut out from our notice, for

    7. Timothy G. Morrison, Gregory Bryan, George W. Chilcoat, "Using student-generated comic books in the classroom," *Journal of Adolescent & Adult Literacy* 45.8 (May 2002), 758–67; 758.
    8. Katherine Keller, "A Superman in King Arthur's Court: Jason Tondro's going Medieval on Comics," *Sequential Tart. http://www.sequentialtart.com/jtondro.shtml.*

they are, perhaps, the last significant community of readers who, despite recent critical efforts to the contrary, still suppose that literature is based on character, plot, and action. These readers, who will one day lead this nation — indeed, since comics are international, this world — still believe in good and evil, in victory and defeat, in winning and losing, and the costs, both material and spiritual, of both. Their heroes stand as the latest and perhaps last monuments to mankind, as spirits capable of great splendor and great sadism, of creating and causing misery as well as happiness. In short, comic book heroes are the inheritors of our civilization, and there is nothing Dopey in recognizing in them our present achievements and our continued failures. For we cannot hail the former without recognizing our collective aspirations, and we cannot condemn the latter without acknowledging those things of darkness within ourselves. In such epiphanies are heroes born.

Index